COLLABORATIVE PRACTITIONERS

COLLABORATIVE SCHOOLS

Second Edition

Marleen C. Pugach
University of Wisconsin, Milwaukee

Lawrence J. Johnson
University of Cincinnati

Foreword by
Stephen Lilly
California State University, San Marcos

LOVE PUBLISHING COMPANY®
Denver • London • Sydney

Published by Love Publishing Company
Denver, Colorado 80222

Second Edition

Library of Congress Catalog Card Number 2001094889

CONTENTS

FOREWORD

Each year the San Diego County Office of Education surveys area school districts to determine hiring and employment patterns for new teachers. In addition to asking districts to report current and future hiring needs, the survey collects information on how often and why districts decline to renew contracts for new teachers who are on probationary appointments. While non-renewal is not a common occurrence, the reasons that districts cite for taking this action are instructive.

The primary reasons for non-renewal of teachers' contracts usually are predictable, with lack of classroom management skills and ineffectiveness in teaching to academic standards topping the list. Another common reason, however, is not so obvious to many people. District personnel directors report that a major reason for contract non-renewal is the inability to work effectively with other teachers and parents.

Teaching is no longer a profession in which one can close the classroom door and perform in isolation. Teaching is more than ever a "public act," with well-defined expectations for both student and teacher performance. Parents, policy makers, and the general public are well aware of student performance prospects and expect teachers to achieve measurable results with all students. It is not acceptable in today's world of education for teachers to achieve success only with the top tier of students in their classes. Rather, it is anticipated that all students will live up to high academic and performance standards. Expectations have never been higher in education, for students and teachers alike.

With these higher expectations and increased public accountability for today's teachers, collaborating with and learning from one's professional peers has taken on greater importance. When students are not learning, it is not acceptable for the teacher to "forge on," thereby leaving students behind. The major public policy focus in the United States on under-performing students and under-performing schools creates a tangible pressure on educators to redouble our efforts when individual students are not learning. The public pressure to do better with low-performing students is reinforcing the professional and moral imperative felt by teachers to be successful with each and every student.

In my view, the "three Rs" for teacher education (that is, the basics for all new teachers) are (1) the ability to teach effectively to rigorous student learning standards, (2) the ability to organize the classroom environment and manage student behavior to optimize student learning, and (3) the willingness and ability to collaborate effectively with parents and fellow teachers. While I am confident that teacher educators and prospective teachers understand the importance of the first two, such is not always the case with the third. In my experience, many prospective teachers are not aware of the importance of collaboration in their chosen profession, and too often teacher education programs approach collaboration as a predilection or disposition, rather than a set of skills to be taught and nurtured.

This book is an important resource for teacher educators and prospective teachers because it is based on the premise that collaborative and cooperative behavior can and should be taught to both prospective and practicing teachers. This is true whether one is preparing to be a classroom teacher or a special educator. While special educators face collaboration challenges based in the rules and regulations governing special education practice, these should not be confused with the simple act of working effectively with peers to increase the quality of teaching and the level of performance of all students. Collaboration with teachers and parents is, purely and simply, a means of using what others know to improve one's own teaching practice, while also helping one's peers to be more effective teachers.

The Zeigarnick Effect is an age-old principle of psychology that holds that human beings tend to remember unfinished tasks over those that are completed. In no profession is this principle more obvious than teaching. The best teachers spend much more time worrying about students who are not learning than they do celebrating those who are. A primary purpose of this book is to help make that worrying productive by preparing teachers to effectively use the single best resource for improving their own performance in teaching all students well: fellow teachers and parents. When a teacher faces a seemingly intractable student learning or behavior issue in the classroom, it is almost certain that one or more fellow teachers in the school have not only faced the problem before, but also solved it. One's fellow teachers are an enormous source of help in planning instructional modifications for students, as are parents, but not if one is trapped in the "Lone Ranger" model of teaching.

This book, then, is a pathway from professional isolation to teacher success with all students. It offers both compelling rationale and practical guidance for improving one's teaching practice through collaboration. The ideas presented in this book provide important building blocks for the foundation of professional teaching. The most important statement for any teacher to be able to make is that each and every student in her or his classroom has learned to high standards. In order to reach the point of being able to make this statement on a regular basis, teachers must be not only masters of pedagogy and classroom management, but also masters of collaboration. This book provides the tools necessary to become the latter. Use it well.

Steve Lilly, Dean
College of Education
California State University, San Marcos

PREFACE

We began working together to consider the dimensions of collaboration nearly 20 years ago. Over that time we have watched collaboration move from a fledgling, almost radical idea to a fully enacted way of conducting professional interactions in the schools. In 1995, when we wrote the first edition of this book, our goal was to transcend the then current arguments about various ways collaboration should be conducted. We wanted instead to present an integrated, multidimensional framework for the practice of collaboration that gave credence to the seemingly contradictory ways collaboration was being practiced in its early stages of implementation. By doing so, we wanted to emphasize that collaboration was an appropriate overarching professional stance for education professionals across the spectrum of their various day-to-day interactions.

Six years later, we still adhere to a multidimensional view of collaboration. However, the context in which collaboration is practiced has changed significantly, and in this second edition we have tried to situate a multidimensional view of collaboration within this new context. Specifically, two years after the first edition was released, the 1997 amendments to the Individuals with Disabilities Education Act (IDEA) were passed. The reauthorization of IDEA overwhelmingly signified the institutionalization of collaboration between special and general education, particularly as it pertains to making the general education curriculum accessible for students with disabilities. Further, in May of 2001, a new set of standards were released from the Interstate New Teacher Assistance and Support Consortium, or INTASC, defining what all teachers need to know and be able to do to educate students with disabilities. These standards for beginning teachers clearly underscore the fundamental role of collaboration in meeting the needs of all students in the schools.

As a result of these developments, we have updated the context of collaboration in relationship to IDEA. Further, we have included a section on the relationship between collaboration and staff development. This was an important change because it is becoming increasingly common for teachers to create and implement professional development opportunities for their peers as a dimension of collaboration. We have also extended the idea of collaborating across institutions to include not only school-university partnerships, which we discussed in the first edition, but also a substantial section on partnerships between schools and social service and/or health agencies. We believe that the broad scope of interagency collaboration better represents the range of school partnerships that exists and provides prospective and practicing teachers with an important perspective on the full range of services their students might require. Finally, we have expanded the chapter on school-family collaboration.

As we prepared this new edition, we purposely framed many of our examples and arguments in the context of an increasingly diverse student population and the routine disparity between students of color and a primarily white teaching force. We believe this is a crucial issue to consider in relationship to collaboration. As teachers work together to improve teaching and learning, it is clear that they will need to address issues of equity in any location in which they work. Our goal in this edition is to create a continuous awareness of the challenges related to providing culturally relevant education and closing the achievement gap in our schools as it relates to race, class, culture, and language.

A few acknowledgements are in order. This second edition was a long time coming, and we are grateful to Stan Love, our publisher, for pressing us to set aside the time to revise our original work. We are grateful as well for the highly professional work that Cathy Mae Nelson of the University of Wisconsin, Milwaukee, did in preparing the manuscript. Also, we greatly appreciate the work of Jenny Carpenter of the University of Cincinnati for her help in identifying appropriate websites that may be of interest to the readers of this book.

Finally, our confidence in the power of collaboration continues to be strengthened by our own involvement in serious, ongoing collaborations that are changing the way education is practiced. With profound respect for the commitment every real collaborative effort in education requires, we dedicate this edition to the teachers and administrators with whom we work, who willingly engage in collaboration because they know it is a means of helping them reach their most important goal: improving the quality learning for the children and youth they serve.

Marleen C. Pugach
Lawrence J. Johnson

PART ONE

The Conceptual Context of Collaboration

1

Collaboration and the Complex Work of Teaching

Teaching is a challenge. This assertion, in all its simplicity, is the reason why professional collaboration finally has come to be recognized and valued as such an important facet of the work adults do in schools. Traditionally, teaching has been considered an occupation that requires a great deal of interaction with children and youth and little with other adults. Often it said about a teacher, "She's great with the kids, but she has a hard time communicating with grown-ups." Being "good" with children and youth, of course, is one of the cornerstones of teaching. But limiting our conception of teaching to how well we interact with children and youth means being content with a definition of teaching that stops at the classroom door. From this traditional perspective, teaching means going it alone and each classroom is seen as an independent entity with few ties to any other classroom, or to the school as a whole. Without professional collaboration, whatever challenges we face as teachers, we face alone within the confines of our classroom's four walls.

If we instead define teaching as working well with children *and* interacting well with adults, we acknowledge the rich intellectual resource provided by all the adults who have a vested interest in schools—teachers, specialists, principals, family members, to name a few—who form the basis of a community of adult learners to support the complex work that schools are expected to perform. This expanded definition acknowledges the power a school derives from being thought of as a whole community in which each adult who works there is responsible for educating the children and youth who attend, adults who are interested not only in their own classrooms but also in what goes on in the school at large.

Most of all, we recognize that, to be a source of vibrant, intellectual stimulation for every student who attends, teachers themselves must work in stimulating, supportive, collegial environments. This is crucial in providing education that is responsive to the vast cultural differences among students and that assists teachers in bridging the gaps between their students' cultures and their own. In collaborative work environments, teachers have the potential to create the collective capacity for initiating and sustaining ongoing improvement in their professional practice so each student they serve—across ethnic, racial, language, and socioeconomic differences—can receive the highest quality of education possible.

Collaboration in Contemporary Educational Practice

Teaching always has been hard work, so why is it now so essential to redefine professional norms of teaching to include collaboration? Why is collaboration receiving so much attention? Many developments in the reform-minded educational scene, which has existed since the early 1980s, have converged to encourage educators to rethink the role of adult-adult relationships in schools, to come to agreement on the value of professional collaboration, and to establish it deliberately as an expectation for all teachers. Although all of these developments are linked to the overarching, fundamental goal of improving the quality of education for students, they contribute to this goal in different ways. Let's consider five in detail.

CHANGES IN THE AUTHORITY STRUCTURE OF SCHOOLS

For as long as many of us can remember, schools were run by principals under the direct guidance and influence of the district office. The reforms of the 1980s, however, introduced the concept of greater local management of each school. Sometimes called *site-based management,* this approach is based on the principle that schools are best managed by those who work at and are invested in the site itself—the teachers, principal, specialist teachers, secretaries, custodians, and family members of students who attend.

This change represents a decentralization of authority. Working as a team, representatives of each of these groups often are charged with decision-making authority for budgeting, hiring and firing, the instructional program, and school policies. At the high school level, students themselves can be included as members of the team. For example, in a school that is managed on site, the decision to integrate instruction thematically across subjects or to teach them separately could be school-based. Adoption of new instructional materials could take into account whether they are relevant to the cultural backgrounds of all the students. The school is the unit of concern for all who work in it; decisions are made with the quality of the school's total educational program in mind.

Collegial management of a school site does not mean that everyone works on every task; that would not be an efficient way to run a school. It does mean, however, that everyone has a stake in every task contributing to overall success of the educational program. Although not all school districts subscribe to decentralized authority, its practice is widespread. Collaboration is essential to successful implementation of local school management; without it, consensus on fundamental decisions could not be reached easily. These changes in the authority structure create the expectation for schoolwide responsibility across all stakeholders.

INCREASED TEACHER RESPONSIBILITY FOR THE PROFESSION

Although teaching commonly is referred to as a profession, historically many things about being a teacher have not been characteristic of how professionals do their work. One of the most important lessons learned from the reforms that began in the 1980s is that, for teaching to gain the professional respect it deserves, teachers themselves will have to be involved actively in professional activities and take responsibility for the quality of the profession. This shift to greater professionalism means that teachers no longer will stand by and receive directives from principals and district supervisors. It means, instead, that teachers and administrators have to work together, as colleagues, to make the best decisions for their schools and for their profession.

For example, teachers historically did not take responsibility for evaluating their peers' performance. Simply by virtue of the fact that each classroom was considered an island of its own, teachers did not tend to talk to their peers about what they do, preferring instead, in some cases, to lock their classroom doors and be free from external scrutiny. Collaboration implies that this kind of individual power is no longer acceptable, and that what goes on behind the classroom door is the responsibility of every adult in the school. Increasingly, teams of teachers may be called upon to visit the classrooms of teachers who are not performing well, offer structured support, and, when necessary, identify teachers who should not be teaching any longer. Another reason, then, why collaboration has become so valued is that one hallmark of professionalism is having teachers themselves take mutual responsibility for the quality of their individual and collective practice. The goal is to make the profession better as a whole—not just one's own isolated practice of it.

Likewise, teachers historically did not have authority for developing or interpreting curriculum themselves. Instead, as a rule they were expected to follow the teacher's manual, use the basal texts, and do what the principal asked. Today, teachers are voicing more and more interest in making their own curriculum decisions—those that best fit the needs of the students in their building in the context of the surrounding community. Along with this kind of curricular responsibility comes the need for teachers to demonstrate high levels of curriculum knowledge in each of the subject areas in which they teach to ensure that decisions are made responsibly and are based on the most current knowledge. Working together, teachers can push themselves to new heights in curriculum expertise.

Another example of this kind of collegial responsibility is the development of formal mentor teaching programs to support new teachers in their induction (first) year—invariably the most difficult year of teaching. Identifying mentors means that, as members of a profession, experienced, accomplished teachers today are taking responsibility for supporting new teachers and helping them bridge the gap from preservice to practicing teaching. Mentoring can take place within a building, across buildings in a district, or via technology. Because one of the major purposes of mentoring is to increase the retention of novice teachers, taking on this responsibility means exerting a positive influence on the stability of the teaching profession as a whole.

Teachers are also taking responsibility for identifying professionals whose skills represent the best of the teaching force. For example, the National Board for Professional Teaching Standards, through its portfolio assessment process, enables teachers to volunteer to have the quality of their teaching assessed by peers to determine whether they meet the criteria for becoming a Board Certified teacher. Most of those who assess the quality of the portfolios, which include videotaped portions of teachers' lessons, are other teachers. This is a significant development in the professionalization of teaching, and recent studies indicate that Board Certified teachers are in fact more highly skilled than those who are not ("Teachers with National Board Certification Outperform," 2000).

Finally, teachers themselves can participate actively in studying their own teaching and sharing their inquiry with colleagues. Networks of teachers who are working to implement specific instructional methods are common today, often aided by technological advances. Teacher researcher study groups, often in collaboration with university partners, enable teachers themselves to ask questions about their work and study it systematically. In this way, collaboration serves to support teachers in understanding and improving their own professional practice.

THE CHANGING DEMOGRAPHIC RELATIONSHIP BETWEEN TEACHERS AND STUDENTS

As our society becomes more diverse, this diversity is reflected in our schools. In the past, students and teachers often came from similar cultural, ethnic, or socioeconomic backgrounds. Today this is not always the case. Two significant issues related to diversity are crucial in the practice of collaboration.

First, when teachers work with students whose backgrounds are different from their own, they may fail to understand the cultures from which their students come. Teachers may not adequately value the strengths their students bring from their cultural backgrounds and life experiences and may make the erroneous assumption that cultural strengths are deficits. Teachers of students who have not yet mastered English may see their students as "problems" instead of challenging themselves to understand the vast cultural and linguistic resources their students bring to the classroom community. Teachers who consistently see these differences as problems or inconveniences will not be able to support their students' learning well. Collaborating with the families of their students and with community cultural organizations is a critical means for teachers to deepen their understanding of their students.

Second, particularly in urban schools, students of color, who also often live in poverty, are in the majority and most often are taught by teachers who are White and who often do not live in the community. The potential for misunderstanding is great and often plays out in teachers' (1) holding low expectations for their students and (2) holding erroneous stereotypical beliefs that parents and families in urban communities place less value on their children's education than do parents and families in other communities. If teachers are to engage in healthy, sustained dialogue about how to provide the most effective education for the students they teach, a trustworthy, collaborative environment is needed within schools and across schools and communities in which such dialogue can take place. Teachers must feel safe confronting their own biases, sharing them with fellow professionals, and taking action to move beyond the negative stereotypical expectations they may hold about students and their families. Of course, collaborating with families themselves is critical to the depth and accuracy of these dialogues.

These are difficult questions—some of the most difficult ones teachers face—but in the context of today's schools, they bear serious attention. Teachers need to know that, as they struggle with the personal reflection necessary to confront their own stereotypes about students who are different from themselves, their professional peers are equally willing to engage in this kind of self-inquiry. As teachers face these issues, the value of a collaborative working environment, one in which support can be expected and found readily, becomes paramount. A collaborative working environment can help to assure that all students are accepted in the schools, are actively supported in accessing the full array of educational experiences, and are achieving success.

INCREASED INTEGRATION OF STUDENTS WITH DISABILITIES

The trend toward greater and greater integration of students with disabilities into schools and classrooms nationwide is unmistakable. Since passage of the

1997 amendments to the Individuals with Disabilities Education Act (IDEA), shared responsibility for educating students with disabilities among special and general education teachers has increased significantly. Some students currently labeled as having disabilities, notably those with mild academic problems, have difficulties that are more similar to than different from their peers. This requires collaboration to change the general instructional program so it is more accommodating of all of the students (Johnson & Bauer, 1992) and, in particular, the general approach to curriculum (Pugach & Warger, 1996). Others have enduring disabilities—such as more serious physical or cognitive impairments or a combination of disabilities—requiring that classroom teachers (or groups of classroom teachers), special education personnel, families, and support agencies work collaboratively on a continual basis. This kind of collaboration also includes collaboration with related-services personnel—for example, specialists who provide physical therapy or mobility training, or transition specialists who assist older students in moving from schools to community settings or jobs.

Professional collaboration between special education teachers and classroom teachers is not new; it has taken place in varying degrees ever since mainstreaming came into common practice in the mid 1970s with passage of the 1975 Education for All Handicapped Children Act. But since IDEA was enacted, the expectation for integration has increased enormously and new forms of collaboration have been developed and implemented—many of them successfully. These collaborative activities include:

- one-to-one consultation between special education teachers and classroom teachers
- small teams of teachers working together
- team teaching, or co-teaching, in which special education teachers and classroom teachers or groups of classroom teachers form permanent teaching teams to allow more complete and ongoing integration

Some of these interactions have a more formal structure than others, but each can be successful only to the extent that the adults who share responsibility for the students—be they students with or without disabilities—work well together, support each other, and learn from each other. As part of their collaboration, special education teachers and general education teachers also must work together actively to stem the inappropriate placement of students of color, students who are English language learners, and students from lower socioeconomic groups into special education.

INCREASED COMPLEXITY OF INSTRUCTION

Goodlad's landmark 1984 study of schools documented the continued predominance of the lecture method. Contemporary researchers who study teaching and learning have made a convincing case for more complex, active forms of instruction that demand much greater and more varied skill by teachers. Most notable is the finding that students learn most effectively when they are actively involved in constructing their own knowledge (for a summary of constructivist learning, see Levine, 1992) rather than simply listening to teachers present material. At the elementary level, the overuse of workbooks and skill-driven curricula has been found wanting, as these approaches rarely give students the opportunity to engage in the kind of high-level problem solving that can challenge them intellectually and prepare them for today's jobs. In addition, prior to the end of the millennium, convincing evidence accumulated to support the power of cooperative learning (Slavin, 1991). Experiments with interdisciplinary approaches to curriculum and project-based learning also are being tried with success, especially at the middle school level (EDC, http://www2.edc.org/fsc/).

In addition to the complexity of providing active, authentic instruction, developments in technology represent a new instructional challenge for teachers. Technology clearly can facilitate goals such as problem-based learning and can provide multimedia formats for students' presenting their work, and teachers should invest in learning the technology that supports these instructional goals. Once learned, teachers must manage classrooms that are becoming more and more complex as technology is integrated. Technology that specifically supports students with disabilities (assistive technology) represents an additional challenge. The integration of technology signals the need for another level of collaboration—with network administrators, with library-media specialists, with assistive technology specialists, and often with students who might know more about computers and software than do teachers themselves.

Teaching according to principles of constructivism, utilizing organizational structures such as cooperative learning, problem-based learning, and integrating technology to enhance instruction, means that teachers no longer can expect to rely on lectures and repetitive drill work if they expect to prepare their students effectively for today's global, information-driven world. No longer can teachers assume that merely by lecturing or by providing individual drill-and-practice worksheets will students gain the capacity to continue learning as adults and meet the expectations of a technologically based work world. Rather, teachers are expected to provide meaningful, challenging, and complex tasks, plan for interactive group activities, and become involved in developing curricula that better match what is known about teaching and learning. This applies to all students, not only those we traditionally have thought of as "more capable."

If these changes in teaching practice are to come about, teachers in general and special education alike will have to support each other in taking risks as they attempt to change what they have done traditionally. Risk-taking and experimentation are far more likely to be found in collegial, collaborative school environments than schools in which the status quo prevails (Little, 1982; Rosenholtz, 1989).

The Complexities of Collaboration

We can see that a wide range of developments at the end of the 20th-century accounts for why collaboration among the adults within a school is coming to be seen as a necessary part of the way teachers do their work. Collaboration is acknowledged to have been one of the most glaring, persistently absent characteristics of the work of teachers—and one much in need of being implemented— whether it is for personal support in a time of changing expectations, for maximizing the kind of results that occur when teachers work with specialists on a given student's problems, for learning to build actively on the cultural and language strengths their students bring, for figuring out together how to implement new approaches to teaching and learning, to develop specific interventions that enable students with disabilities to be educated with their general education peers, or for generating new knowledge derived from classroom practice.

Another way to think about how schools might be different if a collaborative professional ethic were to prevail is that schools would become *communities of learners* in which all participants would contribute to their own and each others' growth. If we think of teachers as members of a community of learners—rather than as isolated individuals performing a narrow set of instructional duties—we shift our thinking to how teachers can both learn from and contribute to the learning of their peers on many counts, be they schoolwide issues or solving the problems of a specific child with a specific set of needs. Each collaborative interaction, although it may occur for multiple reasons in multiple contexts, contributes to building a collaborative school. "The thing that distinguishes collaborative communities from most other communities is the desire to construct new meanings about the world through interaction with others" (Schrage, 1990, p. 48). In schools, these kinds of interdependent intellectual and personal communities also serve as important models for students as they try to make sense of their place in the world.

How does this shift to a collaborative norm of professional interaction come about? If it is so crucial to improving schooling, how do we get there? What do schools look like if collaboration is deeply ingrained? How do we know when a school has become a collaborative work environment? How are the old norms of isolation shed? Because collaboration has quickly become a

A Collaborative School or Not?

Elm Elementary School is located in the inner city of a large, metropolitan school district. The student population is entirely Black, and the majority of students come from low socioeconomic levels and receive free or reduced-price lunches. Most of the students live in the neighborhood, which is considered among the rougher neighborhoods in the city. Student achievement levels at the school are consistently low, and the teachers talk about this as a source of frustration. The teachers appear to care a great deal about their students and want them to do well. The school uses traditional approaches to curriculum and instruction, but various new programs are tried each year to improve the situation. Faculty meetings are the time for a lot of friendly conversation before coming to order. During the meetings everyone listens attentively to specific suggestions. Outside of faculty meetings, few formal professional interactions take place. For example, grade-level meetings are rare. Depending on individual teachers' interests, classes work together occasionally for certain activities.

The teachers like to work in this school. They report that it is a friendly place. Many of the teachers socialize together on Friday afternoons, play volleyball together on weekends, and celebrate one another's birthdays joyfully. Students from the local university also report that the school is a good site for field experiences and student teaching placements; they are accepted quickly and made to feel part of the school. This feeling of acceptance extends to the paraprofessionals who work in the building, as well as to the families. Guests and visitors are welcomed wholeheartedly. Beginning teachers are paired with experienced buddies and fit easily into the social structure of the staff.

In describing the school staff, the phrase "We're all family here" is commonly voiced. In the teachers' lounge, the conversation is friendly, with little negative talk about the students and a feeling of camaraderie. Teachers willingly share ideas they have used successfully in their classrooms. Staff development days almost always feature a shared potluck meal; the administration pitches in actively, and the principal often serves the staff at these festive occasions. When a staff member or one of their family members is sick, the staff rallies around to support their colleague.

buzzword among educators, we should take the time to think critically about what collaboration actually means in a school, what it is, and what it is not.

 To get a sense of the dimensions of collaboration, let's look at how the teachers and staff interact in one elementary school. As you read, be thinking about how well they work together and whether their interactions constitute professional collaboration. Jot down your thoughts about collaboration at Elm Elementary. What are the teachers' strengths as collaborative professionals? Their weaknesses?

THE ROLE OF PERSONAL SUPPORT

Few of us would want to work in a school where, at the least, adults were not congenial with each other. All things being equal, most of us would opt for congeniality as opposed to hostility or benign isolation. The way adults treat each other at work goes a long way toward creating a certain atmosphere, or ethos, in a school building. This atmosphere extends beyond the adults to the students themselves, who usually are quick to pick up on how teachers get along with one another.

Creating a cordial, personally supportive environment is an important goal for all workplaces. Particularly for teachers, this support is crucial. By virtue of the long stretches of time in which one adult works with a group of children each day, personal support is vital. In schools populated by children who live in conditions of poverty, such as those attending Elm Elementary, teachers also might have to deal with the stress of their students' lives outside of school. Without personal support, the day-to-day experience of teaching would likely be much more difficult. Personal support enables the teachers at Elm to deal with these challenges and promotes their personal caring for their students.

SHARING INFORMATION AND IDEAS

In addition to the congenial atmosphere and personal support teachers give each other at Elm Elementary, they share their ideas and talk about what is working for them in their classrooms. In contrast to much talk in other teachers' lounges, these teachers respect their students and help their colleagues by providing specific suggestions about successful lessons, tips for managing classes well, ideas for field trips, and so on. This kind of sharing allows teachers to develop a new bank of ideas to add to their repertoires.

Within each teacher's private world of practice in his or her classroom, exchanging ideas with colleagues is an indication of mutual caring, much like the mutual caring in the personal realm that is evident at Elm. They listen to one another's ideas and are grateful that teachers do not hoard their ideas, as is the case with teachers in some schools. At Elm, this cooperative professional atmosphere is noted with admiration especially by student teachers, beginning teachers, and substitute teachers who work in the building.

IS "BEING NICE" ENOUGH?

Despite the warm personal environment at Elm Elementary and the sharing of ideas that have worked in the past, the students' achievement levels have not improved over the years. Although the teachers seem to work well together, their goals are independent of those of their colleagues. They have no sense of mutual commitment to a common purpose.

This shared commitment to a schoolwide goal is precisely what distinguishes collaboration from simple cooperation. Collaborating with other teachers is not just a matter of being cooperative, of being nice to your colleagues. Being nice is important in creating a pleasant atmosphere, but it can easily exist independent of focused, mutually agreed-upon educational goals. Collegiality should not be confused with congeniality (Barth, 1990).

Likewise, sharing good ideas and information can exist independent of teachers' sharing a common goal. The kind of sharing that goes on at Elm Elementary is really a kind of information swapping; the result is meant to embellish the capacity of each individual teacher. Giving advice has limited capacity to lead to sustained, improved teaching practice. Although it might provide a short-term solution to a specific problem, it does not effectively address the underlying changes that may have to be made to improve the quality of instruction on the part of teachers who are seeking such advice (Aldinger, Warger, & Eavy, 1991; Pugach & Johnson, 1988). When advice is given in the absence of a schoolwide goal, the receiver is not under any obligation to use it; the only context in which it might appear is the individual classroom. Further, sometimes when teachers give advice, they are really saying, "You ought to do it my way."

At Elm Elementary, advice is given freely, but this practice does not seem to have contributed to improved education for its students. Giving advice results in collective awareness of individual actions (Schrage, 1990), but because the teachers can go about their business independently, a school characterized by well-intended advice-giving and exchanges of ideas without a common goal is not truly collaborative.

A distinction also has to be made between communicating well and collaborating. The skills you will learn from Chapters 3, 4, 5, and 6 of this book are skills of good communication—because good communication is necessary for collaboration. But being a good communicator has limited value without first identifying and then sharing a common goal with colleagues. People who collaborate share a vision of where they want to go, of the purpose for which they are communicating (Schrage, 1990). That vision, or goal, transcends individual interests, but the creative energies of the individuals committed to the collaboration are what makes reaching the collective goal possible. Collaboration is a more challenging goal than good communication; it means that you have to negotiate what your common goal is, be able to articulate it, and keep the vision in mind. Communicating well allows you to achieve the vision. In the absence of prior agreement regarding the common goal, however, each participant could have a different reason for communicating.

Despite the pleasant atmosphere the staff at Elm has created, by now it should seem obvious that although it is cooperative, it is not collaborative. No common goal is driving the work of this staff. Although the staff members are empathetic toward each other and their students, they are not making progress toward improving the conditions of learning in their school—even though, as individual teachers, they may be making progress. If the promise of collaboration as an instrument of school reform is to be realized, the question, "Collaborative for what purpose?" must be foremost in our minds.

Participating in a Collaborative School

Now that we have a clearer idea of exactly what collaboration is, let's turn to what kind of people make good collaborative professionals and what collaboration might actually look like in a school. Then you can begin to reflect on your strengths as a collaborative professional and where you might need to grow to take on this role effectively.

QUALITIES OF COLLABORATIVE PROFESSIONALS

The following are characteristics of professionals who are effective collaborators.

1. *People who are effective at collaboration recognize that the goal is complex and requires a joint effort.* Improving the educational process is extraordinarily complex, and the process of change is not always efficient. Teachers can respond in many ways to the new complexity of teaching. One view is to say merely that they are doing the best they can in their classrooms. A more optimistic, realistic, and promising professional response is to acknowledge that if everyone pulls together, schools can more readily become challenging, motivating

places for children and adults alike and places where more students achieve success.

2. *People who are effective at collaboration acknowledge and honor the creativity generated by working with others.* In addition to making tasks more manageable, collaborative interactions lead to results that are more creative than what any one individual can design alone. Collaborative efforts work because they add value to the solution (Schrage, 1990). Accepting this characteristic of collaboration also signifies that the professional is willing to share with all participants the recognition for accomplishments. Valuing the creativity the group generates means taking pride in the group's accomplishments toward the goal. This doesn't mean forgetting the natural human need for individual recognition but, rather, that the needs of individuals do not become obstacles to group achievement.

3. *People who are effective at collaboration value the social nature of joint problem solving.* Collaborative interactions are not always easy; just because people are committed to a common goal does not mean they always get along (Schrage, 1990). But collaboration does not happen when people do not work well together or plainly do not value and enjoy being around other adults. Working well together requires respect for other participants in the collaboration, even if you don't always agree with them. When collaborative interactions begin, participants must establish trust. Then, after the participants trust each other, disagreements that arise do so within a context of respect for others.

4. *People who are effective at collaboration value their growth as a result of participating in the collaboration.* Collaboration would not be an attractive way of dealing with complex problems if the individual did not benefit in some way. Of course, the major benefit is reaching the common goal the participant set out. Professionals who collaborate also value the intellectual growth that results from working with others. Collaboration is intellectually stimulating and can foster intellectual challenge and promote intellectual growth.

5. *People who are effective at collaboration are reflective about their own professional practice.* People who invest time and energy in collaborative efforts are not satisfied with the same routine of teaching day in and day out. Instead, they challenge themselves to grow and improve their practice at the same time as they contribute to the improved practice of the whole school. Teachers cannot contribute to the goal of improved education in schools without being aware of the quality of their own individual practice, and they take responsibility for it. This is what being a reflective teacher means. Without understanding

the effects of your own decisions and actions in the classroom and taking responsibility for them, it is difficult to change them for the better.

Thoughtful, reflective teachers do not change their practice with each successive educational bandwagon that comes along. They deliberate with their colleagues about the merits and pitfalls of new methods and implement them only when the benefits are clear and consistent with their professional knowledge about teaching and learning. Collaboration in schools means change both within individual classrooms and in schoolwide practices in accordance with the common goals identified by the staff at a school site.

John Dewey (1933), the noted progressive educator, defined reflective teaching in terms of three specific qualities.

1. Reflective teachers are *open-minded;* they are accepting of all the students they teach and are flexible about how to work with them.
2. They are *wholehearted;* by this, Dewey meant that these teachers are genuinely enthusiastic about their work, take it seriously, and are aware of new developments that can assist them in their teaching.
3. Dewey believed that reflective teachers are *intellectually responsible;* by this he meant that teachers should be aware that their instructional decisions have consequences for the students they teach and should take responsibility for those consequences.

Together these three qualities encourage teachers to improve their own teaching as a means to reaching the common vision set within a collaborative school.

 Stop for a moment to review these five basic qualities of professional collaborators. They should add another broad dimension to your conception of teaching as a profession. Have you already drawn on these qualities in your experiences in schools? In other situations? Which can you say confidently that you have, and for which do you need additional experiences? Are you comfortable accepting collaboration as an integral part of your professional responsibilities?

ESTABLISHING COLLABORATIVE CULTURES

Another important distinction that has to be made with respect to collaboration is the difference between creating a collaborative culture and implementing various collaborative structures, or specific models, for working together. Hargreaves and Dawe (1990) remind us that, although various collaborative structures (e.g., mentor teachers, peer coaching) have been developed over the past several years, implementing them does not necessarily mean that the staff in a given school is developing into a collaborative culture. They define collaborative cultures as "evolutionary relationships of openness, trust and support among teachers where they define and develop their own purposes as a community" (p. 227). When a school culture becomes collaborative rather than isolated, it promotes the professional growth of all of its teachers and staff members.

But what is the relationship between the goal of establishing a collaborative school *culture* and all of the specific collaborative *structures* that may have sprung up in schools? For example, does instituting peer coaching in a building foster the development of a collaborative culture? What about problem-solving teams to facilitate the integration of students with disabilities? Team teaching? The point Hargreaves and Dawe (1990) make in distinguishing between cultures and structures is that it is easy to think a school is becoming collaborative simply because it mandates a joint activity such as peer coaching. In reality, the district or building administrator might have supported adopting the structure without devoting sufficient time and attention to the overall school context in which the collaboration was supposed to take place. When this happens, collaborative structures too easily can become examples of "contrived collegiality" (p. 230). These contrived structures do not take the place of the challenging work of creating mutual trust among teachers, and when they are mandated, they are not based on the identification and acceptance of common goals.

Collaboration is something people come to accept; it cannot be imposed. Some people seek out collaboration naturally because it fits with the way they feel comfortable working. They already value the joint creativity it unleashes and work willingly with others toward the common purpose of building schools that support the education of all students. Others come to appreciate the benefits of collaboration only after they see it working. Creating a collaborative culture in schools is an evolutionary process, not one that can be mandated. Identifying a common goal establishes the purpose for the collaboration, and building trust among participants who have not engaged in this kind of work before—even if they are committed to the common goal—takes time, patience, and hard work. It also is crucial not to "write off" potential participants just because they do not seem interested at first. Rather than working only with those who volunteer, collaboration should be seen as a *progressively inclusive* effort. It may start with staunch supporters, but those involved in initiating collaborative efforts in schools have to be committed to keeping the door open to those who initially choose not to participate. More than just keeping an open mind, collaboration means continuously inviting expanded participation.

Forcing people to collaborate by mandating artificial structures for interaction and expecting a truly collaborative outcome is not likely to work. Those who are interested in building effective, broad-based collaborative cultures have to be sensitive to the tendency of some administrators, specialists, and teachers themselves to be so taken with a specific collaborative structure that they push for its implementation in a contrived manner, perhaps missing the larger purpose. In these situations, collaboration itself at times becomes the goal, rather than collaboration for the purpose of improving educational achievement for children and youth.

THE PLACE OF COLLABORATIVE STRUCTURES IN FOSTERING COLLABORATIVE CULTURES

We would not want to leave you with the impression that a school must have already developed into a full-blown collaborative culture before any specific collaborative structures can be implemented. Creating professional, collaborative schools is a developmental process. Considering the centuries during which teaching has been an isolated profession, no one can expect the shift to collaboration to be achieved easily or quickly. Change takes time, and those who hope to change the profession of teaching need to accept the pace of change as well as continue to push for it. What is the specific role, if any, for the vast array of collaborative structures that can be implemented in shifting to schoolwide collaborative cultures?

Let's imagine that five general education teachers at Elm Elementary are interested in changing from the use of basal reading texts to literature as the basis of their reading and writing instruction. The principal doesn't mind, and a small budget is available for purchasing the necessary books, many of which reflect the various cultural experiences of the school's students. These teachers have identified their common goal—the basis of their collaboration—and have decided to meet weekly to relate their progress and provide mutual help as they all embark on this new instructional venture in literacy. They also have agreed that at least once a month they will use their preparation time to observe each other's reading and writing instruction to get ideas and to give suggestions. Further, they have agreed to meet once a month to discuss articles related to literature-based instruction and multicultural literature as a means of bringing new information to the group and promoting their own professional development.

At the same time, a group of special education teachers—who serve mostly third, fourth, and fifth graders—have met with the principal to talk about the possibility of trying out team teaching on a limited basis. Although they know teachers who have tried this in other schools and districts, they are apprehensive about the challenge. They talk with two general education teachers who also want to see students with disabilities included on a more permanent basis.

The classroom teachers are somewhat hesitant to change the way they organize their instruction, and all of the teachers are unsure about what team teaching will be like, but they agree to try.

As these teachers review their schedules, they realize that with some judicious juggling of specialists' schedules, they can have at least one 45-minute period of common time per week for joint planning. They decide to begin on a limited basis at the start of the second semester. Their common goal is twofold: (a) integrating students with disabilities, and (b) improving the capacity of the general classroom teachers, through teaming, to reach more children in their classes who are having problems. They have discovered that the district has a small support group made up of special education and general education teachers who are teaming in various schools. The group meets each month to share ideas and help with problem solving, and they make a commitment to begin participating on a regular basis.

These two scenarios represent two separate collaborative efforts that take their direction from two different kinds of collaborative structures that we have seen emerge over the past decade. In the first scenario, the teachers are using a peer support structure. By deciding to observe each other, they are agreeing to break out of their classroom isolation and are taking steps toward peer coaching as a support mechanism for instructional change. In the second scenario, the teachers are implementing one of the many variations of increased integration between special and regular education—namely, collaborative team teaching. Neither of these examples includes the whole school, but each effort constitutes a small collaborative team and follows the basic principles of collaboration. Common goals have been identified, a commitment to those goals has been established beforehand, and there is enough mutual trust to begin the effort. The structures have not been imposed top-down—although in the case of the special education collaboration, the special education teachers did have to seek out classroom teachers who were willing to work with them. They all were a little nervous about the change. By agreeing to attempt this together, however, they implicitly agreed to support each other. These separate collegial activities give participants the opportunity to work with a specific collaborative structure. In the case of the special education teaming effort, the teachers also planned to become part of a larger network of professional collaboration in their district.

Each instance of collaboration can work to sustain the interest of that group of teachers in a building and can add incrementally to eventually establishing a broader collaborative ethos in the school (Fullan & Stiegelbauer, 1991). If one of the foremost goals of collaboration is to professionalize teaching, initial, incremental efforts can contribute substantially to professionalization of the larger group, which in turn can provide leadership for subsequent schoolwide collaborative efforts.

Networks of teachers who come together to support various professional interests are important developmental activities in building collaborative schools. These more limited collaborations based on well-defined structures provide experience in collaboration for small groups of teachers. They also play a crucial role in contributing to the creation of a schoolwide ethos of collaboration by introducing new models for professional interaction for other teachers in the building who may never have conceptualized what real collaboration among teachers looks like.

If you've always gone about your work in relative isolation, if you've thought that sharing good ideas was enough in terms of professional interaction among teachers, if you've never worked toward a clearly defined mutual goal, chances are that you don't have a sense of what collaboration might look like. By having some teachers create new, collaborative models for working together, others can begin to get new mental images of how things can work differently. If these initial, isolated instances of collaboration meet with success, others might begin to view collaborative work in a more positive light. As we make the transition from isolated to collegial professional relationships, the success of these initial collaborative efforts is an extremely important development.

Efforts to transform schools into collaborative workplaces can take place on many levels, and the transition will not look the same in each school or in each district. Some schools might begin by identifying schoolwide goals. Others might let individual collaborative efforts—like those described here—be the catalysts for change. In either case, work in one mode should not preclude work in the other. Multiple collaborative activities can and should take place simultaneously.

A Worthy Challenge

Is making the shift to collaboration as a professional norm worth the effort? The position we take is a resounding "Yes!" This stance is not based on an abstract vision of collaboration. Rather, it emerges from our experiences over the past several years as participants in intensive collaborations for the purpose of reforming teacher education in urban schools. Driven by this goal, the work of each of our institutions has been energized by the collective efforts of its faculty members. The professional and personal satisfaction that results from being part of a successful team that begins to see the payoff for its collective work is extraordinary and energizing.

Some schools are already healthy collaborative environments in which to teach. In others, collaboration is not a widespread expectation. You will have to assess the situation in the school in which you work. Whether you are beginning your career as a education professional or thinking about renewing your commitment to it, collaboration provides the piece that often has been missing for those who work in schools—the collegial community of professionals who work together to support the complex work of teaching.

The challenge is not whether to collaborate. Instead, it is whether, as professionals, we have the collective will to maximize our capacity to meet the needs of the students in our schools and foster their success. This is the common goal for which collaboration is needed. Today's schools leave unmet the needs of too many students. The unrelated efforts of individual teachers, no matter how heroic, will not be enough to meet this challenge. We know more than ever before about the most effective approaches to curriculum and instruction. We can be confident of the potential and vast cultural capital of children of color, youth who live in poverty and students for whom English is not their first language. We know much more today than ever before about supporting students with disabilities. These developments no doubt advance our potential to improve education. To unleash the creative energies of teachers, to kindle the intellectual challenge for teachers as a means of renewing the educational system for all children, collaboration is indeed a worthy goal.

Remember . . .

1. Teaching is more than just working well with your students. It also means working well with your adult colleagues and the adult family members of your students.
2. Among the developments in education that have converged to make collaboration an essential part of a teacher's work are changes in authority structures, a greater teacher responsibility for the profession, changes in the demographic relationship between students and teachers, inclusion of students with disabilities, and more complex instruction.
3. Collaboration provides a way for adults who work in schools to form a community of learners who can grow professionally and improve the school.
4. Collaboration is more than just sharing ideas; it means working together to identify and reach mutually agreed-upon, schoolwide goals so education can be responsive to the diverse student population that schools serve.
5. Collaboration grows out of trust between professionals. It cannot be constructed artificially.

Activities

1. Think of a time when you worked with a group of your peers. Briefly describe the situation and decide whether your interactions were collaborative. Why or why not?

2. Think of a school in which you have worked, either for a field experience if you are a prospective teacher, or in a school where you have taught as a practicing teacher. How would you describe it in terms of being a collaborative workplace? Identify specific examples or nonexamples that support your viewpoint. What changes would have to be made for the school to become collaborative in nature?

3. Rate yourself on the five qualities of a collaborative professional discussed in this chapter. What activities could you name to assist people in developing these qualities as preparation for teaching?

4. Create a list of activities to assist teachers in developing an active, vibrant collaborative relationship with the community in which they teach. Discuss the importance of this issue in schools where teachers and students are from different cultural, ethnic, and socioeconomic groups.

5. Split up into small groups to prepare a mini-debate on the proposition, "A teacher's job is to help children learn, not to help other adults learn."

A Multidimensional Framework for Collaboration

ollaboration in schools means that all members of a school staff are working together and supporting one another to provide the highest quality of education to all the students they serve. Collaboration extends to working with others who have a stake in the school community. This book addresses the various dimensions of collaboration, which skills support collaborative practice in schools, and the context in which those skills are embedded in action in real schools. We have adopted a particular perspective on collaboration that frames our beliefs about the philosophy and practice of collaboration. But before we go any further in defining our own specific conception of collaboration—the conception that drives this book—we would like to give you the opportunity to consider what you think collaboration is and to identify some of the beliefs and biases you might bring to this discussion.

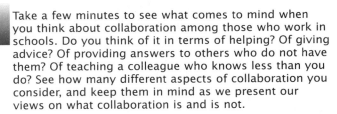
Take a few minutes to see what comes to mind when you think about collaboration among those who work in schools. Do you think of it in terms of helping? Of giving advice? Of providing answers to others who do not have them? Of teaching a colleague who knows less than you do? See how many different aspects of collaboration you consider, and keep them in mind as we present our views on what collaboration is and is not.

A Historical Perspective on Professional Collaboration

To understand the role of collaboration in the schools, we must understand the prevailing norms of professional interaction and also how collaboration has been dealt with in the past. Where has collaboration been practiced? To what degree of success? How are the norms associated with professional interaction in schools changing? This brief historical look at collaboration will serve as a backdrop against which we will introduce a guiding framework for thinking about collaboration throughout the book.

FROM ISOLATION TO INTERACTION

Although the word *collaboration* is part of the educational parlance today, historically teaching has been a highly isolated rather than a collaborative profession. In his landmark study of teacher socialization, Lortie (1975) identified the distinguishing organizational factor of schooling as "the persistence of separation and low task interdependence" (p. 15) in "egg-crate" schools. As long as teachers were not interdependent, what they did in their own classrooms did not affect their colleagues' work. With the exception of a brief and limited foray into team teaching during the late 1960s and early 1970s (Cohen, 1981), which never caught on nationwide, teaching until recently has been marked by the absence of collaboration. Not until major reform efforts that began in the 1980s did collaboration begin to be viewed as one of the critical goals of educational reform.

Consultation Model

In the fields of special education and school psychology, the history of collaboration has been a bit different. In the early 1970s, consultation started to be seen as a logical extension of the service delivery continuum for special education students. Until this point, resource rooms offering pull-out services had been the option that afforded the most interaction with general education. Although consultation had long been a feature of the services that school psychologists offered, its appearance in special education heralded the recognition that certain features of the general education environment often were problematic for students labeled as having disabilities. The purpose of shifting to a consultation model was to encourage special education teachers to provide training to general classroom teachers (Lilly, 1971). Therefore, consultation was designed as an *indirect service* to students. In this model, special education teachers began to work with classroom teachers, and the results of that work were thought to benefit students with disabilities in those general education classrooms.

The appearance of the consultation model definitely signified an increase in interaction between special and general education teachers. What soon became obvious, though, was that more often than not, these interactions were not actually collaborative. The early practice of consultation was based on the hierarchical notion that special education teachers and school psychologists had the answers to the problems that classroom teachers were describing. The solutions that were offered often reflected a one-sided view of how to help—namely, to adopt the behavioral methods used in special education. For example, the heavy use of extrinsic reinforcement often was seen as the only credible approach to solving behavioral problems that teachers might be encountering. Special educators and school psychologists began to be seen (and often saw themselves) as experts who brought a new set of solutions that, if followed, would make general education more like special education and thereby clear the way for students with disabilities to be successful in the general classroom.

This highly directive model, which over time became known as the *expert model of consultation*, was characterized by a one-way channel of communication in which the consultant provided the expertise to develop an implementation plan and the classroom teacher adopted it. Input from general education teachers typically was not sought because as a group they were not thought to possess adequate expertise to contribute to problem solving. No other option was considered, primarily because of the role of specialists in the school staff hierarchy, with classroom teachers traditionally at its lower end.

Collaborative Consultation

Throughout the late 1970s and 1980s, it became apparent that classroom teachers were not readily implementing the suggestions of their colleagues in special education and school psychology, and more and more special educators and school psychologists recognized the need for greater parity among specialists and general classroom teachers if consultation was to be effective (Idol, Paolucci-Whitcomb, & Nevin, 1986; Johnson, Pugach, & Hammitte, 1988; Pugach & Johnson, 1988b). This change was needed not only to promote ownership on the part of classroom teachers for whatever interventions were designed, but also to capitalize on the expertise of general education teachers.

As a result, the term *collaboration* began to be used to describe the need for more parity among participants in professional interactions. This eventually evolved into the term *collaborative consultation*, which for a time became the new, acceptable model of professional interaction, one in which specialists refrained from prescribing solutions hierarchically and instead worked as equal partners with classroom teachers. Increasingly, the concept of providing direct prescriptions to classroom teachers began to be seen as inappropriate precisely because it did not seem to fit the basic tenets of collaboration— namely, that teachers with different kinds of expertise come together as equals to solve problems, and that their joint efforts are more powerful than the efforts of either one in isolation.

 Stop for a minute to consider the various strengths that classroom teachers bring to a collaborative school. Special education teachers? Administrators? Make a list of strengths for each. How does each kind of expertise complement the other?

One other important idea introduced during this transitional period was that special education teachers might not always have to be present to solve the classroom problems that general education teachers were experiencing with students with disabilities. For many problems, classroom teachers themselves might have enough collective expertise to do the job (Chalfant, Pysh, & Moultrie, 1979; Pugach & Johnson, 1988a). This became an important consideration because, with the growing expectation that special education teachers would work with more and more students (those labeled as having disabilities and those without), it was inefficient as well as illogical to develop models of service delivery that would require the participation of special educators in every problem-solving interaction. To make good on the belief that classroom teachers did, in truth, possess valuable expertise to bring to bear on classroom problems, part of the collaboration trend had to acknowledge that expertise overtly. Simultaneously, others argued for a much more direct, prescriptive, and consultative approach by part of special educators and school psychologists (e.g., Fuchs, Fuchs, & Bahr, 1990). The majority, however, accepted what came to be called a collaborative form of consultation, in which highly prescriptive forms of problem solving were considered inappropriate forms of practice.

This period of argumentation dominated the last half of the decade of the 1980s. Today, the terms *consultation* and *collaboration* often are used interchangeably to describe the broad class of activities in which specialists work with classroom teachers to provide assistance. Because it evokes the expert model, however, the preference has shifted away from the term *consultation*. Today, what typifies the relationship between special and general education is a desire for collaborative interactions in which special education teachers and school psychologists refrain from providing expert advice to avoid being overly prescriptive and in which specialists and teachers work together to meet the needs not only of children who are formally labeled but also of all children in need of assistance.

Legislative Underpinnings

Recognizing the problems with conventional consultation was not the only thing that contributed to the shift in how the relationships between specialists and general education teachers came to be defined. In 1986, a landmark document issued by the Office of Special Education and Rehabilitative Services, which has since come to be known as the *regular education initiative* (REI) (Will, 1986), ushered in the shift from mainstreaming to a view of special education that promoted much more interaction between special education and classroom teachers. In this document, then OSERS Assistant Secretary Madeleine Will described the problems with the prevailing special education delivery system and supported the need to identify new, dynamic models of special education that would better serve those labeled as having disabilities and also children who were regarded as being at risk for school failure—most often students of color or of low socioeconomic classes who were (and often continue to be) poorly served by the education system. The appearance of this document signaled another level of support for the changes being advocated in the form and substance of a consultation model of special education service delivery and, in essence, marked the advent of inclusion as the new model for special education.

Between the appearance of the REI in 1986 and reauthorization of the Individuals with Disabilities Education Act (IDEA, Public Law 105–17) passed in 1997, collaboration flourished as a means of professional interaction. During this period, various approaches to collaboration competed with each other as special education professionals attempted to redefine their work in relationship to general education. This period of time was marked by heated arguments over the definitions of *consultation, collaboration,* and *collaborative consultation.* Those who favored a *consultation* approach generally saw the expertise of special educators as primary. Those who favored *collaboration* generally argued for more participation by general education teachers and serious acknowledgment of their professional expertise. Those who used the term *collaborative consultation* tried to walk a middle ground, acknowledging the expertise of special educators but encouraging them to be wary of holding their general education colleagues in lower esteem.

As a historical development in changing the way special education services are delivered, these arguments about the nature and purpose of collaboration probably were inevitable and helped to clarify the direction in which the field would finally go. With the passage of the 1997 IDEA amendments, collaboration became a virtual necessity to be able to carry out the mandates of the law, which strongly favor the general education classroom and the general education curriculum as the appropriate context for many students with disabilities. Special and general education teachers now must work together to create and sustain general education classrooms that are welcoming of students with a wide range of abilities and whose curriculum accommodates a much wider continuum of students.

Today collaboration no longer is a contested form of special education service delivery. Special education teachers collaborate with their general education colleagues without hesitation and as a regular part of their work, so much so that nearly every current introductory textbook in special education includes collaboration as a basic professional responsibility. Nevertheless, the specific practices of collaboration that are best suited to supporting the major goals of IDEA continue to evolve, particularly with regard to curriculum modification and accommodation—the newest and perhaps most challenging goals of IDEA (for a discussion of curriculum-centered collaboration, see Pugach & Warger, 1996; Warger & Pugach, 1993).

What these historical developments in defining collaboration illustrate is that in practical terms the relationship between teachers and specialists cannot be limited exclusively to one kind of interaction or another. Today *collaboration* is the umbrella covering a wide range of activities. Collaboration is not unidimensional but, rather, exists along a continuum that spans the range from teachers' developing solutions together to specialists' prescribing solutions in situations when unique expertise is clearly needed. Further, every collaborative interaction does not require a formal, step-by-step approach to problem solving. Collaboration is not synonymous with problem solving, although to be sure, problem solving is common in collaboration.

Different situations require different kinds of collegial interactions, and all professionals in a school should be prepared to engage in a multidimensional range of collaborative interactions in their work. When teachers collaborate, they are called upon at various times to support their colleagues, to help colleagues recognize their own problem-solving capacities, to provide expert information on a variety of issues, and sometimes even to suggest a specific path for a colleague to take. This is true for special and general education teachers alike. If collaboration is defined in this multidimensional manner, the specific characteristics of the situation for any given interaction determine which kind of collaboration will best fit an interaction. Until professionals in general and special education begin talking together about a specific situation, they are not likely to be able to predict which kind of collaborative interaction may be required.

COLLABORATION AS A SCHOOLWIDE COMMITMENT

The real promise of collaboration lies first in creating work environments in schools where an ethic of care (Noddings, 1992) is present among colleagues and dominates professional interactions to attain the goal of educating children and youth well. This ethic of care extends to developing common schoolwide goals for learning, for curriculum, and for instruction. One way of demonstrating this sense of caring and commitment is for adults to work together to meet the needs of the students they serve. Interactions that fall under the general practice of collaboration ought to emanate from a philosophical framework in which all professionals in a school are valued as having skills and expertise to contribute to the collaborative process, and thus, to their schools' success.

In contrast to how collaboration has been discussed in the special education literature, the literature on collaboration emerging from general school reform contains little discussion of which is more appropriate—to provide a colleague with a direct solution for a specific problem or to work together to develop a solution. Instead, talk in general education focuses on supporting continuous improvement for *everyone's* practice: teachers, administrators, teacher education students, specialists, and the students themselves. The assumption is that all teachers and staff members need to develop professionally and that everyone is a potential source of expertise on some subject and can contribute to schoolwide improvement. There are no preconceived prohibitions for what kinds of interactions are appropriate.

By taking a schoolwide, professional-development perspective, collaboration can be more broadly defined. Within this broader definition, the roles of professionals when they interact are not seen as absolute but, rather, are acceptable as long as they support the schoolwide goal of building effective relationships between the adults who work there for the purpose of fostering students' learning. Therefore, to prepare professionals for a single collaborative role seems to miss the point. Education professionals need to know how to shift from role to role depending on the situation they are addressing within the larger framework of schoolwide collaboration. And even within a given situation they might shift from role to role. Instead of worrying about whether they are permitted to give advice directly or to assist in problem solving, professionals need to feel comfortable moving back and forth among various forms of collaboration.

Once the focus of professional interaction shifts to developing a schoolwide norm of responsible mutual interaction, we can see how the term *consultation* seems too limited to describe how teachers and other school staff members work together in schools. In addition to the emphasis it places on a hierarchical approach to problem solving, this hierarchical approach itself devalues the classroom teacher's general education expertise. Further, using the term *consultation* seems to have led special educators and school psychologists in the wrong direction with its exclusive focus on individual interactions and rarely, if ever, on schoolwide goals on which professionals work together. Even the term *collaborative consultation*, while clearly promoting greater parity among participants, fails to capture the wider intentions of schoolwide collaboration and still places collaboration exclusively in the context of special education/school psychology—the education specializations from which the term arose in the first place. In a school setting, where classroom teachers, specialists, and administrators all bring a specific form of expertise to the table, the general term *collaboration* covers a broad spectrum of appropriate professional interactions and seems to be a more accurate descriptor of the dynamics that take place (or should take place) among all the stakeholders involved in a student's education.

An Example of Schoolwide Collaboration

East Central High School, in a large urban school district, is a multiracial school with students who are White, African American, Latino, and Asian. Teachers and administrators at East Central have been concerned that students enrolled in the Advanced Placement (AP) classes are primarily White and, to a lesser extent, Asian. White students make up 20 percent of the school's enrollment and 80 percent of all AP classes. Asian students, primarily Chinese and Japanese, make up 10 percent of the school and 15 percent of AP classes. African American and Latino students, who each make up 35 percent of total enrollment, are extremely underrepresented in these classes.

At the start of the fall semester, the teachers, administrators, and other staff members set a schoolwide goal of increasing the enrollment of African American and Latino students in AP classes beginning in the next school year. Together the entire staff constructed a plan of action to reach this goal. The following activities were planned and implemented to inform the school's collective consideration of the AP situation.

First, during the spring semester the principal and a group of teacher volunteers organized data on the representation of various groups of students in AP classes for the past 10 years. Next, a small group of teachers began conducting research into other high schools in the region and nationally that had successfully increased the representation of students of color in AP classes and identified two schools the team would visit before the end of the year. At the same time, teachers who instructed AP classes formed a group with other teachers to identify African American and Latino students who showed great academic promise but who were not yet prepared for AP classes. The teachers

Defining a Multidimensional Framework for Collaboration

In this book we have elected to adopt a multidimensional framework based on the term *collaboration* alone, primarily to honor the broad-based, multidimensional nature of professional interactions in schools and to stress the need for nesting the goals of special educators and school psychologists with also prepared a plan for academic support services during the summer to help the identified students gain the skills they would need to begin AP classes in the fall.

This group of teachers also communicated with the school's special education teacher to identify any students whom they might have overlooked in their considerations. At the same time, the principal began to consider whether more sections of AP classes might be needed in the future if the plan would result in the desired increase of students taking these classes. She also worked with another group of teachers to prepare a grant application to a local foundation for funds for the summer program they believed would be necessary this year to jumpstart their commitment to increasing the number of African American and Latino students in AP classes.

While these activities were taking place, the entire staff, at staff meetings throughout the spring, engaged in sustained dialogue with an external facilitator about expectations for African American and Latino students and how low expectations affect the issue of which students seek and are counseled into AP classes. The staff paid special attention to the counseling process and how guidance counselors might either make decisions based on their own low expectations or translate low expectations of classroom teachers into students' schedules.

At the start of the spring semester, the school was notified that it had received the grant to hold the special summer session. A team of teachers and guidance counselors began meeting with identified students and working with their families to discuss the summer program and fall AP classes. By the end of the spring term, 30 African American and Latino students had been identified and signed up for the summer program and were enrolled across the eight AP classes in the fall.

respect to collaboration within the larger educational community in which they work.

As we have indicated thus far, in collaborative schools people are committed to working together for school improvement. But how specifically shall we define "working together?" What are the different ways adults actually interact in schools in the broad context of collaboration that we described in Chapter 1? How do the various kinds of interactions relate to one another, if at all? As we have noted, suggestions from the general education reform literature are general with respect to collaboration. Although collaboration is held as an overriding goal for all professionals, it lacks specificity. The literature in special education/school psychology has moved toward a unidimensional interpretation of collaboration, favoring the joint solution of problems involving specialists and general education teachers.

A multidimensional framework for collaboration, in contrast, encompasses a broad range of professional interactions that take place among a collaborative staff in schools. In this framework professionals draw on and move between four basic roles when interacting with their peers—all of which represent appropriate dimensions of collaboration. The ultimate purpose of these four roles is to improve the practice of teaching to serve a wider range of students in all classrooms. The four roles that form the underlying framework we have adopted for schoolwide collaboration are (Johnson & Pugach, 1992):

1. Supportive role
2. Facilitative role
3. Informative role
4. Prescriptive role.

Within a multidimensional framework these fundamental roles make up the continuum of collaborative relationships. The nature of the relationship between any two individuals in a school will change depending on the situation in which they are collaborating. Further, the roles often overlap, and during a single meeting a teacher might draw on more than one of the dimensions of collaboration.

By creating a multidimensional framework, we are stressing the point that engaging in each of these forms of interaction is more than all right—it is natural in the course of a school year. Fundamental to this multidimensional framework is the principle that all education professionals who work in schools potentially act in any of these four roles depending on the situation. No one role is reserved for a given person by virtue of his or her title. And if any one of these dimensions is missing, the full potential of collaboration as a means of creating a school where students learn and learn well is not likely to be realized.

SUPPORTIVE DIMENSION

To maintain a healthy work environment in schools—which tend to be complex and often hectic places to be—one of the most important and fundamental dimensions of collaboration is support. The support function is defined conventionally as *caring and "being there" for colleagues professionally and often personally* to share in times of need and in times of joy. In a school that is striving to become a caring community of learners, support takes different forms.

Interpersonal Support

Interpersonal support is needed because, in schools as in all workplaces, many people work together and go through life experiences and life cycles together. Staffs show interpersonal support by celebrating together events such as marriages, births, and graduations. Staff members who are experiencing difficulties such as family deaths or divorces need support, too. Interpersonal support may be found in groups or it may be manifested between individuals. Interpersonal support represents a basic level of caring between staff members. This is the dimension of collaboration that we saw in our hypothetical sketch of Elm Elementary School in Chapter 1.

Interpersonal support also comes in recognition for work well done. Many schools seem to have a curious, often unspoken ethic against too much public recognition when, for example, a teacher has been cited for some kind of award or has participated in a professional presentation outside of school. Achievements ought to be celebrated in collaborative schools, primarily because these schools usually evidence professional growth and effort—precisely the kind of practices to which all education professionals ought to aspire.

Professional Support

Collaborative schools have a professional support function as well. Those who have taught school are aware that teachers have more challenging classes in some years than in others. Likewise, in some years a teacher might have one or two especially challenging students. In a collaborative school colleagues absolutely must support one another to get through tough situations. This might mean asking a colleague how things are going, agreeing to work with a targeted student as a guest in your own classroom from time to time, or stopping by the classroom when you have a free minute to provide a bit of relief.

Another form of professional support comes when a teacher or groups of teachers are trying out new methods of instruction or new conceptions of curriculum. For example, if a school is shifting to a fully integrated, thematic approach to teaching science, support is needed for people to share their instructional successes and to provide a place for teachers to air the problems they are facing as they struggle with new approaches. If a school is adopting a social justice curriculum to engage students in authentic problem solving, teachers need support to develop curricular units and instructional activities. This means devoting time to talking purposefully with one another about what has worked, what mutual problems can be identified, and what strategies might best meet students' needs.

Support for instructional or curricular innovation also might include participating in peer coaching as a means of providing specific feedback when teachers are attempting to use new instructional models. The history of special education consultation suggests that these conversations often have taken place only on a one-to-one basis, usually placing only one of the partners—the general education teacher—in the position of facing challenges as he or she attempts to implement a technique that a special education colleague has suggested. We are suggesting that those conversations ought to have a much larger context across colleagues in a school, and that all teachers should be challenged to improve their practice and learn new methods.

Still another form of professional support is in mentoring beginning teachers. New teachers often are given the most challenging classrooms but have the same responsibilities as experienced, veteran teachers. Sometimes mentoring relationships are formally established and are structured so that a beginning teacher is expected to work closely only with his or her mentor. In a collaborative school, however, beginning teachers should feel comfortable seeking out whatever sources of assistance they need.

For some professionals, giving support comes easily and intuitively. Others will have to learn how to provide it. Although it may seem like a fairly simple aspect of collaboration, providing support is a challenging role because it has to be given in ways that are genuine. The support function is not enough, though. Other situations demand that professionals draw upon different dimensions of collaboration.

FACILITATIVE DIMENSION

Colleagues take on the role of facilitators when they help their peers develop the capacity to solve problems, engage in tasks, or deal with professional challenges independently. As such, the facilitative dimension of collaboration is related to the concept of *scaffolded instruction* (Palincsar, 1986), in which those with more knowledge and skill support those who cannot yet function independently on that specific task. The facilitative dimension of collaboration is a growth dimension; it "nudges" teachers who may not realize they have the capacity to move forward. This is the dimension of collaboration that provides just enough modeling or demonstration to enable peers to master a new approach, to come up with a new solution, and to gain confidence in their own skills. Examples of the facilitative dimension are:

- *Demonstration.* When skilled peers demonstrate a specific methodology for a colleague, they are providing the opportunity for their colleague to see a new methodology in action and to model it.
- *Peer coaching.* One person provides feedback to another after observing that person as he or she implements a new methodology. This feedback enables a better understanding of how to improve the next lesson.

Finally, in peer collaboration (Johnson & Pugach, 1991), teachers who want assistance with a classroom-based problem work with colleagues whose role is to help them utilize all of the information and expertise they already have to develop and implement practical, creative solutions.

The facilitative role differs substantially from advice giving or support in that facilitation is directed specifically at assisting peers in developing their own skills to a greater extent than before. Suppose one of your colleagues wishes to implement cooperative learning and is experimenting with how to structure her classes according to those principles. You are well-trained in cooperative learning techniques and have much to offer. You might agree to demonstrate a cooperative learning lesson during one of your planning periods, or you might agree to review a videotape of your colleague's first try at using cooperative learning in the classroom. You also might agree to co-teach a lesson, taking the lead while your colleague works closely with you. To be sure, playing a facilitative role offers an important element of support. Acquiring the new teaching skill, strategy, or methodology, however, is what distinguishes this dimension of professional collaboration.

INFORMATION-GIVING DIMENSION

Within a collaborative school, teachers and other staff members provide information as a means of helping each other with challenging situations. The goal is to provide direct assistance to colleagues so they are better equipped to address new situations or pressing problems on an ongoing basis. As a dimension of collaboration, information-giving can take many forms. In one, a colleague might simply pass along knowledge of appropriate resources—for example, instructional materials or professional literature pertinent to a specific situation. A Black teacher who is familiar with the community in which an inner-city school is located might relate valuable information about the community to a White teacher who is new to the school and is unfamiliar with the community. A veteran teacher might describe what has worked in his or her own classroom.

Information-giving is a relatively direct form of collaboration, and the colleague who receives the information does not necessarily have to utilize it. The information-giving dimension of collaboration acknowledges the wide range of professionals in a school who have invaluable expertise to share. This expertise should not be foisted upon colleagues (a problem discussed in greater detail in Chapter Five) but, instead, should be tapped only when some kind of external knowledge or resource clearly is needed. Information-giving should be thought of as suggestions.

Perhaps one of the most beneficial aspects of information-giving is putting colleagues in touch with other professionals who might be able to assist them, or *networking*. As a form of collaboration, networking enables the iden-tification of human resources—both within the school and without—who can assist with specific issues. This means knowing who has what expertise within a school or community. The source of expertise might be other teachers, spe-cialists, family members, or community activists, to name a few.

Networking comes more easily to some teachers and school staffs than others. Successful networking requires professionals to include colleagues in networking activities and make sure they feel comfortable contacting people they may not have met. In some situations—for example, a low-incidence dis-ability or a serious mental health problem—a teacher might initiate a formal referral for assistance. In this situation, a collaborative colleague can help a peer access the appropriate assistance, whether it is within the school system or by connecting to an outside agency.

PRESCRIPTIVE DIMENSION

The fourth and final dimension of collaboration—prescribing a path of action to a colleague—is the most directive aspect. In the traditional hierarchical model of consultation dominant during the 1970s and the early 1980s, pre-scriptive approaches were considered the best way to ensure that special edu-cation methodology was transferred readily to general education classrooms and implemented by general education teachers. The predominance of this approach signaled a long period during which classroom teachers were viewed primarily as recipients of these prescriptions for practice, and not as having expertise themselves. This often led to teachers' not implementing the pre-scriptions they were given. The reason most often cited for this outcome was that the teacher did not have real ownership of the prescription.

Moving away from prescription as the dominant collaborative activity does not mean that it should be abandoned. In a multidimensional approach to collaboration, a certain methodology or practice might be "just right" for the situation you are encountering with a colleague. How do you know when to be prescriptive? Given the problematic experiences with prescriptive approaches in the past, an important rule of thumb is that dimensions of collaboration other than direct prescription are more likely to encourage teachers to take ownership of the changes they are trying to implement. When teachers are supported in their efforts to change what they are doing to better accommodate the range of students they teach, when colleagues facilitate their use of new methodologies, and when teachers can network with others who are attempt-ing the same changes or who have valuable information, significant change seems more probable than when someone simply tells them what to do. The rule of thumb, then, is to be ever attentive to the way teachers do change their teaching practice—namely, through day-to-day practice of new teaching methods and practices and feedback from skilled peers.

If a colleague has been trying in good faith to make the changes needed to accommodate the student population and requests direct assistance, prescription may be in order. Prescription also might be needed when a teacher is struggling with a new methodology and really needs assistance to get back on track after a setback. This might call for moving back and forth between prescription and facilitation to provide the most complete collaboration possible.

Putting Multidimensional Collaboration to Work

Although the four dimensions of collaboration have been presented separately here to point out their contrasting elements, in practice those who work in schools go back and forth among them rather than select one, use it in a pure form, and ignore the other three. Collaboration is based on building healthy working relationships for the purpose of promoting learning for children and youth in schools. Building relationships requires that all adults who work in a school engage in continuous collaboration for a variety of purposes related to this goal. Although not everyone engages in all forms of collaboration all of the time, each of the four dimensions has to be present if collaboration is to transcend the simple goal of making school a nice place for the adults who work there. The kind of support that collaboration offers must be accompanied by a clear set of schoolwide goals that make the investment in these multiple activities worthwhile.

Remember . . .

1. Collaboration is a multidimensional activity that combines supporting, facilitating, informing, and prescribing.
2. The four dimensions of collaboration usually are not used in their pure forms; teachers move back and forth among them in any given collaborative interaction.
3. Historically, collaboration was not part of the job of teaching.
4. Within special education and school psychology, a tradition of consultation has shifted from an expert model to a collaborative model.
5. Collaboration among school professionals is based on the philosophy that all professionals have something important to contribute to the collaborative process.

Activities

1. Reconsider the thoughts you had on collaboration when you began to read this chapter. Jot them down. Divide into small groups and discuss your original thoughts, compare them with your peers' ideas, and see how your thinking has shifted, if at all. Are the shifts important? Why?

2. Prepare a brief presentation on the benefits of a multidimensional approach to collaboration.

3. Describe a collaborative interaction you have observed or participated in. Was the interaction successful? Which of the four dimensions of collaboration came into play?

4. In each of four small groups, discuss one of the four dimensions of collaboration and create examples in writing. After 10 to 15 minutes of brainstorming, post, read, and then discuss the examples. Which rely on one of the four dimensions of collaboration exclusively and which rely on a combination?

The Basis for Collaboration: Communication Skills

3

Communication:
The Foundation
of Collaboration

I n Chapters 1 and 2 we provided a framework for thinking about collaboration from a multidimensional perspective. Essentially we presented collaboration as a way of being and not limited to isolated actions. Before we continue with this line of thought, we have to understand that certain foundational skills must be acquired to collaborate effectively. Perhaps the most important skill of effective collaborators is the ability to communicate ideas effectively. Communication is the foundation of all interactions between humans. Without the ability to communicate, our lives would be barren. Effective communication enables us to share experiences and establish a sense of unity with others (Hames & Joseph, 1986) and it is the sharing and sense of unity that define us as people.

In this chapter and in the following three chapters in this section, we present a communication model and explore verbal and nonverbal aspects, continuous feedback, practices that facilitate or inhibit communication, and group processing as it relates to collaboration.

Before you read on, consider the last time you had a conversation with someone with whom you felt you were not connecting. What aspects of this conversation led you to believe you weren't connecting? How could you have changed the way you participated in the conversation to feel more connected? When you read the next section, reflect on this conversation and ask yourself if part of the problem was a result of incomplete communication cycles.

The Communication Cycle

Communication is a deceptively simple process made up of four components: a sender, a channel, an environment, and a receiver. A communication cycle begins when the sender sends a message by some kind of channel through an environment (i.e., a setting) to a receiver of that message. In human relationships, the channel for these messages is typically auditory or visual. A verbal message consists of words, whereas a nonverbal message consists of things such as gestures, facial expression, and even pitch or tone of voice. Senders simultaneously send verbal and nonverbal messages through the environment to the receiver. The environment may be conducive to communication, or it may contain distracters that make communication difficult (e.g., noise). The receiver picks up the message through a combination of visual and auditory means and gains meaning by interpreting the combined visual and auditory message. The receiver then becomes a sender and provides direct or indirect, verbal or nonverbal, feedback to the original sender (who now becomes a receiver), which helps the original sender understand that the original message was understood. This cycle continues throughout the interaction, and through continuous feedback participants in the interaction communicate. Figure 3.1 illustrates the communication cycle.

When people send messages to their colleagues, they often believe they are communicating automatically, regardless of whether their colleagues

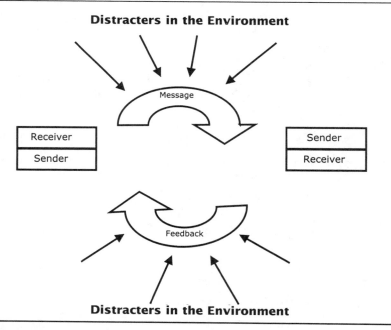

FIGURE 3.1   Communication Cycle

understand the message. This often leads to problems. Communication is a cyclical process that requires all individuals participating in the process to understand the message. Sending a message is not enough. The receiver must accurately understand the message. Often, two individuals engage in an interaction with little communication taking place.

Raul Alvarez, an 8th-grade science teacher, has been working hard to integrate Jason into his class. Jason receives special education services because of his behavior. Although he is bright, Jason is often belligerent and at times aggressive, which has often inhibited his learning. During science Jason had a blow-up and ran out of the class. Mr. Alvarez decides to call Ms. Jackson, Jason's mother, about Jason's behavior in class.

Mr. Alvarez:	*I'm sorry to have to bother you at home, but you asked that I call you if Jason had any problems in class.*
Ms. Jackson:	*Don't be silly. I'm glad you called. I've been having trouble with Jason's behavior myself lately.*
Mr. Alvarez:	*Today in class Jason got upset with one of the students and shoved him, knocking over some expensive equipment.*
Ms. Jackson:	*I'm also upset with Jason. Last night he yelled at his sister during dinner for no apparent reason. I just don't know what to do with him when he gets like that.*
Mr. Alvarez:	*This isn't the first time that something like this has happened, and if we can't get this under control, we may have to reassess his placement in my class.*
Ms. Jackson:	*I know just what you mean. He yells at his sister or me all the time and I don't know why he gets angry so easily.*
Mr. Alvarez:	*Ms. Jackson, I appreciate the your willingness to talk to me about my concern with Jason's behavior in class. Maybe we can get together to develop some kind of plan.*
Ms. Jackson:	*No problem. Any time you want to talk, just give me a call.*

On the surface, this seems to be a positive interaction, but in reality the two parties are not communicating. Mr. Alvarez is talking about Jason's behavior in school, and Ms. Jackson is talking about his behavior at home. They are engaged in a parallel conversation with little understanding of each other's messages. As a result, they are talking but not communicating. The effectiveness of communication between individuals is determined by the extent to which the sender and the receiver have the same understanding of the message being sent.

By engaging in continuous feedback, individuals exchange information and modify messages or clarify misunderstood messages. Continuous feedback is a process by which individuals constantly receive feedback about how their messages are being received. For example, when we speak, we hear ourselves talking. As a result, we hear what we're saying and, more important, how we're saying it. We can determine if our verbal and visual messages are consistent with our intentions and we must judge whether the tone and intonation of the message we are sending matches our intended message. In addition to hearing ourselves, we pick up subtle reactions from the receiver, such as nods, a raised eyebrow, a frown, and the like. All of these actions on the part of the receiver indicate that our message is being received in the way we had intended. A frown, a look of disgust, or a smile can be an indicator that we need to change our message in some way or that our message is not being understood.

The feedback we receive is both direct and indirect. When receivers demonstrate by their actions that they have understood the message, the feedback is characterized as direct. Consider the following example.

Terry is a school psychologist and Jim is a classroom teacher. They have scheduled a meeting with Mr. Jackson to talk about a home-management plan. They run into each other in the hall and the following interaction occurs:

Terry: Jim, do you know what time we'll meet with Mr. Jackson?"

Jim: On Tuesday at four o'clock.

In this example, Jim's verbal response or *direct feedback* to Terry clearly indicates that he understands the message being sent. Direct feedback also can be provided through nonverbal means. Consider the following example:

Tara is excited about Ian's birthday and is sitting at the breakfast table talking to her mother about his gift. All of a sudden, her mom squints her eyes and gives Tara a stern look. Tara immediately stops talking. Just at that moment, Ian comes into the room.

Tara's mother sends a nonverbal message—a stern look—indicating that Tara should stop talking. Tara's actions provide direct feedback indicating that she understands the message.

Indirect feedback, in contrast, is the case when the receiver indicates that he or she is aware that a message has been sent but that the message is not well understood. Consider the following example:

While sitting in the teacher's lounge at lunch, two third-grade teachers had this exchange:

Tom: *Sue, would you please pass the ketchup?*
Sue: *(looking at Tom, puzzled) Huh?*

Sue's question to Tom provides indirect feedback that she does not understand his message and needs clarification. Even in this brief response, she indicates clearly that she doesn't understand what Tom said. The problem may be that she is not paying attention or is thinking of something else. Indirect feedback can come without a great deal of verbal exchange.

Tom: *Sue, would you please pass the ketchup?*
Sue: *(Looking at Tom, puzzled) Huh?*
Tom: *I said, 'Please pass the ketchup.'*
Sue: *(Hands him the mustard).*

This time Sue's actions clearly indicate that she is aware that a message was sent. Equally clear, however, is that she does not understand the message. Obviously, Tom and Sue do not have the same understanding of the message, and Tom is going to have to send his message in a different way to complete the communication cycle. When someone is having trouble understanding your message, a good strategy is to change how you are sending the message.

Kate and Shauna are both second-grade teachers, and their classes join together for certain activities. In preparation for the upcoming meeting with Molly's parents, Kate and Shauna are talking about some of Molly's strengths.

Kate: *One aspect we should emphasize is Molly's ability to share with the other kids during reading.*
Shauna: *You think Molly shares well? I always thought she was a little possessive with her things.*
Kate: *No that's not what I mean—I was referring to her ability to share during reading.*
Shauna: *Now I'm really confused. If you don't mean sharing her things, what kind of sharing do you mean?*
Kate: *I'm referring to the way she shares! You know how she shares from the stories she reads!*

The problem in this interaction is that when Kate realizes that Shauna is confused, she repeats essentially the same phrase that caused the confusion ("her ability to share") in an attempt to clarify the misunderstanding. As one might expect, repeating the phrase that caused the confusion typically just intensifies the receiver's confusion. Rather than clarifying the miscommunication, the two individuals may become frustrated, further inhibiting communication. A better strategy is to send the message using different words or emphasis.

> *Kate:* One aspect we should emphasize is Molly's ability to share with the other kids during reading.
>
> *Shauna:* You think Molly shares well? I always thought she was a little possessive with her things.
>
> *Kate:* No that's not what I mean—I was referring to her ability to relate key ideas from stories.
>
> *Shauna:* Oh, yes! She can be very insightful.

This is a more efficient interaction that avoids needless confusion. The receiver can ask the sender to say the statement or question in another way because the receiver is having trouble understanding the intent of the message. This is a powerful technique that can help clarify a confusing message quickly. Let's return to the first example and see how Shauna could have used this technique to help Kate provide a clear message.

> *Kate:* One aspect we should emphasize is Molly's ability to share with the other kids during reading.
>
> *Shauna:* You think Molly shares well? I always thought she was a little possessive with her things.
>
> *Kate:* No that's not what I mean—I was referring to her ability to share during reading.
>
> *Shauna:* Now I'm really confused. If you don't mean sharing her things, I don't understand what you mean. Can you say it another way?
>
> *Kate:* I think we should emphasize how Molly is able to relate her interpretations of stories and ideas to her peers.

Asking colleagues to repeat the message in another way forces them to think through the essential ideas of the message and other words that will convey its meaning. In this way, the receiver hears the message with different words than those that initially were misunderstood. As a result, the confusion can be bypassed and the communication cycle can be closed.

Finally, the messages we send pass through an environment. Often this environment is noisy and includes other messages that can complete and interfere with the receiver's understanding of the message. The framework of the environment also can have an effect. For example, if two teachers are in the lounge talking about a student of one of the teachers and a third teacher is also sitting in the lounge, the way messages are sent and received is likely to be different than if the two were alone. Carrying this further, the same message spoken in a classroom with other students around would take on a third form.

Distracters in the environment can be intense or mild. The intensity of the distracter is proportional to its inhibiting impact on the communication. Noise, for example, is an obvious distracter. All of us have experienced the futility of trying to talk over a loud band. Many other distracters are more subtle, such as accents, voice tone, other conversations in the room, other activities in the room, the temperature or room comfort, and even the appearance of the room.

The way the sender constructs and sends the message can serve as a distracter as well. If the speaker uses sentences of great length, the complexity of the structure can confuse the listener and prevent him or her from interpreting the meaning accurately. If the sender speaks too quickly or interprets the same word or words differently than the receiver does, confusion can be the result. Finally, if words are used in an inappropriate context, they can inhibit the listener's understanding. In a similar way, being unaware of body language and how it can inhibit or enhance the message being sent is problematic as well.

VERBAL COMMUNICATION

Verbal communication is transmitted through an arbitrary set of codes that we call language. These arbitrary sets of codes are agreed upon by people that use those codes. Generally, it is accepted that language is made up of four components: phonology, syntax, semantics, and pragmatics.

Phonology

Phonology refers to the variety of individual sounds that comprise our language. The word *pet*, for example, is made up of three sounds or *phonemes:* the consonant *p*, the vowel sound *e*, and the consonant *t*. Based on regional dialects and different accents, these sounds can be slightly different. As long as the sounds have sufficient similarity, however, the sender and the receiver recognize them as the same and the word is recognizable. At times, though, dialects can inhibit our ability to communicate.

Syntax

The rules of the language for how words go together are called syntax. These rules are arbitrary and again, they are agreed upon by the users of the language. These rules include parts of speech, grammar, and sentence structure. Each language has its own set of syntactical rules that allow for a wide variety of meanings. When we make grammatical errors or use long, complex sentence structures, we can inhibit our ability to communicate our ideas.

Semantics

The meaning of words and their connection to the arbitrary set of symbols and sounds that make up words is called semantics. To communicate effectively, both the sender and the receiver must have a common understanding of the words being used. Words have both a *denotation* definition, which can be thought of as the dictionary definition, and a *connotation* definition, which is the implied meaning of the word from context. How the word is used in a sentence, the body language of the person using the word, and the sentences that precede and follow the word are all indicators of the intended meaning of the word.

Semantics is an area of particular concern to individuals who are trying to collaborate with their colleagues. We must have a common understanding of the words we use. Education is full of jargon. We talk about linkages, networking, and integration, to name just a few. Typically, all of us have a slightly different meaning for these words. We cannot assume that we all have the same understanding; rather, we must check each other's understanding to be sure that we are on the same wavelength.

Pragmatics

How language is used in different environments and contexts is called pragmatics. We all have expectations for communicating in certain environments. For example, people watching a football game together appropriately hoot, holler, and scream. Watching a tennis match, in contrast, requires a whole different set of behaviors.

Those who interact inappropriately for the environment send a confused message. Someone screaming at a tennis match to show support for a player will bring the ire of the referee, the players, and other spectators. An individual watching an exciting football game quietly and calmly may be thought to be unengaged and uncaring about the outcome. These same kinds of roles can affect the way we interact in collaborative relationships. Saying to your partner something unexpected and inappropriate for the circumstances can inhibit communication and understanding.

NONVERBAL COMMUNICATION

Nonverbal communication is extremely powerful. Often the nonverbal messages we send are a more accurate representation of our actual intent than what we actually say. We all know people who say they are fine while frowning and sighing. Their whole body and orientation indicate that they are not at all fine. Although nonverbal messages can be confusing, nonverbal language often is what imparts real understanding of the intended message. Like verbal communication, nonverbal communication has several components. These have been defined in different ways, but we have organized them into three components: physical, temporal, and surroundings.

Physical

The speaker's age, physical condition, and vocal inflection add to our understanding of the message. For example, when a teacher says to students, "Would you please be quiet?" they usually understand that this is not a question. It is a command. In a similar fashion, the way we respond to our colleagues can send a very different message from what we intended. The distance between individuals in the interaction also has an impact on the interaction. Generally, the more informal and intimate the interaction, the smaller the *distance zone*. When we violate someone's distance zone, we make that person uncomfortable and can communicate lack of respect toward his or her own needs.

Our physical posture when interacting also sends an important message to the receiver. Maintaining eye contact and an open stance while leaning forward slightly communicates to listeners that you are attending to them. Looking at your watch, not making eye contact, sitting back away from the individual with your eyes forward, and other disengaged behaviors can communicate that you are not interested in what the person is saying.

Temporal

Temporal factors relate to the amount of time we are willing to spend with a person. Time is an interesting factor, and how we spend it on one another can communicate powerful expectations. If people are always left waiting for you to come to meetings, for example, you are communicating that your time is more valuable than their time is. Similarly, the amount of time scheduled for an interaction indicates the importance placed on that interaction. The shorter the time, the less important is the interaction.

This is an important message to keep in mind when scheduling meetings with teachers or family members. For example, because of time constraints, schools commonly schedule conferences with parents or family members at 15-minute intervals, which may communicate—despite school rhetoric that parental and family input is important—that these meetings are unimportant to the professionals at the school. When scheduling important meetings, participants must be on time, and plenty of time must be allotted for the meeting.

Surroundings

The setting in which an interaction takes place and the appearance we bring to an interaction are also important. A meeting held in a classroom with bolted-down desks and attached seats makes open communication between participants difficult. On the other hand, desks that are easily moved to form a circle help to facilitate communication. Further, uncomfortable surroundings can inhibit communication because individuals can become distracted by their discomfort. A room with poor acoustics or plagued by noise can have a similar negative impact on communication.

Finally, clothes can indicate difference in status. An individual who "dresses down" communicates a very different status than someone who wears formal dress, which may imply that he or she is in authority.

 Before you read about congruent and incongruent messages, think about the last time that you had an emotion you wanted to keep secret. Were you able to keep it secret? Did some people see through your facade, or were you able to fool everyone? If people found out about your secret, what part of your behavior gave you away?

Congruent and Incongruent Messages

Our messages are rarely single-channeled (Molyneaux & Lane, 1982), and most messages come across in multiple ways. While we are talking, we also are sending a whole series of nonverbal messages. A multidimensional message can improve understanding if the various dimensions are congruent—if the facial expressions, the body, the verbal and nonverbal messages are essentially communicating the same idea. Conversely, when the verbal and nonverbal messages are communicating different ideas, the overall message can be confusing.

Jack walks into the office to check his mailbox and has the following interaction with June, the school secretary.

Jack: *Hey, June!... How was your weekend?*
June: *(With a deep frown and a slight sigh) Great.*

Although her verbal message indicates that her weekend was great, June's nonverbal message clearly reveals that her weekend was anything but great. Incongruent messages can confuse the receiver because the receiver then must decide which of these two messages is the most accurate. On the other hand, if June had responded to Jack's question with a congruent message, he would have little doubt about the message being sent.

Jack:	*Hey, June!... How was your weekend?*
June:	*(A big smile comes across her face and her eyes light up) Great.*

This message is much clearer because the verbal and nonverbal messages are consistent. When the verbal and nonverbal messages being sent are consistent, the combined message is congruent. When the verbal and nonverbal messages disagree, the combined message is incongruent.

Congruent messages are much clearer and more easily understood than incongruent messages. Participants do not have to sort out the differences between verbal and nonverbal messages and then make decisions as to which is most accurate. Conversely, incongruent messages are made up of different verbal and nonverbal messages that can be confusing and are ripe for misinterpretation.

Typically, our nonverbal behavior supplements and augments what we say verbally. When nonverbal and verbal messages are congruent, the nonverbal message enhances and facilitates understanding. When the verbal and nonverbal messages are incongruent or different, the nonverbal message typically provides more insight. As a result, if a speaker is sending an incongruent message, the receiver should look to the nonverbal message to gain understanding. Nonverbal aspects of our behavior are under less conscious control than the verbal aspects. Sometimes we are unaware of the nonverbal messages we are sending. Therefore, astute listeners listen not only with their ears but also with their eyes. Pointing out the inconsistency to the person sending the message and asking for some clarification may be helpful.

A word of caution is in order. When individuals from different cultures are interacting with one another, they may try to use nonverbal aspects of behavior that their own culture does not use. Therefore "typical" interpretations of nonverbal aspects of behavior from individuals engaging in crosscultural communication can be misleading. We must be extremely sensitive to cultural differences and not make assumptions about expected behavior.

Communication for Collaboration

Communication is the foundation upon which effective collaboration is built. Good communication skills are a prerequisite for collaboration. If we cannot communicate effectively with our colleagues and others, a collaborative relationship is not possible. Communication involves a sender, a message, and a receiver. In Chapters 4 and 5 we will provide specific suggestions regarding skills to facilitate communication and obstacles that can inhibit communication.

Remember . . .

1. Communication is a cyclical process that involves a sender, a message, and a receiver.
2. For the cycle to be complete, a sender must send a message and a receiver must provide feedback to the sender indicating that the message was understood accurately. This feedback can be direct or indirect.
3. Messages are transmitted through verbal and nonverbal means.
4. The environment or setting can introduce distracters that impede the understanding of messages and the communication process.
5. When verbal and nonverbal messages are not in agreement, the message is incongruent. When messages are mixed, the nonverbal message tends to be most reflective of the true message.

Activities

1. Using a brief case study of a child, engage in the following activity with four or more individuals. One person reads the case study silently and whispers it from memory to another member of the group. Each group member, in turn, then whispers the key components of the case study to another member of the group. The last member of the group relays the case study aloud. Then the first member of the group reads the case study. Discuss differences between the key components in the original case study and those in the case study finally read aloud. Discuss factors that contributed to the differences. In particular, focus on the absence of feedback in reaching the outcome of this activity.
2. Keep a list of all of the incongruent messages students receive over the next week. Discuss these lists in class and generate an overall list. Describe the situation and the clues that suggest the communication was incongruent.
3. Select five or more pictures from magazines or other sources that depict clear emotions. Write down the emotion being expressed. After all the group members show their pictures, discuss the emotions that each of the pictures depicts. Discuss differences and similarities in interpretations of emotions. Describe aspects of the pictures that led them to their interpretation.

4

Skills to Facilitate Effective Communication

D eveloping good listening skills is a key step toward collaborating with colleagues and families. Listening skills will help you clarify and understand the messages that are being sent to you. When you are first learning these skills, they likely will seem artificial. As you use these active listening skills, though, they will become more comfortable to you and you will incorporate them into your repertoire of communication. But they can be learned only through practice. Through this practice you will develop your own style of communication and natural ways to utilize active listening skills to enhance the understanding of others.

In this chapter we identify active listening skills that can help you understand the messages a speaker sends to you. To be a successful collaborating professional, you must understand the intent of those with whom you interact. The skills covered in this chapter include offering support, general openings, reflecting, stating the implied, clarifying, silence, placing the event in time or sequence, and summarizing. The chapter concludes with suggestions about ways to develop your own communication style so you can include these skills as part of your natural style of communication.

Think about the an individual you consider to be a good listener. Visualize the last time that you had a conversation with this person. What aspects of this individual's behavior contributes to his or her skills as a listener? Is it body position and eye contact? Is it how he or she responds to what you are saying? Is it a combination of nonverbal and verbal language? As you read this chapter reflect on the actions of the individuals you have selected as good listeners and see if you can identify which practices they have incorporated into their repertoire of communication skills.

Offering Support

Offering support means indicating to colleagues that you are there to listen and try to help them work through their concerns. Letting colleagues know that you are ready to help and will make time for them is an important message in itself and indicates that you are supportive. Clear expectations, however, must be established with regard to an appropriate time and place for collaborative interactions. For example, the teacher's lounge with a lot of teachers around the table may not be the best time to discuss a student's problem; nor is it appropriate to discuss the problem in the hallway when other children might be around.

Time to talk is equally important. Sometimes colleagues begin engaging in a collaborative dialogue when they clearly do not have enough time to finish the discussion. A better strategy is to let your colleague know that you have an engagement in a few minutes and to suggest a time when both of you would be available for a longer time. For example, if you have classroom responsibilities and only 10 minutes before the children return, you don't want to begin a collaborative problem-solving session. If you find yourself in this situation, you might listen a while and before things go too far, say, "I think this is an important problem, and I'm glad you came to talk to me, but I have students coming in five minutes. Is there a time when you and I can get together and continue to talk about this more?" In this way, you indicate to colleagues that you care about them and that you will make the time to engage in a serious discussion. Colleagues can easily recognize why this isn't the most appropriate time. If, on the other hand, you try to rush to try to get the conversation completed before the bell rings, your colleague may interpret the interaction to mean that you don't care and are not willing to spend the time to help.

You and the school psychologist have an IEP meeting in 15 minutes. Sandy, with whom you have been working to develop a behavior management plan for Jack, stops by before the meeting. Sandy comes in to tell you about an idea she has. You and Sandy talk for about 5 minutes. It becomes clear to you that this is a complex intervention and that it is going to require some careful discussion to identify possible pitfalls. Rather than rushing Sandy or supporting her artificially by telling her that it sounds like a great idea before you have had a chance to think through all the options, you should find a way to (a) indicate your interest, (b) explain why now is not a good time for a discussion, and (c) settle on a better time to meet. You might say the following:

> *You:* Sandy, on the surface this sounds like a great idea,
> but I just want to make sure you've got the time to
> do this and you can use Evelyn to help you put the
> plan into place. But I have to go to an IEP meeting
> in five minutes. What if I meet you in the morning
> and bring in coffee and doughnuts, and we can think
> this through when we're both fresh?
>
> *Sandy:* Sure. Sounds great. Make sure you get French
> crullers—you know those are my favorite!

In this scenario, Sandy is asking you for your opinion about what you are planning to do. You might have given her quick, and perhaps careless, feedback. If the plan didn't work, careless feedback could have hindered your relationship later on. It is important to be honest about immediate limitations on your time and not try to rush the situation. Equally important is for you to show up the next day. If you don't, you will communicate to Sandy that you really don't care or have the time for her. We must recognize that we cannot be available 24 hours a day to help others sort through problems. We must be honest when we don't have the time to interact.

General Openings

When first engaging in collaborative dialogue, the communicators should avoid getting too specific too soon. Statements such as, "Let's talk—tell me a little bit more about yesterday" or, "How are things going?" are broad statements that allow a colleague the opportunity to begin focusing on the issues and to begin defining problems. Subtle differences in the way you start the communication can create either a sense of openness or a sense of enclosure.

> *June is a first-year teacher who has just completed her first
> month of school. She has a difficult and challenging class and
> is trying to work on management skills. You have been asked
> to serve as an in-house mentor to her. As you enter her class-
> room, you notice that she is staring out the window and it
> looks as if she has been crying. Consider the following four
> opening statements.*
>
> *Response 1:* June, why are you so upset?
>
> *Response 2:* Oh, June, don't worry about your students' act-
> ing up. We all have trouble our first year. It will
> get a lot better.

Response 3:   *(Seeing that June is upset, you decide to put on*
                 a good face and pretend you don't notice.)
                 "Hey, June, let's get some grub."
Response 4:   Hi, June. How are things going?

Response 1 is far too specific and can make June defensive. First, June may not want to discuss the fact that she seems upset. It might even upset her more that it is so obvious to you that she is upset. Being so direct with her can make her uncomfortable and make it unlikely that she will provide you with information to better understand what is wrong. Without understanding why she is so upset, you are likely to make her withdraw rather than open up. This is an inappropriate opening statement.

Response 2 makes a critical assumption that may or may not be true. The assumption is that June is upset because her students are acting up. Although this may be a plausible assumption, many other factors may be contributing to why June is upset. This initial assumption could be unwarranted and derail the communication. In addition, it provides false reassurance that things will get better when in reality things don't always get better by themselves. Sometimes we need to work hard on changing activities or instruction. False reassurances can hinder the process.

Response 3 could be a successful response depending on what follows this opening. At times it is better not to address a problem or a concern, thereby providing your colleague with some "space." This kind of approach also may provide an opportunity for your colleague to make the first move and indicate that there is a concern about which he or she would like to talk. Your colleague, however, most likely is aware that you sense something is wrong but have chosen not to voice your concern. If this becomes an interactional pattern, you and your colleague are not likely to become effective collaborators.

Response 4 is the most appropriate. It is broad enough to provide an avenue for June to begin talking about what is happening in the classroom. It does not provide false reassurances, nor does it directly move to the emotions that June may be uncomfortable addressing. This response allows June to set the stage for the discussion and gain greater understanding.

Reflecting

Reflection is a technique in which the receiver restates key information the sender has sent for the purpose of gaining clarity. This enhances the receiver's understanding of the message and provides the sender with the opportunity to reflect on the received interpretation and modify the message to be consistent with the sender's intent. Key information must be paraphrased and communicated back to the sender. In this way, the sender gets a clearer understanding of the problem and the message he or she is sending to the receiver about the problem. This is a critical dynamic because reflection clarifies the message for the receiver and also provides an opportunity for the sender to reflect on the problem and better understand critical factors related to it.

Typically, individuals beginning to use active listening skills have little trouble incorporating reflection into their repertoires. Incorporating reflection in a natural way, however, is difficult and requires practice. Taking two or three key phrases from the previous statement and restating them to your colleagues is easy, but this often results in a stilted form of conversation. Although reflection is a powerful tool, it should be used sparingly because it can create a sense of phoniness when overused.

Cory and Tom are close friends and have taught fifth grade for the past 4 years. They do a lot of planning together and often share ideas and frustrations. Tom is grading papers after school one day when Cory walks in, obviously upset over something.

Cory:	*I'm so upset. My lesson fell flat on its face.*
Tom:	*You're upset.*
Cory:	*Yes. I thought this would be a great lesson.*
Tom:	*You thought you had planned well.*
Cory:	*Yes. I spent a lot of time in this lesson. I'm not sure what happened.*

In this example, Tom is using reflection for the dual purpose previously described. First, he is helping Cory gain understanding of his intended message and the problem that is bothering him. At the same time, Tom is identifying key words within each sentence and feeding those back to Cory to make sure that the interpretation he is obtaining from the message is the same as the intended message. Note that Tom's first reflection is a direct paraphrase of words Cory said and provides the opportunity for Cory to go into more depth as to why she is upset. In the second reflection, Cory restates the implied meaning of her statement and the conversation further. Now consider another example.

Sarah and Binh are first-grade teachers serving on the districtwide curriculum committee to pick a new reading series. The two have agreed to meet to discuss some unique concerns of the primary grades. Before they can get down to business, however, Sarah is upset and Binh tries to help her find out why.

Sarah:	I've had it with these kids! Every time I go back to the reading group, the kids act out and do nothing. I don't care how hard I try, they're always disruptive.
Binh:	You're upset with the children.
Sarah:	Yes, I'm upset with the children. They don't listen to me. They act out and they don't value the time I spend preparing for these lessons.
Binh:	The children don't value the time you spend.
Sarah:	Yes! I told you I'm upset with them. These kids just don't listen.

In this example, Binh is paraphrasing only a surface level of the conversation and not the key intent. The first reflection, although not particularly deep, could have been appropriate if Binh had followed with a reflection that helped move Sarah's understanding of the problem farther. Both of the reflections, however, focus on the message that Sarah is upset. That message is clear, and the second reflection only serves to exasperate Sarah. Even though Binh has good intentions, he probably is making the situation worse. Focusing on factors that contributed to Sarah being upset would have been more helpful.

José and Chelsea are third and fourth grade teachers, respectively. They often combine their classes and team-teach. José has asked Chelsea if she would meet with him to discuss some problems he was having with Danielle.

José:	I don't know what to do with Danielle. She seems so bored in class. No matter what I give her to do, it just doesn't seem like she's interested in what's going on.
Chelsea:	She seems bored?
José:	Yes. The other day I did a story on dinosaurs. All kids like dinosaurs. It seems like she just doesn't get into it. I'm not sure what else to do. I don't think Danielle is ever going to learn anything.
Chelsea:	Danielle can't learn?
José:	Well, it sure seems that way. I spend extra time with her. I give her feedback. I try to reinforce her. I just don't know what to do.
Chelsea:	So you spend extra time?
José:	Yes. At the end of each lesson, I try to call her up to my desk and go over the information that she is supposed to do on her own. But it doesn't seem to help.

The first time that Chelsea reflects on José's messages, she is generally indicating that she's interested in listening but hasn't really helped José to clarify his conversation. In the second instance, Chelsea picks a specific aspect of what José said to follow up. By picking a specific phrase, Chelsea is beginning to focus the conversation. José then goes on to indicate his frustration with the situation. Chelsea could have chosen to follow up on José's frustration by saying, "You seem frustrated." This would have been an equally good response and might have helped José to focus on his frustration. Chelsea, however, chose to focus on the child and reflect José's frustration by saying, "Danielle can't learn?" This gives José an opportunity to begin to discuss what he's tried with Danielle to get her to learn. When Chelsea focuses on the brief phrase, "You spend extra time," José goes into greater detail. Chelsea has successfully moved José from indicating some general frustration to talking about strategies that he has tried and why they may or may not have been effective. This is a good use of reflection that helps José to narrow down what he is trying to communicate to Chelsea and begin to reflect on things he has tried.

After reading the descriptions of these practices and the corresponding examples, think about your own interaction style. Are any of these practices in your current repertoire of interacting? Do some practices seem more natural than others? Do you think these practices would be effective if they were applied artificially? What steps can you take to incorporate some of these practices into your repertoire of interacting?

Stating the Implied

One method to move the conversation along is to state the implied. This technique is particularly effective when it is used with reflection because it can help make the conversation feel more natural. With this technique, rather than stating exactly what has been said, the receiver verbalizes what he or she understands as the underlying message being sent. This provides the sender with an opportunity to concur or to further refine the message. Although reflection and verbalization of the implied are similar skills, there are key differences between them.

It's before school on a brisk November day, and Carlos decides to go into the teacher's lounge to get a cup of coffee before the students come. When he enters, he sees Rebecca sitting at a table by herself looking obviously disappointed.

Carlos fills his coffee cup and goes over to sit by Rebecca.
They engage in conversation.

Carlos:	*Hey, Rebecca, what's up?*
Rebecca:	*Oh, not much.*
Carlos :	*Come on, you don't seem like yourself. What's the deal?*
Rebecca :	*Oh, I don't know. Sometimes I wonder if teaching is all it's cut out to be.*
Carlos :	*Teaching all it's cut out to be? That seems a little dramatic.*
Rebecca :	*Perhaps it's just Monday blues or . . . I don't know.*
Carlos :	*This seems like a little more than Monday blues to me. I haven't seen you this down since you missed that shopping trip to New York.*
Rebecca :	*Well, it's Ian. I thought I'd really made progress. He seemed to be getting his work done. He seemed to be getting his assignments in and really changing his whole attitude about school.*
Carlos :	*So you're concerned about Ian.*
Rebecca:	*Well, yes, I'm concerned . . . but . . . no, I've been really discouraged. I thought with all the hard work we do, he would get a passing grade in social studies. But I just talked to his social studies teacher and he's not getting a passing grade.*

It was clear to Carlos that Rebecca was upset. Rather than reflecting Rebecca's words, Carlos verbalized the messages he was receiving from Rebecca's body language and gave her the chance to clarify if this secondary message was accurate. For example, when Rebecca indicated that "perhaps it's just Monday blues . . . ," Carlos could have used reflection and said, "So you think it's just Monday blues?" but this would have been inefficient, and Carlos's choice to verbalize the implied moved the conversation to the source of the concern quickly.

What also should be clear from this example is that Rebecca and Carlos had a friendship and a rapport that allowed Carlos to probe into Rebecca's feelings in the way he did. Verbalizing implied messages can be threatening when two individuals have not established rapport. On the other hand, when Carlos verbalized the messages he was receiving through nonverbal channels, he was able to get Rebecca to talk about her real concern: the amount of time she had put in working with Ian and Ian's apparent setback in social studies. Reflection probably would not have resulted in the same outcome.

Clarifying

When engaged in a collaborative dialogue, you will seek clarification at times to gain understanding of the information being sent to you. When you become confused about what you are being told, you should stop your partner and ask for clarification. Although admitting that you are confused might be difficult and you might not want to indicate to your partner that you had not been listening, you must put aside those feelings and seek clarification. If you allow your partner to continue when you are confused about the message, the confusion will escalate.

How do people become confused? *First*, the manner in which your partner is sending the message can lead to confusion. When people are upset or concerned, they tend to flit between several different thoughts and send messages that contain parts of each of these thoughts. When this happens, you should slow down your colleague, ask some key questions, and in the process, help the person to begin to sort out what is really important about the situation.

Second, you may need to seek clarification because of your own lack of attention. All of us are human, and after listening to a person for a while, you may find that you have begun to think about issues unrelated to what the individual is saying. All of a sudden, you may realize that you aren't sure what was really said in the last couple of minutes. Trying to bluff through this situation is a mistake. Although you may be concerned that you will be communicating to your partner that you are not listening, asking for clarification is far better than pretending you were listening. By your responses, your partner will become aware that you had not been listening to what he or she said.

Being honest and expressing that you have lost track of the conversation, asking for repetition, identifying the last thing you remembered clearly, and asking for the rest of the content is a far better strategy than bluffing. Furthermore, if you do try to bluff through the situation, you are likely to become more confused and will be less able to help your partner.

La Tonya, a third-grade teacher, comes storming into Isaac's classroom after the students have left. La Tonya appears to be extremely upset, and the following dialogue ensues.

Isaac: *Wow! You look angry. What's got your goat?*

La Tonya: *Angry? You have no idea! I thought Sue was supposed to go to the resource room today, but she was in my class all day long.*

Isaac: *Oh?*

> *La Tonya:*   *I'm so mad at the principal. Did you know that yesterday he changed the morning bell without telling us third-grade teachers.*
>
> *Isaac:*   *So you're upset with the principal?*
>
> *La Tonya:*   *Ever since he's come here, I don't know what's going on. You know I really liked Mr. Jones and wish he hadn't left. He was the kind of principal who always let us know what was going on.*

In the above interaction La Tonya is clearly upset. Isaac appropriately starts with a broad opening statement that allows La Tonya to indicate why she is upset. Early in the conversation, however, La Tonya brings in the principal and talks about being upset about the bell schedule. This is confusing, and it is unclear from the conversation why the principal is important to La Tonya's concern about Sue going to the resource room. This is where Isaac makes his mistake. Rather than following up and seeking clarification, Isaac uses reflection and asks La Tonya if she is upset with the principal. In the subsequent conversation, La Tonya's response to Isaac's original reflection takes the conversation farther away from La Tonya's original concern—that Sue was supposed to go to the resource room today. This would have been a critical point for Isaac to seek clarification and to ask what the principal and bell scheduling has to do with being concerned about Sue going to the resource room. Let's consider a scenario in which clarification is sought.

> *Isaac:*   *Wow! You look angry. What's got your goat?*
>
> *La Tonya:*   *Angry! You have no idea! I thought Sue was supposed to go to the resource room today, but she was in my class all day long. I'm so mad at the principal. Do you know that yesterday he changed the second morning bell without telling any of us third-grade teachers?*
>
> *Isaac:*   *Wait a minute. I'm a little confused. What does the principal not letting you know about the bells have to do with Sue?*
>
> *La Tonya:*   *Well, I'll tell you how. It's just another example of the information that he doesn't tell us. As I understand it, Sue couldn't go into the classroom until next week because her mother is indicating some concern, but no one told me this until I went to the special education teacher.*

By seeking clarification, it becomes clear why La Tonya brought the principal into this situation. Actually, the real locus of the problem seems not to be that Sue did not go to the resource room. Rather, it may be the lack communication between La Tonya and the principal. Now that the real problem has been revealed, Isaac can help La Tonya come up with some possible solutions.

Silence

One of your most powerful tools as a collaborative colleague is the appropriate use of silence to indicate that you need more information from your colleague. Unfortunately, silence is a technique that is frequently overlooked. Humans have an incredible need to fill in the gap when others are silent. A certain amount of uneasiness sets in when you are in a group and nobody is saying anything or when you are sitting with someone who is not saying anything. Ironically, only when people are extremely comfortable with each other, such as husbands and wives or in other kinds of intense relationships, are they able to be silent together.

As a collaborative practitioner, you can use silence to your advantage. If you avoid falling into the trap of being uncomfortable and speaking just because no one else is speaking, the silence can create a sense of uneasiness on the part of your colleague that, when combined with the appropriate body language, will indicate that you need more information, and your colleague will likely oblige.

Another reason why silence is such an important technique is that you don't have to worry about sounding phony. Many of the techniques we have discussed so far, such as reflection and seeking clarification, can sound stilted and unnatural unless you are an accomplished reflective listener. Another benefit of incorporating silence into your collaborative interaction style is that it provides you and your colleague a moment to think and reflect upon what is being said. From this reflection, the most salient aspects of the conversation often are selected and help the interaction go forward.

You go to pick up your mail in the main office and overhear two fifth-grade teachers talking about Maggie, a sixth-grade science teacher. It seems that one of her students, when she wasn't paying attention, poked his pen through all of her slides from Egypt. Some of the negatives were damaged in processing the slides, so Maggie isn't sure if these slides are replaceable. The two teachers are talking about how upset Maggie is and how she is sitting in the room alone staring out of the window. You decide to go and talk with Maggie. You walk over to her, pull up a chair next to her, and say:

You: I just heard what happened. You must be furious. (At this point you sit quietly and allow a moment or two for Maggie to respond).

> *Maggie:*   *I don't think furious is the right word.*
> *You:*   *You're not furious?*
> *Maggie:*   *I think I'm really hurt. I don't know why Roger*
>   *would try to hurt me.*

In this situation, you use silence appropriately. You are a good friend of Maggie and know how important these slides of Egypt are to her. By allowing the silence, you indicate that you are there for Maggie and that you are ready to listen if she has something to say. By giving Maggie space and time, she is able to think through her feelings on the issue and take time to reflect on her feelings. Eventually Maggie is able to articulate that she is hurt. The time provided is important. If a colleague had been in your place, had been uncomfortable with the silence, and had added a lot more information, Maggie probably would not have had this revelation and the conversation would have gone a very different way.

> *Maggie acknowledges that Derek has come in. He pulls up a chair and sits down.*
>
> *Derek:*   *You must be really angry.*
> *Maggie:*   *(Continues to stare out of the window.)*
> *Derek:*   *(After a few moments) I would have killed him if he*
>   *had done the same thing to my stuff. I don't know*
>   *how you kept your temper.*
> *Maggie:*   *I don't know. I just didn't think I should yell at him.*
>   *I didn't know the right thing to do.*
> *Derek:*   *When I brought my pottery in from Mexico last*
>   *year and Anne dropped it on the floor, I know*
>   *everybody said it was a mistake, but I'll tell you I*
>   *wasn't so sure it was a mistake and I let her parents know what I really thought.*
> *Maggie:*   *I'm not sure what I'm going to do.*

In this example Derek is uncomfortable with the silence and, in an attempt to show that similar events have happened in his own life, he talks about his past situation and how he dealt with the problem. He does not help Maggie come to grips with the key events about this situation and how she feels about it. As was apparent in the first situation, Maggie's feeling is not anger but, rather, a feeling of hurt. Derek's response to a similar situation in the past was anger, and he wrongly assumes that Maggie probably has a similar reaction. This mistaken assumption guides Derek's subsequent questions and inhibits Maggie's understanding of her own feelings.

Used appropriately, silence is a natural means to integrate active listening skills into your style of communication. As a word of caution: Using silence advantageously is difficult and requires some sophistication. As we will discuss in Chapter 5, the inappropriate use of silence can inhibit communication.

Placing Events in Context

As a conversation develops, the need to place events in time or sequence, *in context,* becomes increasingly important. This skill is used when the collaborative dialogue involves some substantial or complex information. It places events in their proper order and helps identify events that are unrelated to the issue under examination.

Yvette stops by Shenice's class one morning and asks Shenice if she has a moment to talk. They are both seventh-grade teachers with the luxury of not having a homeroom. They have a little time before the first class begins. Shenice and Yvette begin talking about what's happening in Yvette's classroom. After a while, it becomes clear that Shenice is still having problems with Damon.

Shenice: *I just can't figure it out. No matter what happens, Damon is throwing spit wads, yelling, or doing something annoying. [Note the use of some reflection to expand on the conversation.]*

Yvette: *What were you doing the last time Damon threw a spit wad?*

Shenice: *Yesterday he started throwing spit wads when they were putting their homework problems up on the board.*

Yvette: *Where were you when he was throwing spit wads?*

Shenice: *Well, I usually go over and sit on the side.*

Yvette: *How far away were you from Damon when this happened?*

Although Damon's disruptive behavior during math period is what is causing concern to Shenice, knowing the specifics related to this concern is difficult at first. Yvette begins placing the event into some kind of time and sequence. This strategy reveals that the disruptive behavior occurs when Shenice selects students to put their math problems on the board and after she moves to the side of the room to monitor the problems. In this dialogue, Yvette is facilitating Shenice's understanding of when and where the problem arises.

Summarizing

Every collaborative interaction should end with a summary of what has taken place during the interaction and the actions to be taken as a result of the interaction. The summary is important for two reasons:

1. It allows both individuals in the interaction a chance to hear the key points and to agree about what was said or to disagree and revise the content of the interaction and clarify key events.
2. It makes public the action that everybody is to take, thereby avoiding misunderstandings about agreements or next steps.

Selina has been working with Saundra on ways to help Maria complete her independent seatwork. The two agree that Saundra is going to spend an extra couple of minutes with Maria alone, making sure that she understands what she is supposed to do and going over the directions. Selina ends the conversation like this:

Selina: *Sounds like you have worked out a good plan. As I understand it, every day you are going to mark in your plan book whether you spent five minutes talking with Maria about her directions. You're going to determine the effectiveness of the interactions based on whether Maria gets her work done or not, so what you will be looking for is incompletion of work or completion of work.*

Saundra: *Yes, that's what we talked about. I'm going to spend five minutes with Maria, and I'll mark in my book every day whether I did it or not. I think it will be easy to talk to Maria about her completion of these activities.*

Selina: *Sounds great. Let's get together in a couple of weeks and see how it's going.*

Selina summarizes the key actions that Saundra is going to take as a result of their collaborative relationship. Afterward, Saundra confirms that Selina's understanding is the same as her understanding, and they set a time to get together and discuss how things are progressing.

Practicing

The communication skills discussed in this chapter require practice if they are to become part of your repertoire of collaborative interaction skills. You will have to work on these skills and try to develop your own style in using them. When conversations sound stilted and contrived, collaborative interaction is inhibited. The more you work on these skills to make them part of your repertoire, the more natural they will become and the more effective you will become as a collaborative practitioner. Identifying practices that you now use only partially and those that seem comfortable to you will help you as you incorporate these into your own communication style. By consciously practicing with your friends and family, these skills will gradually become part of your interaction style.

You do not have to learn to use all of these practices at once, nor is any one used in isolation the most effective. Rather, a combination of these practices will become your style of interacting. People who combine these practices in a natural manner are characterized as being good listeners.

Remember . . .

1. Don't try to get into the meat of a conversation too quickly. Start with some broad opening statements and ease into important information.
2. Offering support is the key first step. You must make clear to the other person that you are ready and willing to listen, and you can provide the parameters around when this should occur. When you offer your support to a colleague, you follow through on your commitments and set realistic time frames and reactions.
3. Reflection is a skill in which you restate key elements of your colleague's statement into a question. This allows your colleague to hear what you are hearing as if you were an "audio mirror," and gives the colleague a chance to further refine and develop his or her thoughts.
4. Stating the implied is important because the implied message being sent is often the most important message.
5. If for some reason you become confused or your concentration wanes, you should seek clarification to get yourself back into the conversation.

6. Silence is a powerful tool that, if incorporated appropriately, should help you develop a natural interaction style.
7. As conversations move forward, you must place information into a context that orders it into the proper time and sequence.
8. The information gained from an interaction should be summarized so those involved are clear as to the information shared and the actions to be taken as a result of the interaction.

Activities

1. Participate in role-play situations that depict a teacher interacting with (a) a parent, (b) a specialist, (c) an administrator, and (d) others. Work in pairs and videotape the role plays. One person in the pair plays a teacher and the other interacts with the teacher. Show these videotapes to a small group or the class (depending on the class size). The individual playing the teacher describes everything he or she did to facilitate communication and then asks the viewers to elaborate or expand on the positive. (Our experience with this activity indicates that viewers typically focus on the negative aspects of this interaction.)
2. To expand on the above activity, have pairs of students engage in two role playing activities. The first role play occurs prior to receiving the information on communication and skills that facilitate or inhibit communication. The second role play occurs after the information has been presented. Students can meet in small groups or as a whole class (depending on the size of the class) to discuss differences between the first role play and the final role play.
3. Ask students to keep a list of incidents over the next week in which someone used one or more of the communication skills addressed in this chapter to facilitate communication. Discuss these lists in class, and generate a combined class list. Ask students to describe the impact this experience had on them.

5

Barriers to Effective Communication

In Chapters 3 and 4 we presented techniques to enhance your ability to listen to and communicate with your colleagues. These are extremely important skills that, if practiced and incorporated into your standard style of interaction, will enhance your ability to be effective in collaborative interactions. Unfortunately, we all sometimes engage in an interactional style that lessens our ability to listen and thereby communicate. Usually this results from poor habits that we have unknowingly adopted over a period of time. Without an understanding of communication as a cycle involving both a receiver and a sender, we might assume that we communicated successfully because we sent the message. Without feedback from the receiver indicating that the message we sent was accurately understood, this is a faulty assumption. The communication cycle must be completed before we communicate.

To communicate effectively, we also must recognize barriers to communication and eliminate them systematically from our interaction style. Recognizing these barriers and becoming aware of how easily they can become a part of your interactional style is the first step to eliminating them from your style of communication.

As you read through the common barriers to communication, think about conversations in which you and a colleague have run into one of these barriers. In retrospect, do you believe you and your colleague ever really completed the communication? Were you and your colleague able to recover and eventually communicate? If so, how did you do this? Did the interchange result in anger, frustration, or other negative emotions?

Advice Giving

Perhaps the most common error in a collaborative relationship is to give advice too quickly. We walk a fine line when trying to help our colleagues. Often they are seeking a suggestion or an alternative strategy to help them solve a problem. Making a suggestion that a colleague may choose to implement is quite different from giving a colleague advice that implies that the advice giver has the correct and only answer. If pressed too strongly, giving advice can negate the professionalism of our colleague by dictating a specific course of action.

Compounding this problem, when we give advice too strongly, we make suggestions that come from our own repertoire of effective strategies but may not be within our colleague's repertoire. These actions may foster dependence; we may be treating our colleagues not as professionals but instead as individuals who do not have the capacity to act on their own—even if the resulting intervention is successful.

Advice giving that results in professional disenfranchisement is a strategy to be avoided. Suggesting alternatives to consider, however, is different and is something we would want to do. Our colleagues, though, should be the ones to decide what they wish to implement in their own classrooms.

Amelia is an eighth-grade English teacher whose school is embarking on a full inclusion model. Amelia's class has been targeted to incorporate some of the children that have been in the self-contained special education classroom. These children have mild to moderate disabilities, and Amelia is trying to figure out a way to differentiate instructions and incorporate all of these children. She goes to Keiko, the resource room teacher, and they begin discussing some possibilities.

Amelia: *I really care about these kids, and I'm excited about the opportunities, but at the same time I'm scared and wondering if I can really handle such differences in abilities.*

Keiko: *Sounds like you're concerned about the wide range of abilities you are going to have in your classroom.*

Amelia: *I am. I've never had such differences before, and I don't know how to construct a lesson so both groups of kids will survive.*

Keiko: *If I were you, I would get away from the idea that all these kids are going to be involved equally in the classroom and recognize that the best you are going*

*to do in some cases is to socially integrate these
kids.*

Amelia: *So you don't think I should try to develop lessons to
incorporate all of the kids.*

Keiko: *No. I wouldn't try that. I would recognize some of
their limitations and with half of the kids in the
classroom, that's the best you're going to do. You
might want to have two sets of lessons that all the
kids can work on individually and then work on
some group topics that will allow you to include all
the students.*

Amelia: *Huh! You have some interesting ideas. Maybe I'll
try that. Would you mind helping me with my first
lesson?*

On the surface this looks like a helpful interaction. Keiko begins by facilitating Amelia's reflection and elaboration on her concern. The fatal flaw in this interaction is that Keiko quickly gives Amelia advice. Keiko tells Amelia to recognize that some of the children are never going to be integrated completely into her classroom and that Amelia should regard social integration as sufficient. This caution may be warranted, but at the same time it now is more probable that Keiko's suggestions may set lower expectations on Amelia's part and may limit the possibilities for her students. Other strategies, such as cooperative learning, might be considered.

Amelia: *I really care about these kids, and I'm excited about
the opportunities, but at the same time I'm scared
and wondering if I can really handle such differences in abilities.*

Keiko: *Sounds like you're concerned about the wide range
of abilities you're going to have in your classroom.*

Amelia: *That's probably it. There are so many kids and such
differences between the kids that I'm just not sure
how things are going to work out.*

Keiko: *Are you concerned about everything? Or just specific parts of the classroom or your routine?*

Amelia: *Well, now that you've mentioned it, I guess I'm most
concerned about having the kids work independently.
I don't know how I'm going to incorporate these kids
into my reading groups, and I worry that it will take
too much of my time.*

Keiko: *Let's focus on your reading groups. Maybe there's a
way to incorporate these kids that you haven't
thought about.*

In this example Amelia and Keiko have an interaction similar to the previous one, but Keiko avoids the enticing lure to offer advice and instead encourages reflection and seeks clarification from Amelia to gain a greater understanding of her concerns. Once the concerns begin to be identified, Keiko helps to facilitate Amelia's thinking by beginning to explore possible ways to modify her approach to reading.

False Reassurances

Perhaps one of the most well intentioned errors that results in the most serious consequences is giving false reassurances. This is the case when you indicate to your colleague that everything is going to work out and there is nothing to worry about or that you are sure the problem is going to be solved. In an attempt to ease your colleague's concern, you dismiss the problem. Providing false reassurances also puts you in a difficult spot because, although we would all like every problem to be resolved, some problems do not have an easy solution. In addition, if we assure a colleague that it's all going to work out, this could minimize the motivation to work toward a successful resolution. Finally, if the person thinks perhaps the problem wasn't so intense after all, he or she may feel uncomfortable talking about it, which inhibits further communication.

Esteban is a brand new eighth-grade science teacher. The school feels fortunate to get Esteban. He comes highly recommended and brings a strong science background to the school. During the first couple of weeks of the year, the principal, Ms. Jones, notices that Esteban seems distant and preoccupied. She decides that perhaps it is time to sit down with Esteban and talk about what might be happening in his class.

Mrs. Jones: Hi, Esteban. I thought I'd stop by this morning and see how things are going for you as the new teacher. You may not be aware of this, but I make it a practice to stop in and see what's up.

Esteban: Oh, that's a good idea, I'm really glad you stopped by.

Ms. Jones: Well, Esteban, what's up? Seems like you've got some neat activities planned for the kids.

Esteban: Well, I guess. But I don't know. I guess they're neat activities. I don't know if the kids will like them.

Ms. Jones: Esteban, you sound unsure. Is something going on that's bothering you?

Esteban:	*Well, not really but . . . everything seems to be fine. It's just . . .*
Ms. Jones:	*Esteban, I know you say everything is just fine, but I can't help but hear some doubt.*
Esteban:	*Well, I guess you're right. It just seems that I spend so much time planning for each of these lessons. I work sometimes three and four hours after school. I plan to get married soon, and I'm having a hard time trying to balance personal life and school. And even though I spend a lot of time preparing, it seems I'm just not getting it right. Sometimes the lesson seems to be over the kids' heads. Other times the lesson seems to be too simple. Sometimes I have too much time; sometimes I don't have enough.*
Ms. Jones:	*Oh, is that all? Esteban, you're just going to have to come to grips with your first year of teaching. You came highly recommended. I'm sure you're going to be a great teacher! It's your first year, and I wouldn't worry. It's not really a big deal.*

In this example, the principal does an excellent job of using broad opening statements and getting to the discussion of what apparently is wrong. The principal follows with some good reflective statements to help Esteban clarify his feelings and then eventually to be able to share his concern. At that point the conversation breaks down. The principal minimizes Esteban's feelings as if they are not important and gives him false reassurances that he is not to worry, that everything will work out fine.

The danger in this interaction is twofold. *First*, because Ms. Jones minimizes Esteban's feelings, he is led to believe that this is a trivial matter and that in similar situations others would not worry as much. If he has other similar issues or problems, he is unlikely to bring them forward because what he thinks is a problem seems trivial to someone he respects. He is not likely to want to be told a second time that his concerns are unimportant. *Second*, this problem may not work itself out and may continue to be a problem for Esteban. He might have real difficulty organizing his time to provide effective lessons and to create a balance between his personal and professional life. His problem may be compounded because he has been led to believe that this is something that typically works itself out. If it doesn't, he might begin to question not only why he is having a problem but also why it isn't working itself out.

Misdirected Questions

In a collaborative relationship one of the most important roles is to ask questions and to help the individual reflect upon what's happening in his or her situation to gain greater understanding. Questions are the primary means of directing such conversations and developing mutual understanding. If too many questions are asked or these questions lack a consistent direction, however, they will inhibit the conversation. These questions will lead your colleague to focus on different aspects of the communication without clearly developing a meaningful dialogue about the situation. This is another reason why reflective listening must become a natural part of your conversation. On the one hand, you must ask questions to guide your colleagues and facilitate their understanding. On the other hand, too many questions or irrelevant questions prevent your colleague from developing a clear line of thought and will inhibit communication.

Shakeel is an elementary-school gym teacher who has been trying to find a way to incorporate Terry into gym classes. Terry seems angry all the time. He is tall and has a good sense of coordination, so Shakeel thinks that athletics may be an opportunity for Terry. Martha is Terry's homeroom teacher and one day Shakeel stops by Martha's class with a couple of cups of coffee.

Shakeel: *Hey, Martha, I thought I'd bring you some coffee and ask for a piece of your wisdom—that is, if you've got the time.*

Martha: *For coffee, your time is my time.*

Shakeel: *I'm struggling with Terry in class and I'm not quite sure about what I should try— to help him be less angry and not so interested in fighting.*

Martha :   *So you're concerned about Terry.*

Shakeel: *Yes, he seems . . .*

Martha :   *You're worried about his attention span.*

Shakeel: *No, I'm not worried about Terry's attention span.*

Martha :   *Does he come in late for class?*

Shakeel: *Well, yes. Sometimes he comes in late for class.*

Martha :   *You're not worried about his being late for class?*

Shakeel: *Yes, I'm worried about his being late for class, but there are other problems.*

Martha :   *There are other problems?*

Shakeel: *Yes. There are other problems. I'm worried about how Terry gets along with other students.*

Martha :   *Is he absent a lot?*

This dialogue exemplifies many of the problems with misdirected questioning. First, questions come in a rapid-fire pace that does not give Shakeel an opportunity to think. At one point Shakeel is interrupted before he can even complete his thought. When too many questions are asked too quickly, the colleague likely will start responding to the questions and will not have the time to reflect on what is happening in the classroom or the concerns that led the colleague to seek your help.

Another problem in this example is that the questions are not particularly focused, and they lack any consistent line of thought. For example, raising questions about Terry's tardiness may be relevant, but to keep dwelling on his tardiness when Shakeel seems concerned about other issues is inhibiting, too. Focusing on Terry's tardiness and then on his potential absences may take Shakeel so far off track that he will not be able to get to the problem concerning him.

Asking too many questions is often a problem when someone is uncomfortable with reflective listening or is concentrating more on potential questions than listening. Any time you are trying to help a colleague gain understanding about what is happening in the classroom and you are doing most of the talking, something is wrong. If you pay attention and listen, questions will flow naturally. The important trends within the conversation will become apparent, and you will have a naturally flowing conversation rather than a choppy interaction confused with a lot of questions.

Wandering Interactions

Similar to misdirected questions are interactions that wander and do not follow a logical progression. If we are interacting with a colleague, the interaction can wander and we unknowingly may change the subject. This abruptly inhibits the communication and clearly indicates that you have not been listening and perhaps do not care about what is being said. When you find your attention wandering, you should bring it to the attention of your colleague immediately and seek clarification of the subject at hand. The more engaged and skilled we become as listeners, the easier it is to avoid this pitfall.

Concha is a primary-level special education teacher, and Maria is a first grade teacher. In her classroom, Maria has Todd, classified as having mild mental retardation. Todd spends a half hour with Concha in the resource room and the remainder of his day in the general classroom. Maria has been troubled by Todd's feelings of inadequacy when he is

*involved in any academics in the classroom. She has asked
Concha to come in and help her sort through some issues.*

Concha: *Well, Maria, I'm glad we have this chance to get
together and talk about Todd. I know you are concerned about how Todd is feeling in comparison
with the other kids.*

Maria: *Yes. Todd's a good kid. I really like him and the
kids like him, but it hurts me when we're working
on math facts or any other academically oriented
activity. Although I try to get Todd involved in
meaningful ways, he just doesn't understand things
at the same level as the other kids, and he knows it.*

Concha: *You know, I really think Todd is a good kid, too. Do
you know that the other day one of the fifth-grade
boys was teasing a first-grade girl and Todd
stepped in and stopped those kids?*

Maria: *Really! I've seen Todd take risks in other ways and
go out of his way to help kids. That's why I'm so
concerned about his feelings when we're involved
in academic activities.*

Concha: *Speaking of risk-taking, I think that Todd needs to
take more risks and should be encouraged to take a
risk at any opportunity that presents itself.*

In this example Maria is trying to talk about ways to help Todd feel more
comfortable in her classroom when the ability levels between Todd and the
other students differ. She is concerned about his feelings and self-esteem.
Concha, though, changes the subject and in the end gives some advice that
isn't related to the problem Maria is concerned about. Changing the subject
like this is problematic for several reasons. *First,* it breaks Maria's conversation about Todd and inhibits her ability to reflect on the situation and gain
understanding. *Second,* it suggests to Maria that she is not being listened to
and may even suggest to her that Concha is not interested in her problem. This
situation is likely to discourage Maria from seeking Concha's help in the
future. *Third* this kind of conversation is frustrating, which is another reason
for Maria not to be interested in talking with Concha in the future.

Interruptions

When we are engaging in a collaborative interaction that is leading toward better understanding, interruptions can disrupt the flow of the conversation and

seriously hinder our colleagues' abilities to gain full understanding of the situation. Interruption is closely linked to changing the subject because frequently we interrupt when we have lost our train of thought. This also can happen when time becomes an issue and we interrupt to try to get to the heart of the problem too quickly. That is why setting realistic time parameters for collaborative interactions is so important.

Tony and Darrell are seventh and eighth grade science teachers, respectively. They carpool together and find it a good time to talk about what happens in the classroom. Darrell is incredibly quiet during the drive to school today.

Tony: *You seem a little quiet today. Did you get enough sleep last night?*

Darrell: *Yeah, I got enough sleep. It's just that . . .*

Tony: *So you got enough sleep and you didn't watch movies like you usually do, huh?*

Darrell: *No, I didn't watch movies last night, but I'm really concerned about Jill.*

Tony: *Jill?*

Darrell: *Yeah. I'm really concerned about Jill. She . . .*

Tony: *How could you be concerned about Jill? She seems to have everything together.*

Darrell: *Well, I know she seems to have it all together . . .*

Tony: *Seems to have it together? I've never seen a student her age so sure of her future and how to get there.*

In this situation, Darrell is having a hard time getting his thoughts heard. The interruptions are frustrating and do not lead to greater understanding. To the contrary, they communicate to Darrell that Tony is not listening, nor does he seem to care about the problem that Darrell is facing. The interruptions inhibit this interaction and also can discourage Darrell from bringing other concerns to Tony for discussion.

Clichés

Responding to a colleague's problem with a cliché is a sure-fire way to inhibit the communication. Clichés clearly diminish the feelings of the person with whom you are interacting. They often are used without thought and can be part of regional speech patterns. In virtually no situation is a cliché an appropriate response. If you hear yourself using a cliché, you should backtrack immediately and clarify your response.

Pete comes storming out of his classroom and bumps into Tom in the hallway. It is obvious that Pete is upset. Tom carpools with Pete and is an old high school buddy.

Tom:　*Hey, what's the matter with you, pal? You look really upset.*

Pete:　*I've had it with these kids. No matter how hard I work, they don't seem to care about anything. Last period three of the kids were fooling around and broke my last box of micro slides. I've got to go the supply room and get more. I've just had it.*

Tom:　*Hey, Pete, don't make a mountain out of a molehill. Kids will be kids.*

At this point, Pete probably is ready to hit Tom, and Tom has done nothing to help diffuse the situation. If anything, Pete now is probably angry at his friend, as well as frustrated about what happened in the classroom. The two clichés minimized his feelings and made the situation worse by increasing Pete's anger and frustration. Let's take the conversation a little further.

Tom:　*Hey, what's the matter with you, pal? You look really upset.*

Pete:　*I've had it with these kids. No matter how hard I work, they don't seem to care about anything. Last period three of the kids were fooling around and broke my last box of micro slides. I've got to go the supply room and get more. I've just had it.*

Tom:　*Hey, Pete, don't make a mountain out of a molehill. Kids will be kids.*

Pete:　*Don't give me that garbage! You have no idea how I feel.*

Tom:　*You're right. That was a stupid statement. I tell you what. I'll get the slides for you, and why don't you get a cup of coffee.*

Pete:　*Thanks, I could use a cup of coffee.*

Tom:　*If you like, maybe we can talk about it on the way home.*

As the conversation progresses, Tom is able to recover from his error and successfully diffuse the situation. More important, he offers his help to Pete in an appropriate way, laying the groundwork for helping Pete sort out his concerns and develop a solution.

As you read these common barriers, have you recognized any of which you or a colleague have been guilty? Did you see any barriers that may be recurring in your interaction style? If so, what steps can you take to eliminate or avoid these barriers? When you are with a colleague and he or she puts up one of these barriers, what can you do to try to get the conversation back on track?

Minimizing Feelings

We have talked about a number of ways that minimize the feelings of someone with whom you are interacting. False reassurances, changing the subject, interrupting, and clichés are all examples of ways in which you can minimize feelings and inhibit colleagues from interacting further with you. Feelings can be minimized in other, more subtle ways, too.

Merle has always taught third grade: This year she was transferred to a kindergarten class and is having difficulty trying to organize the free flow of kindergarten and maintain some sense of order. John, the principal of the school, recognizes that Merle is having problems and stops by one morning with doughnuts and coffee.

John: *I thought you might like to have a doughnut and coffee on the three-month anniversary of our hiring you.*

Merle: *That's really nice, John. I appreciate the coffee and doughnut.*

John: *How are things going?*

Merle: *Well, I don't know. I get here at seven every morning to make sure I have everything set up for the kids, and I stay until four-thirty every day going over everything I've done, reviewing the students' work and planning for the next day. But I'm still not hitting it. It seems like I have lessons that are either too short and not challenging enough or lessons that are way over the head of these kids.*

John: *Merle, I wouldn't take it so seriously. Any teacher who shifts grade levels has trouble adjusting to a new age group.*

In this example, John begins by doing some positive things. Bringing coffee and doughnuts is a real show of support and a clear offering of his willingness to help. He uses broad opening statements to begin the interaction and is being attentive as Merle explains her concerns. As soon as John tells her not to worry because this is a problem all teachers face, however, he devalues her as an individual and makes her feel as if her concerns are not important. Because she may be reluctant to be devalued a second time, Merle probably will not continue to share her concerns or problems with John. If colleagues think they have a problem, they do have a problem, no matter how trivial the problem may seem to us. As effective collaborative colleagues, our role is not to make judgments regarding the worth or value of a problem. Rather, it is to help colleagues gain understanding of the problem so they can identify and implement a solution.

Quick Fixes

Moving too quickly to fix a problem is a barrier similar to giving advice. Actually, two barriers often arise at the same time. People often make assumptions about a situation when they do not spend the time with a colleague to really help him or her explore what is happening in the classroom and what may be causing concern. By not spending adequate time to consider all the factors related to a problem, you and your colleague might end up working on a symptom of the problem instead of the actual problem. When this happens, you and your colleague are unlikely to change whatever was causing the problem that led to your interaction in the first place. Furthermore, spending time and effort working on something that is not the real problem can frustrate your colleague and lead him or her to believe that collaboration is an inadequate way to solve problems.

Vanessa is a first grader who has not had opportunities similar to other children in her new school, in that she hasn't been in preschool or kindergarten. Nonetheless, she is a bright little girl who has just moved into the area. Because she is new to the school and hasn't attended school before, Kerry asks Will to observe. The following conversation takes place after Will has observed Kerry's class several times.

Will: *Do you have some time when we can talk? I've visited several times in the last three days, and I have some ideas.*

Kerry: *Great. This is a good time for me. The kids won't be here for another thirty minutes.*

Will: *In my opinion, we have a little girl who has some*

cognitive delays. I believe we ought to refer her to
special education for a full diagnostic.

Kerry: *That's strange. She seems to be really insightful*
when I talk to her.

Will: *Well, that may be, but don't you notice all the diffi-*
culty she has describing the pictures in the stories you
read? She doesn't seem to know the common pictures.
I also believe she has no idea of any letters. Anything
the least bit abstract is beyond her comprehension.

In this case, Will makes an assumption without adequate reflection. As a result, he begins to plan for something that is not a problem. Upon testing, it turns out that Vanessa's real problem is that she needs glasses. Vanessa has not had good medical care during her early years, and no one thought to test her vision. Jumping to the conclusions Will makes so quickly can seriously hurt Vanessa. In the process of getting her tested, negative biases could form, and expectations for her performance could be seriously diminished. Kerry provides some information that conflicts with Will's observations, but Will does not listen to her words. He is more interested in making a case to support his position. Had Will used good listening skills, he and Kerry could have explored Kerry's observations and may have reached a different conclusion about Vanessa's problems.

Avoiding Barriers to Good Communication

When people are attempting to communicate, barriers to communication often arise, and these barriers can result in miscommunication. You should learn to recognize these barriers and discipline yourself to remove them from your interactional style. In this way, your effectiveness as a collaborative colleague will be enhanced.

Remember . . .

1. The kind of advice giving that encourages dependency and disenfranchises a colleague professionally is different from making suggestions that your colleague may or may not choose to implement.
2. Giving a colleague false reassurances minimizes the importance of the problem and can compound the problem if things don't work out as you predict.

3. Too many or unfocused questions inhibit a consistent train of thought and understanding.

4. Wandering and changing topics in a dialogue communicate that you are not listening and shift the attention of your colleague away from the problem being discussed.

5. Interrupting is frustrating and can thwart a colleague's ability to express concerns and explore the problem.

6. Using a cliché as a response trivializes the conversation and impedes further discussion.

7. Responding to colleagues in ways that minimize their feelings can make them feel inadequate professionally. As a result, problems are less likely to be solved and your colleagues will be less inclined to approach you to discuss other concerns in the future.

8. Jumping to a quick fix based on false assumptions can result in working on symptoms of the problem rather than getting at the root of the problem.

Activities

1. Expand the role-playing activity described in Chapter 4 to include barriers to effective communication. After discussing strengths or positive aspects of the interaction, suggest ways to enhance the interaction.

2. Engage in the role playing twice: (a) prior to the information on communication skills, and (b) again after the information on communication skills has been presented. Students can meet in small groups or as a whole class (depending on the size of the class) to discuss differences between their first role play and their second role play.

3. Over the next week keep a list of incidents in which someone put up a barrier to communication. Exchange the lists in class and generate a general class list. How did this activity affect your perception of your own interaction style?

6

Working With and Supporting Groups

T he previous three chapters dealt with the communication process and factors that facilitate or inhibit effective communication. Most of the examples focused on interactions between two individuals as a way of illustrating communication facilitators or inhibitors. Many of the concepts presented in Chapters 3, 4, and 5 apply to group interactions as well. The group is a common unit of interaction within schools, and communication within the context of a group of more than two people has unique dimensions. When more than two individuals interact, a set of dynamics comes into play that adds complexity to the communication process. In this chapter we describe those dynamics and provide examples to illustrate key concepts.

As you read this chapter, think about the discussions you have had in class. What kind of group functioning was in play? Has the class functioned like a different group during different activities (e.g., breaks, discussions, projects)? When you are part of different types of groups, can you identify differences in communication styles, formality, proximal distance between group members, or body language?

Types of Groups

Humans interact in an endless number of groups. The typical teacher is at once a member of a faculty, a family member, possibly a student, a club member, and so on. A group is defined as having more than two individuals who are working toward a unified purpose (Hames, 1980). The basic types of groups are conversational, instructional, decision-making, problem-solving, and discovery (Combs, Avila, & Purkey, 1971).

CONVERSATIONAL GROUPS

Informal groups in which individuals exchange information in a casual manner fit the conversational category. Conversational groups usually lack an articulated purpose other than to share information, and they are characterized by extensive participation by group members. These groups tend to be composed of individuals who are interpersonally compatible and have joined the group voluntarily. Conversational groups at school meet during lunch, after school, and at other times when they come together to interact informally.

INSTRUCTIONAL GROUPS

Instructional groups meet formally to learn new information or skills. Instructional groups almost always have a leader or facilitator who orchestrates the group's activities. Although instructional groups can be participatory—in which all members exchange information and contribute to others' learning—they also can be unidimensional in that certain types of information flow in one direction. Typically, the leader or facilitator presents new ideas or techniques and members generate questions or concerns. Membership in these groups can be voluntary or mandatory. Inservices, faculty meetings, coursework, and other forms of staff development are examples of instructional groups in the educational milieu.

DECISION-MAKING GROUPS

Like instructional groups, decision-making groups tend to be formal in nature. Although in rare instances the group has no clear leader or facilitator, an individual usually orchestrates the group discussion. This type of group is participatory and is based on a collection of information from a variety of sources related to the decision to be made. Sometimes all members of the group make the decision jointly, such as in a library-selection committee or a group that determines a student's eligibility for special education. Other groups make recommendations to decision makers, such as a school board or local school administrators. Examples of an advisory group are textbook-selection committees and search committees.

PROBLEM-SOLVING GROUPS

The problem-solving group is often considered to be a form of a decision-making group. The important difference is that the main purpose of this group is to solve a problem. As a result, this group makes a decision regarding the problem to be solved and also continues to work together to develop a plan to solve the problem. Like decision-making groups, problem-solving groups tend to be formal in nature and a leader or facilitator usually orchestrates the problem solving. Teacher-assistance teams, building-support teams, and intervention-assistance teams are examples of problem-solving groups. These groups tend to take two forms, each of which can be mandatory or voluntary. Sometimes they are structured so problems are brought to the group and the group makes suggestions as to how the problem can be solved. In other cases groups are formed as a means of support, in which all members of the group bring problems and participate in developing plans to solve the problems.

DISCOVERY GROUPS

As with most of the groups discussed so far, discovery groups, too, are formal. The main purpose of this type of group is for members to gain more self-awareness or understanding. This group tends to have a highly skilled leader with expertise in therapeutic communication. Within schools these groups are voluntary. Examples are stress-management groups and other self-help groups.

Although professionals within the school are likely to find themselves in all five types of groups, three—instructional, problem solving, and discovery—are those in which school problems typically are addressed.

Have you ever wondered why you feel comfortable in some groups and uncomfortable in other groups? What factors led you to feel this way? Was it the size of the group, group members, where the group met, what the group was discussing, how you were feeling, or some other issue that contributed to your comfort level? When you have been a part of a group over a long period, how did the dynamics change over time, and what factors contributed to these changes?

Group Functioning

Good communication among group members is essential to success. Therefore, collaborative professionals must have a good sense of group functioning. Without open and honest lines of communication, the group will not be able to maximize its effectiveness because norms, roles, and goals of the group cannot be defined appropriately. Group facilitators and group members alike should use the communication skills described in Chapter 3 to encourage effective communication. In this section we will delineate responsibilities of various group members in establishing effective groups. We also will describe general components of effective groups, responsibilities of group members, sources of group conflict, and techniques to address group conflict.

GROUP DYNAMICS

Group dynamics determines whether the group will be effective and positive. Improper group dynamics can deter productivity and impede the group from achieving its objectives. The three components of group dynamics are: structure, process, and function (Hames & Joseph, 1986). *Structure* relates to the framework of the group. *Process* refers to the developmental growth pattern of groups. *Function* incorporates the tasks that a group undertakes to achieve its purpose.

Group Structure

Group structure pertains to the overall building blocks of the group—the components or elements that provide the framework from which the group operates. Structure is not static; it can change. The facilitator has to be aware of how the components of the structure can affect group dynamics and the group's ability to be effective. Components of group structure include its size, composition, physical environment, and format (Hames & Joseph, 1986).

Size. In organizing a group, one of the most important considerations for a facilitator is the size of the group. Groups that are too large inhibit communication and the free flow of ideas. Small groups, on the other hand, can narrow the possibilities of discussion because of the limited number of individuals involved. Although the literature is inconsistent with regard to the optimal size of a group, there is some consensus. Generally, groups smaller than four place undue burdens on group members and can inhibit the group's effectiveness. Groups larger than 10 tend to inhibit the free sharing of ideas and place greater demands on the leadership abilities of the group facilitator. Groups of six to nine members tend to have more participation, greater member satisfaction, more intense relationships between members, and member consensus is established more readily.

Composition. Positive characteristics of effective individual group members include (a) the ability to resolve conflicts, (b) the ability to communicate clearly, (c) stability and openness, and (d) willingness to take risks (Abelson & Woodman, 1983). Each group member brings individual competencies that can contribute to the group's success as a unit.

Physical environment. An often overlooked concern in groups is the environment in which they will be functioning. The environment, or setting, can facilitate or inhibit the participation of members. The size of the room, lighting, atmosphere, comfort, location, and acoustics are all important. Think of the times you have been in large conference rooms for a small-group meeting and had difficulty hearing those around you. If you cannot hear what is going on, you have a hard time participating. If the room is uncomfortable, either because of temperature control or seating, group members might attend to their discomfort instead of the purpose of the group. The seating arrangement can facilitate group participation when members are sitting so they face one another and can see each other or can inhibit participation if the lines of view are blocked. Having a table large enough to allow members to have their own space to spread out and take notes also facilitates discussion.

Format. The manner in which a group conducts its business is called the format. Format exists along a continuum, from highly structured groups that rely on Robert's Rules of Order to informal social gatherings with few rules. Well organized groups are apt to be more efficient in accomplishing their tasks. More informal groups usually are less efficient but provide more opportunities for all members to participate and share. A delicate balance must be maintained between the rigidity of the group and permissiveness of a unstructured format. The structure must be formal enough to propel the group toward accomplishing its task, but this must be balanced with an inclusive or participatory style in which members are encouraged to share information in a more permissive manner.

Group Process

Like individuals, groups proceed through a relatively predictable sequence as they attempt to accomplish their objectives. Tuckman and Jensen (1977) have described a model of group functioning that has five stages of development: forming, storming, norming, performing, and adjourning.

1. *Forming.* The forming phase consists of a general orientation to the group. Relationships are begun and established at a superficial level. The initial purpose for the group is discussed. The complete structure of group activities is not yet determined, and communication networks are just beginning to be established. During this stage group members are trying to understand the group's purpose, leadership of the group, and group members, as well as how the group will undertake its task. In the forming stage a group is often quiet and members speak hesitantly. This stage is characterized by continual examination of the goals, norms, and relationships within the group.

2. *Storming.* The second stage, storming, is characterized by conflict and disagreement. The intensity of conflict can range from almost nonexistent to fairly intense. The conflict that may emerge at this stage is normal in groups. It results from group members' questioning their roles, others' roles, and the purpose of the group. As potential conflicts begin to get resolved, group members reestablish relationships and make a transition to the next stage.

3. *Norming.* During the norming stage group members become comfortable with role expectations, relationships, and the group's purpose. Communication networks and structural characteristics are solidified. Group cohesiveness, trust, and leadership are developed, along with a new commitment to the group's goals. At the conclusion of this stage, group members are ready to undertake the task the group is to accomplish.

4. *Performing.* In the performing stage group members work on the tasks of the group. Discussion includes pertinent feedback, which allows for appropriate decision making.

5. *Adjourning.* The final stage, adjourning, marks task completion, and relationships are redefined as closure approaches. This last stage is accompanied by an increase in self-esteem if the goals are met.

Although these stages are linear in their description, they are manifested in a dynamic manner. Groups can move back and forth across these levels of development as they confront new issues or the membership changes. If group membership changes often, the group may have difficulty carrying out its business because of the continuing need to repeat the developmental sequence of group process.

Group Function

For a group to function satisfactorily, all group members should possess several skills. Many of these skills or functions can be categorized into *task functions* and *maintenance functions*.

Task Functions. *Task functions* allow a group to move toward completion of the task. These functions are (Hames & Joseph, 1986):

- *Initiation.* Initiation is a skill related to establishing a group. It includes things such as imposing an agenda and defining group goals.
- *Seeking information.* In seeking information, one requests facts, ideas, beliefs, and suggestions to expand upon information being provided or to ensure accurate representation of the group members.
- *Providing information.* In providing information, one offers facts, ideas, and/or new information related to the group's task.
- *Clarifying.* When seeking clarification, one requests elaboration or new information from group members.
- *Consensus testing.* Group members are checked to determine whether they are ready to reach a decision or to see if a unified position—consensus—is emerging.
- *Summarizing.* Restating ideas or information generated in the group should produce a concise summary of what the group has accomplished.

Maintenance Functions. In addition to these task functions are maintenance functions. They facilitate the group process and keep the group members focused on the task. These are as follows:

■ *Gatekeeping.* Gatekeeping is a process that ensures the participation of all group members. If one or more individuals are dominating the group discussion, they are called upon to curtail their discussion so other group members can participate more fully.

■ *Encouraging.* Comments and information shared by group members are accepted and, when appropriate, praised. Encouraging facilitates full participation by all group members.

■ *Harmonizing.* In harmonizing, differences among group members are arbitrated or mediated. The intent is to reduce tensions among group members and to create an atmosphere in which all members feel supported.

■ *Standard setting.* Standard setting means reinforcing the group's intent. It includes reminders of group goals and progress toward reaching these goals.

RESPONSIBILITIES OF GROUP MEMBERS

Group members might believe that task and maintenance functions are the primary role of the leader or facilitator. This is unfortunate because, although the leader or facilitator must be skilled in task and maintenance functions, groups are far more effective if all members assume these responsibilities. When all members share responsibility for these functions, they take ownership of the group process and this ownership contributes to the group's being able to accomplish its purpose.

Role of Facilitator

Perhaps the most important member of a group is the facilitator. The facilitator must have strong leadership characteristics. The group's success depends on the facilitator's ability to organize group activities, create the communicative environment, and synthesize outcomes. The facilitator is responsible for maintaining a positive, cohesive atmosphere among a diverse group of people embodying varying levels and types of knowledge and personal biases. The leader also must have a clear sense of the purpose of the group and be able to communicate it clearly. Group facilitators should be trustworthy, skilled listeners who can motivate and empower group members to accomplish group goals (Bennis, 1984).

A *participatory* style of leadership is the most effective approach. In this style, group members are encouraged to participate and take on meaningful roles as the group carries out its tasks. The facilitator's skill impacts on both the quality and the timeliness of decisions that groups make (Abelson &

Woodman, 1983). When conflicts arise, appropriate problem-solving techniques must be applied to guide the group through difficulties in meeting the defined goals in a timely manner (Margolis & Shapiro, 1988). The facilitator has the following traits and roles:

- Skill in group facilitation, arbitration, and conflict resolution.
- Ability and willingness to deal with complex issues simultaneously while generating an atmosphere of comfort and flexibility for all members of the group.
- Skill in group development with individuals from various disciplines, as well as the capability of developing true group rapport.
- Projection of unity of concern for group members, with each addressing a problem from the unique perspective of disciplinary or individual orientation.
- Facilitator of group interactions, with enough strength to maintain group cohesion if conflict arises within the group.
- Ability to engender humility of spirit in group members so their own needs do not compete with those of the group.

As the stages of group functioning evolve, the role of the facilitator must change to match the group's needs. At the onset of group functioning, the facilitator should serve as a guide and administrator, but in time this role should become less and less directive. In a group's *forming* stage, the facilitator must serve as a director and administrator to orient the group to the tasks at hand. As the group moves into the *storming* stage, the facilitator must handle difficulties that arise, such as role ambiguity, questioning of authority, conflicting goals, and other potential problems. In this stage the facilitator uses problem-solving skills to negotiate arbitration and mediation among group members. In the *norming* stage, a sense of group cohesiveness and trust is established and the facilitator can become less directive and more able to serve as a fellow collaborator in solving problems and completing tasks.

Although facilitators are responsible primarily for leadership of the group, their decision-making role is equal to any of the group members. After the group's task has been accomplished, it enters the *adjourning* stage. The facilitator should bring the meeting to a close by summarizing the results of the discussion. The leader should state specifically which group members will be responsible for carrying out each recommendation, and before the meeting adjourns dates should be set for initiation and completion of those tasks. This step is critical to allow for opportunities for correction or clarification.

Role of Group Members

The strength of the group approach relies on the participation of all group members. Effective use of members' skills and resources should be one of the primary objectives of group functioning (Abelson & Woodman, 1983). Efficiency is more likely when group members realize their collective purpose and the specific short term and long term goals of the group (Zander, 1971).

Group effectiveness can be enhanced by collaborative goal setting that results in appropriate short- and long-term goals. Frequently, specific goals are not apparent immediately, but members usually can agree on abstract goals. Abstraction allows group members to interpret the goal in various ways. Because premature discussion of specific goals is more likely to divide the group, development of goals should proceed from abstract to concrete and general to precise. Agreement on specific goals is most likely when cooperative interaction has taken place and abstract, general goals are agreed upon (Margolis & Shapiro, 1988). Groups will confront two issues during the procedure of setting goals: content and process.

Content issues deal with specific tasks at hand, such as discussing a classroom concern, whereas *process issues* focus on the means of achieving these specific tasks, such as the most appropriate means of addressing the classroom concern. After agreeing about content, problems that will interfere with process are identified and considered (Abelson & Woodman, 1983). Decisions must be practical, appropriate, and logistically efficient for all group members, including any child and family involved. If members are unwilling to reveal all pertinent information, inappropriate decisions may result. Group members should be encouraged to express their opinions in an accepting environment. If defensiveness, power struggles, or past interpersonal problems cause conflicts, these should be dealt with as they arise and before they become more intense.

Establishing role relationships and norms that define individual and group functioning is of paramount importance. Most group members have a specific repertoire of skills and knowledge that accounts for their membership in the group and helps define their role within the group. Effective group functioning requires clear role expectations. Undefined or unrealistic role expectations can prevent group members from contributing positively to the group process. In contrast, clearly delineated roles with realistic demands provide opportunities for successful interaction. When the group is made up of individuals from a variety of disciplines, a transdisciplinary approach is crucial to successful sharing and problem solving. This approach draws on the differential expertise that all participants bring to the group.

Group members should have a clear understanding of the process of group functioning and of the organizational and decision-making process of the group. They need to understand and anticipate the dynamics of group processes, such as the stages of group development, common characteristics of groups, specific problems that group members face, and strategies to diminish the effects of those problems.

POTENTIAL SOURCES OF GROUP CONFLICT

Conflict is a force that must be reckoned with in most groups. Although conflict can affect a group negatively by preventing the group from undertaking its task—for example, implementing a new curriculum—it also can have a healthy effect on a group by allowing differences among group members to be addressed and resolved, thereby building consensus and commitment among group members. Butler and Maher (1981) defined two types of conflict: *intrapersonal* and *interpersonal*. Although one thinks of the latter most often, it is not always the case that two parties are involved in conflict.

Intrapersonal Conflict

Intrapersonal conflict arises when an individual has one or more concerns that are mutually contradictory (Margolis & Shapiro, 1988). *Role ambiguity* occurs when a member is uncertain about his or her purpose for being in the group. *Role conflict* occurs when a group member has been given incompatible expectations about his or her role in the group (Butler & Maher, 1981; Hebert & Miller, 1985). For instance, if one member of the group views a psychologist as a therapist and another member of the group views the psychologist as a psychometrist, conflicting signals are being sent and the psychologist is likely to be confused and frustrated. This frustration may escalate and turn into an interpersonal conflict.

Additional sources of internal conflict can result from irrational ideas, overgeneralization, and dichotomous reasoning. These conflicts can cause a group member to perceive group goals as incompatible.

Conditions of the organization can reinforce intrapersonal conflict. For example, when an institution requires more from a person than is possible, *role overload* is the result. A person experiencing role overload can become frustrated and feel unsupported by group members who do not seem to be undertaking their share of the tasks. In groups with a facilitator who is experiencing role overload, members may feel frustrated because the leader does not share tasks. These feelings can be compounded if group members interpret the facilitator's behavior as resulting from a lack of trust in their abilities or views. In addition, group facilitators can experience intrapersonal conflict because of their competing roles within a group. On the one hand, the facilitator must be responsible for the product of the group, but on the other hand, the facilitator's decision-making role is equal to others in the group. As with many intrapersonal conflicts, if this overload is not resolved, it may intensify and become an interpersonal conflict.

Differentiation of function leads to dissonance and increases the likelihood of intrapersonal conflict. Individuals may be uncomfortable with new modes of operation or lack appreciation of different ways of operating. As a result, the new way of performing can precipitate an internal conflict with the way things used to be done. This also may happen when group members are unable to adjust to changes in the structure of the group, such as adding new members, losing a member, or introducing new issues or topics for the group to address.

Interpersonal Conflict

The more familiar type of conflict is interpersonal conflict. This type of conflict is a situation in which a person perceives that another person is frustrating to deal with or is complicating a situation or concern (Thomas, 1976). Role conflict and role ambiguity also can lead to this type of conflict. Unless roles are defined clearly, group members will not know their individual responsibilities or the responsibilities of others. Interdependence among group members also may contribute to interpersonal conflicts. The greater the interdependency, the greater is the impact of the relationships on the process outcome.

Personality characteristics of individual group members have a significant influence on interpersonal relationships and conflicts within the group. One of the most challenging tasks a leader must take on is to try to encourage members who are providing a disruptive influence to the group to become functioning members of the group. In most situations preventive action is the best strategy for addressing disruptions. By following good leadership etiquette, the leader can neutralize disruptive interaction styles. In some instances the leader might talk to group members outside of the group's activities to understand concerns of a personal nature and not as part of the group dynamics.

Five common types of disruptive interaction styles are consensus blocking, power seeking, recognition seeking, time dominating, and clowning (Hames & Joseph, 1986).

1. *Consensus blocking.* In this style of interaction, an individual consciously or unconsciously attempts to bring in extreme or extraneous information to inhibit or block group consensus. This individual may become angry or aggressive, change the topic, or go back to reexamine previously established parameters. When a group disagrees with this individual, he or she will not accept compromise and will continue the argument.

Several strategies are possible to counteract consensus blocking. If a member raises issues that have been addressed previously, he or she can be told that the group has addressed the issues and it is time to move on to another topic. If the individual brings extraneous information to the attention of the group, he or she should be told firmly that it is irrelevant to the issue being discussed and it will be considered after the current issue under discussion has been addressed.

Finally, extreme emotional displays cannot be ignored. Sometimes the meeting has to end and the emotional matter discussed in private. If any of these distractions becomes a recurring pattern, the group should bring this to the individual's attention.

2. *Power seeking*. Individuals other than the designated leader sometimes attempt to seek control of the group. They might do this to gain authority, or it can be a personal trait in which the person feels a need to be in control. This problem also surfaces if the leader is not fulfilling his or her role adequately. Someone within the group then may attempt to take over the leader's role, trying to help the group function. The result tends to be counterproductive because the group is being led dually with no one in real control. Then the group becomes dysfunctional.

Having clear role definitions within the group helps to avoid this problem. If it continues, a frank discussion among group members regarding role expectations can clear the air and help the group get back on track. Sometimes if the group leader makes a concerted effort to seek the opinion of the individual who is seeking power, this can diffuse his or her need to take control.

3. *Recognition seeking*. Someone in the group may make inappropriate statements or display inappropriate behavior to bring attention to himself or herself. This individual may talk for a long time, and other group members are unaware of what contribution this discussion will make. These departures may be in the form of story telling that makes the speaker a star. Setting limits on the amount of time each member "has the floor" can help to avoid this problem. Another strategy is to talk to these individuals outside of the group to help them understand how their behavior is being perceived.

If recognition seekers are interested in changing, the leader may be able to establish a subtle signal that will let them know when their peers are perceiving them as seeking recognition. The signal is especially helpful when individuals who engage in power seeking are unaware of how their behavior is being perceived.

4. *Time dominating*. Dominating time is related to recognition seeking. This individual monopolizes the communication by making long speeches that are, at best, tangentially related to the conversation. This person cannot seem to say anything concisely. Time dominators are different from power seekers and recognition seekers in that they seem to dominate because they can. They are not seeking authority, nor are they seeking personal attention. The strategies for working with recognition seekers can be effective with time dominators.

5. *Clowning*. A clown is an individual who actually is nervous in the situation and uses jokes or puns as a way to deal with it. Although it frequently can relieve the intensity of the group, persistent joking can be distracting and

can communicate to others that the group's work is unimportant. Helping the individual feel more at ease can relieve anxiety and the need to clown around. Having a frank, discreet discussion with the person also can help.

Lack of commitment of members within a group also can do much to harm effective group functioning and may lead to interpersonal conflicts. Commitment to the task at hand is a requirement for all group members. Everyone should be actively involved in the tasks of the group. All members of the group must share responsibility in developing and delivering tasks (Abelson & Woodman, 1983).

Finally, time is an important factor in group decision making that, if not carefully managed, can result in conflict. Differing schedules must be adjusted, and flexibility often cannot be stretched far enough. Groups typically take longer than individuals to reach decisions on issues. Time constraints are an unfortunate reality, and on occasion time limits affect the facilitator's management style, potentially decreasing the group's effectiveness (Abelson & Woodman, 1983).

CONFLICT RESOLUTION

Solutions must be reached through discussion and then consensus. Imposing decisions on group members creates resistance, lack of commitment, and withdrawal from further group interactions. Resolving conflicts in an open and supportive manner, on the other hand, typically strengthens commitment and group cohesion. Two requirements are necessary for group members to invest in a solution to a problem: (1) They must believe that the solution will bring about the desired conditions, and (2) they must have a vested interest in the outcome (Margolis & Shapiro, 1988).

Arbitration and mediation are two useful techniques that can be used to resolve conflicts. These may be new concepts to you because they are derived from the field of industrial relations. They have their place in all group dynamics.

Arbitration

When a conflict arises, the facilitator can structure the discussion to allow for arbitration. Kolb and Glidden (1986) define arbitration as a formal decision making procedure that identifies specific, immediate issues presented by the competing parties. As positions are defended and supporting arguments are presented, the facilitator may intervene with questions or clarifications, but the facilitator primarily listens. After the different viewpoints are presented and after all positions have been articulated, the group votes, and the majority position is the one that prevails.

A new program is being introduced into a privately funded preschool program to support families that have been adjudicated for abuse or neglect. The agencies involved in funding this program are Head Start, Children's Services, and the local schools. The facilitator of this group is Bonnie (the preschool director), and the other group members are Arlene (Head Start), Peggy (local schools), and Bob (Children's Services).

A disagreement emerges between Peggy and Bob that prevents the group from moving forward. Bob would like the children to be grouped together in their own class, and Peggy would like them to be integrated across the current classes in the program. Arlene and Bonnie are neutral on the issue. Bonnie decides that unless this issue is resolved, the group will not be able to settle on other issues associated with this collaboration. Bonnie decides to arbitrate this issue and the following discussion occurs.

Bonnie:	*It's clear that we have to settle this issue on integration before we can do anything else. I would like Peggy and Bob to provide concise statements in support of their positions. Each also will have the opportunity to respond to each other's position. Please limit your discussion to the issue of integration. Once their positions are clear, we will vote on the issue. The majority will prevail, and we can put this issue to rest. Can we all agree on this approach?*
Group:	*(Everyone nods in agreement.)*
Bonnie:	*Bob, why don't you start?*
Bob:	*Look, I'm all in favor of integrated programs, but we must face the reality of funding and expertise. Our agency has limited funds, and we must be sure the funds we are providing for this effort are used for our students and not for the general program. Moreover, these kids and their families have unique needs, and I don't believe your teachers have that expertise.*
Bonnie:	*Bob, it seems your main concerns relate to keeping funds isolated from general program funds and the ability of the current teachers to meet the needs of the children and their families. (Bob's body language indicates that Bonnie got the essence of his position.) Peggy, where do you stand on this issue?*
Peggy:	*I'm concerned that if we segregate the kids, they will be in an artificial environment that at best will*

> *be sheltered and inhibiting. At worst, I worry that they will model each other's inappropriate behavior, making it harder for them to make the transition to a general classroom. I agree with Bob that funds are limited, but I believe that with some work we can ensure that funds are spent where they are intended. I also think the teachers are knowledgeable and we can find ways to support them as they work with these kids and their families.*
>
> Bonnie: *Peggy, you're concerned that segregation is harmful to the kids. Also, you believe we can keep funds straight and find ways to support teachers.*
> *(Peggy's body language indicates that Bonnie got the essence of her position.) Does everyone understand the two positions? . . . Okay, let's vote.*

In this example Bonnie sets up a situation that allows Bob and Peggy to state their positions before the group. By voting on the issue, the group can make a decision and move on to other issues. In most cases arbitration should be limited to issues that are fairly simple or for which no compromise is possible.

Mediation

The previous example represents a complex situation, and some compromise may have been possible. Mediation might have been better strategy. Mediation adds the dimension of compromise to the decision-making process. Concerns other than those at hand can be introduced into the discussion as long as they are relevant to the decisions to be made. Because all of the issues are not equally important to everyone, the facilitator structures the discussion in such a way that the adversaries are accommodated to some extent on their issue of most concern and are convinced to concede on issues of lesser importance. Proposals then can be made that will form the basis for agreement (Kolb & Glidden, 1986). When initial positions are being presented, the facilitator's role in structuring the dialogue is similar to that of the arbitrator. After the positions have been presented, however, the facilitator becomes active with individuals, isolating key issues and finding ways to compromise. Consider the previous example with a mediation twist.

> *Instead of voting, the facilitator (Bonnie) begins to mediate between Peggy's and Bob's positions.*
>
> Bonnie: *Bob, do you agree that segregating the kids has potentially harmful effects?*

Bob:	*Of course. That would be like being against Mom, apple pie, and the flag. I don't think we'll be able to keep the funds straight and who has the resources to support these teachers! Peggy is always coming up with suggestions that ignore reality.*
Bonnie:	*We need to limit our discussion to the potential harmful impact of segregation. We'll examine the other points one by one. Can I surmise from your comments that, like Peggy, you see problems with segregating the kids?*
Bob:	*Yes.*
Bonnie:	*If we can find a way to keep the funds straight and to support the teachers adequately, would you consider supporting an integrated approach?*
Bob:	*If those concerns can be addressed, I'm willing to talk.*

In this example Bonnie is able to identify the key issue to be addressed and reach a compromise. She does this by getting everyone to agree on the most important issue—what is best for the children and their families. This agreement establishes the context for a compromise. Although much more has to be discussed and negotiated, the group is well on its way to a compromise. In this example, Bob initially resorts to a personal attack, which is a common way to derail a mediation. Bonnie and the group ignore the attack, which allows the group to get to the point. If the group had been unable to ignore the attack, Bonnie should have intervened and said something like, "If we're going to solve this issue, we must refrain from personal issues and stick to the problem." When engaging in mediation or arbitration, the facilitator must listen carefully and use summarization to clarify conflicting positions.

Working Effectively in Groups

Groups are a basic organizational structure in which humans participate. In schools a great deal of work takes place within groups. If you are going to be a competent collaborative professional, you must have the ability to function as a productive group member. Whether you are the leader, facilitator, or a participant, you have a responsibility to participate in the group in a way that will help the group achieve its goal. Groups are not effective by chance. They result from hard work and commitment on the part of group members.

Acquiring the skills described in this chapter can help you to be a contributing member to an effective group.

Remember . . .

1. The four types of groups are conversational, instructional, decision making, and discovery. A specific form of decision-making groups is the problem-solving group.
2. Good communication among group members is the foundation of a successful group. Without open and honest communication, the group is not likely to maximize its effectiveness. Open channels of communication are the means by which groups establish norms, role expectations, and group goals.
3. The three critical components of group dynamics are structure, process, and function. Structure refers to the framework of the group. Process is the group's developmental growth pattern. Function relates to the tasks a group undertakes to achieve its purpose.
4. As they attempt to accomplish their purpose, groups proceed through a relatively predictable sequence: forming, storming, norming, performing, and adjourning.
5. Skills that group members should have for a group to function effectively are typically categorized into task and maintenance functions.
6. Conflict is an important force that can inhibit or facilitate group development.
7. Efforts to resolve group conflict should move from the abstract to the concrete and from the general to the specific. Conflict resolution should be seen as a problem-solving endeavor that results in group members become mutually satisfied with the outcome.
8. Two techniques used in conflict resolution are arbitration and mediation.

Activities

1. Get three or four primary level puzzles, with 6–10 pieces, and randomly hand out these pieces in class. Have students work together to solve the puzzles without speaking to one another or taking a piece from another student. Students must give their piece freely to another

group member. Once the puzzles have been completed, have the students discuss how they worked together to solve the puzzles. Point out aspects that inhibited or facilitated the group process. Also discuss the roles that individuals assumed in the activity.

2. During the next week have the students record the types of groups in which they participate.

3. Describe any disruptive group members they have observed, and reflect on how group members dealt with these individuals.

4. Reflect on the groups in which they participated and describe the role that conflict played within the group. Have the students try to focus on the positive aspects of this conflict.

PART THREE

Collaboration
in Practice

7

Collaboration as Classroom and Schoolwide Problem Solving

When we think about what collaboration looks like in practice in the schools, we most often think about small groups of teachers getting together to address specific challenges they are facing. Historically, this kind of collaboration has focused on the needs of a specific student who is having trouble achieving in general education classrooms because of behavior or learning problems. Probably the first image most of us call up is two teachers—most likely a classroom teacher and a special education teacher or a classroom teacher and a school psychologist—putting their heads together to develop classroom-based interventions that will increase the student's chances for success.

In contrast to team teaching, which will be addressed in Chapter 8, collaboration as specific problem solving is based on the notion that bringing together pairs or small groups of teachers temporarily to pool their varied expertise is a valuable way of dealing with a wide variety of challenges that teachers face. Ideally, such collaboration engenders a sense of mutual responsibility in the entire school staff for the full range of students who attend and helps to develop all teachers' capacities for and confidence in working well with every student for whom they are responsible.

Groups of teachers that form for the purpose of collaborative problem solving may meet only once, or they may get together at regular intervals to consider the progress of the situation in which they are interested. These groups may be made up of only two teachers, or a larger group of teachers, staff members, or other appropriate individuals (for example, family members). Some groups may adopt formal structures or models to facilitate their work, and others might prefer to work informally. And once the immediate situation is addressed effectively—or at least is on its way to being addressed effectively—that particular configuration of individuals teachers might be dissolved and different groups might be formed to address other issues. The specific form and duration of the pair or group of individuals who undertake problem solving depends chiefly upon the problem that is being addressed.

What approaches to collaborative problem solving have you observed or participated in during your field experiences or in your teaching? What was the purpose of the collaboration? How comfortable do you think the participants were? How well did the process seem to be working? What problems did you observe?

Differentiating Classroom-Specific and Schoolwide Collaborative Problem Solving

In general, collaborative interactions fall into two broad categories of problem solving: *classroom-specific* and *schoolwide*. Collaboration as we usually know it is initiated because of a specific challenging situation within a teacher's classroom. The student clearly is the focus of the interaction. Although the real source of the problem may not be clear until the problem-solving process is initiated, initially the student often is considered to be the one with the problem. This is what we mean by classroom-specific collaborative problem solving.

In contrast, every school has many issues that the staff has to address that transcend individual classrooms and individual students. When teachers get together to work on these more far-reaching issues—which, might for example, be to move from a negative disciplinary climate to a positive school community, or to address a persistent achievement gap between white students and students of color—their interaction is a form of collaborative problem solving as well, but on a schoolwide basis.

The dynamics that participants bring to bear on these one-on-one, small-group, or schoolwide collaborative interactions are similar, even if the sources of the problems differ in origin, size, or scope. Perhaps more important is the consideration that, although distinguishing between classroom-specific and schoolwide issues that require collaborative problem solving might seem easy enough, more often than not the two are closely related. That is, classroom-specific problems often emerge out of pervasive, schoolwide practices that themselves might be diminishing students' chances for success in school.

CLASSROOM-SPECIFIC COLLABORATIVE PROBLEM SOLVING

Although you might think of classroom-specific problem solving as something that takes place primarily in relationship to special education, that is far from the case in today's schools. Historically, consultation and collaboration first gained prominence in the late 1970s as special education activities, but today teachers collaborate to address many situations that may or may not be tied directly to the provision of special education services to students. What these various situations have in common is that the focus of teachers' problem solving is usually the needs of an individual student or a small group of students within their classrooms.

Collaborating to Review Student Progress

One kind of collaboration involves general education teachers' discussion and review of the progress of specific students in their classes as a regular feature of their teaching responsibilities. For example, Patricia Carini (Himley & Carini, 2000) has developed a process called *descriptive review*. In a descriptive review, teachers focus on an individual child. The child's teacher presents the case and raises questions as the departure point for colleagues' responses. Reviewing samples of student work is a critical part of the process. Teachers use descriptive review not because they are targeting specific problems for which they believe they need the input of a specialist but, rather, because they take time to consider in depth the progress of each of their students. Cochran-Smith and Lytle (1993) identify descriptive review as an example of "systematic intentional inquiry" (p. 32), reflecting teachers' capacities to engage in sustained professional reflection.

Teachers who review students' progress regularly in a collaborative fashion do not necessarily rely on a structured model such as Carini's. But the idea of spending time over the course of a semester to consider how each student is doing, and engaging in this practice with colleagues as members of an informal sounding board, is an important professional development in the world of teaching.

Collaborating With Bilingual Education or Content Area Specialists

Teachers also may engage in collaboration with their professional colleagues who have expertise in specific subjects or areas. For example, a general education teacher who has a number of students whose first language is not English might work regularly with a bilingual teacher or a teacher of English Language Learners (ELL) to get advice about methods that will best support the students. The bilingual education or ELL teacher might come into the general education classroom to demonstrate methods for the teacher in question. *Teachers must not make the mistake of seeing students whose first language is not English as having a deficit or a disability.* Instead, they represent students who have a rich resource in their first language and native culture that can serve as a strong basis for learning English. Unfortunately, many teachers have difficulty making proper distinctions between students who are struggling to achieve because they have not yet mastered English and those who really have disabilities and also are learning English. Bilingual education teachers and special education teachers who enter collaborative relationships with general education teachers have to be on the lookout for this problem, making sure that no teacher (specialist or general education teacher alike) supports the practice of assigning disability labels to students whose problems do not warrant this action.

Content-area specialists also might enter into collaborative relationships with general education teachers. For example, a reading specialist may be called upon to work with a classroom teacher if a child is struggling with comprehension. Together these teachers consider different instructional materials and different assignments, demonstrate new methods, or are responsible for shoring up a whole new approach to literacy instruction in the school (Bean, 2001; Lyons, 2001). Mathematics and science specialists may serve similar roles (Huinker & Pearson, 1997).

Again, these kinds of collaborations are formed not to solve problems related to students with disabilities (although students with disabilities are likely to be in the classrooms of teachers with whom they collaborate). Rather, they serve a professional development function in terms of supporting new instructional skills of general classroom teachers as they work to improve their teaching in and across various subject areas. In more recent developments, many classroom teachers are beginning to collaborate with technology specialists to improve their skills in applying technology to the delivery of instruction and thereby enhance student learning.

Collaborating as a Function of Special Education

These examples attest to the broad range of situations for which collaboration is an appropriate means of interaction among professionals in schools. What differs when general education teachers engage in collaborative interactions with special education teachers is that (a) they already may be considering whether the student in question has a disability and requires formal special education services, or (b) they already may be working with a student who is formally labeled, has an IEP, and is receiving special education services.

In the first case, teachers might seek assistance initially from a speech and language specialist, counselor, school psychologist, specialist in vision or hearing impairment, or the professional charged with the education of students who have mild to moderate disabilities. If the student in question is not formally labeled as having a disability, the collaboration may fall into the category of *prereferral intervention*. This term means that teachers are seeking assistance to improve the behavior or learning of a student before a formal referral is warranted. This is an important aspect of collaboration in special education. Why? For many decades students who were referred for special education usually were labeled as having a disability—whether this was or was not the appropriate course of action, and usually as a result of a teacher's referral. Today, in contrast, we recognize that some disability categories—notably learning disabilities and behavior disorders—can be highly subjective in terms of who is and who is not labeled, and we take much more care to try to curb the inappropriate use of special education labels. Prereferral intervention refers to collaborative activities that take place to ensure, as much as possible, that students' problems are addressed *before* resorting unnecessarily to formal special education identification procedures.

Various names are used to denote the formal structures for prereferral intervention within any school or district. These include, for example, Child Study Teams and School Assistance Teams among others. No matter what the name, if the purpose of these teams is to bring general and special education teachers and other school-based professionals together to address student problems in a collaborative manner as a means of stemming the tide of referrals for special education, they are, in essence, serving a prereferral function.

Despite the widespread existence of prereferral activities, however, there continues to be a specific problem with overrepresentation of students of color in special education (Artiles & Trent, 1994), especially in the categories of learning disabilities and behavior disorders. So an important responsibility of those who participate in prereferral activities as a form of collaboration—and this refers equally to specialists and general education teachers—is to make sure that the special education referral system does not continue this damaging pattern (Pugach & Seidl, 1998).

In the second case—when students already have been identified as having a disability—collaboration serves the function of providing ongoing support to general education teachers, whether they are working with students with mild-to-moderate disabilities or significant disabilities. Their collaboration is not the result of reacting to a specific or unusual problem that requires immediate action. Rather, it stems from the agreement to work collegially over time to maintain a high-quality, maximally inclusive program for the student in question, even though the specialist and the classroom teacher might not be team teaching per se. In this kind of collaborative relationship, the two teachers involved may meet regularly over the course of the year to monitor the student's progress, to make any necessary adjustments in the program or curriculum, or to plan for future activities. These meetings typically include the students' family or, in the case of adolescents, the students themselves.

In the following example of classroom-specific problem solving, a classroom teacher relies on a trusted colleague to help construct a solution. Which dimension of collaboration is operating here?

SCHOOLWIDE COLLABORATIVE PROBLEM SOLVING

What kinds of problems deserve schoolwide attention? Perhaps a school's reading teachers find that the methodology used with a certain grade level is

Helping Sarah

Carol is a third-grade teacher at Lincoln Elementary School. Considered to be one of the stronger teachers in her district, she has been working at Lincoln for 7 years. This year, however, she is challenged by Sarah, a child about whom the second-grade teachers have warned her. Sarah did not act out but, rather, was isolated and got little work done. She came from a home marked by poverty.

Colleagues suggested that Carol should expect little from Sarah, although Sarah was identified as a student having potential. At the start of the year, Carol had begun to see the same pattern in Sarah's behavior. She wasn't getting her work done and seemed to have few friends. Determined not to buy into the views of her colleagues, Carol enlisted the support of the reading teacher, Nathan, whom she always trusted to provide a sympathetic ear. In explaining the situation to him, Carol focused on her desire to help Sarah break out of her isolation and reach her potential.

Nathan posed several questions for Sarah to think about, and Sarah posed several more to herself. They talked about Sarah's interaction patterns, her reluctance to talk in a large group, and her unkempt look, which seemed to isolate her even more. Carol also noted the sparkle in Sarah's eye when Carol had the time to work with her one-on-one. As Carol and Nathan talked, Carol

not achieving results; they might engage in problem solving collaboratively with their peers to identify the specific dimensions of the problems and develop new directions for improving students' literacy. Other groups may develop informally around similar interests, working to iron out the bugs as new methods of teaching mathematics, or interdisciplinary approaches to curriculum, are implemented.

Sometimes the school staff might meet as a whole to discuss a general problem—for example, schoolwide discipline—and splinter off into temporary working groups to come up with ways of addressing the challenge. Classroom teachers also might meet to discuss problems with the existing curriculum at a certain grade level and its impact on the achievement of specific students. Other groups may form when the staff realizes, for example, that a disproportionate number of students of color are being referred for special education.

began to see that if Sarah were going to succeed, Carol herself would have to structure some sort of peer interaction carefully and slowly—and select a peer who wouldn't push Sarah too fast.

As Carol discussed these issues with Nathan, they both identified Lilly as a student who would be ideal in this role. Lilly was a bit more mature than the other students, always willing to help, and a good worker. She was a leader, but in a quiet way. With Nathan's encouragement, Carol decided to talk with Lilly about being her special helper for Sarah. Carol would rearrange the cooperative groups so Sarah and Lilly were together, and she would give the two some private time each day to talk about their work. Sarah would know that she could ask Lilly for help, and Lilly's job would be to encourage Sarah.

Carol would talk to the girls together periodically and in addition would plan a time each week to meet privately with Sarah to keep track of her assignments. The other element of this plan was that Carol would buy Sarah a comb and brush to keep at school, along with a few hair ribbons. Sarah could come in a few minutes early each morning to fix her hair.

During the first weeks, Nathan often stopped by to talk to Carol about Sarah's progress. Sarah was beginning to come around after a few weeks, and Carol felt confident that she was now on the right track.

When a school staff undertakes problem solving about issues that affect the entire school, one of the most important things they must do is to fully understand dimensions of the problem. Rather than identifying a problem based on only a few examples that may or may not be pervasive throughout the school, these data should be collected on the whole situation as a starting point for making changes. Say, for example, that a high school staff is thinking of moving to block scheduling. Prior to making any changes, it is a good idea to study block scheduling and collect data on a pilot study in the school. Similarly, if a school staff wishes to increase the number of students with disabilities who participate in clubs and other extracurricular activities, current participation is important to know. Further, students might be interviewed to find out why they are not participating more in this type of activity.

The point is that instituting a data-collection or information-gathering phase for schoolwide problems before acting on them provides a realistic view of the situation. In the case of adopting a new methodology or curriculum, the data-collection phase instead may consist of a careful study of the new approaches, in which a subgroup of staff members brings this information to their colleagues for consideration.

In short, schoolwide collaborative problem solving is initiated when a school staff recognizes that it holds responsibility for improving the entire educational program the school offers. Thus collaboration underlies a school's capacity to move forward—even if the status quo seems to be working. It also creates an atmosphere in which teachers are encouraged to take the risks associated with raising important questions, trying out new practices, and seeing if

---

Block Scheduling

At Cosby High the teachers are in their first meetings of the year. At the end of the previous year, they had begun to discuss their frustration with the short, 45-minute period specified for each class. The principal, Ms. Clanton, remembers their frustration and brings up this issue as one potential goal for the year. In their discussions today, they are reviewing the problems they had talked about last spring. Although everyone is in agreement about the problem, finding an acceptable solution seems to be much more difficult. Some teachers want to use this opportunity to undertake a complete overhaul of the curriculum; others basically like their class periods the way they are, although they do admit that having more time with each class would be helpful.

To move the process forward, Ms. Clanton asks that a set of study groups be set up, each including teachers from various subject areas. Four small groups are formed, each of which is assigned the task of finding out how other schools have moved away from the traditional schedule. Each group includes teachers who are "gung-ho" for radical change and some who are less inclined. Their tasks include talking with teachers from other schools, reading articles about secondary school reform (and curriculum reform specifically), and polling their colleagues about specific aspects of block scheduling and curriculum reform. These study groups are designed to meet during the fall semester and report to the faculty monthly for discussion and debate.

they are truly an improvement. With schoolwide collaborative problem solving in place, problems stemming from ineffective practices across the school have the potential to be acknowledged, minimized, or completely overcome.

THE RELATIONSHIP BETWEEN CLASSROOM-SPECIFIC AND SCHOOLWIDE COLLABORATIVE PROBLEM SOLVING

In most discussions of teacher collaboration, these two general categories of collaborative problem solving—*classroom specific* and *schoolwide*—are not addressed in relationship to one another. From our perspective, though, they are inextricably linked, are not mutually exclusive, and ideally should coexist within a building. If one of the major goals of collaborative problem solving

Through these meetings, the teachers as a whole become well informed about options. It becomes clear that, though many are interested in the opportunities for curriculum reform as represented by interdisciplinary instruction that link, for example, social studies/literature and math/ science, some are far more ready than others to shift to block scheduling to make this possible. Given all of the options studied, at the start of the spring semester, the faculty decides to plan for implementing a double-period block schedule to start the next fall. In this format only four classes meet each day. Given the current seven-period schedule, each class would meet for double the time, but only every other day. The new eighth period would be used for talent-development groups, enabling students to choose activities in which they have a specific skill or interest.

Under this plan, the extended time per class would allow for faculty members who wish to team to do so but would force those who are not interested in interdisciplinary work to create new forms of instruction that lend themselves to the extended time period. Through their conversations, each faculty member agrees to identify one aspect of their teaching to work on changing in the coming fall to better match the proposed new schedule. The spring semester is to be devoted to developing individual or interdisciplinary plans. Also, it is agreed that in the coming year, monthly faculty meetings are to be devoted to sharing the progress of interdisciplinary teaching teams. In the early spring the original study groups disband and give way to pairs of teachers working together to develop individual plans for the coming year.

is to improve the broader educational climate for a wider range of students, education professionals must recognize the delicate interplay between teachers' improving their own classroom-based teaching practices and schools' recognizing what has to be accomplished at a schoolwide level to improve teaching and learning. One would not want to create structures for collaborative problem solving for specific classroom problems without the complementary idea of schoolwide collaboration, which is designed to stop problems from arising in the first place.

Schoolwide collaboration began to emerge as a professional expectation in the context of the educational reforms of the mid-1980s and 1990s, when school staffs were encouraged to engage in collegial deliberation about the school's curriculum and instructional practices. In contrast, collaborative problem solving initiated in reaction to a specific student's academic or behavior problems—which often is seen as requiring the involvement of a specialist working together with a classroom teacher—is a far more common practice that began in the late 1970s and in most cases preceded large-scale collaborative school reform efforts. In schools that practice the inclusion of students with more significant disabilities, collaborative problem solving to support their continued inclusion is also becoming far more widespread than in the past.

To foster classroom-specific and schoolwide collaboration alike, teachers need to be skilled in the four dimensions of collaboration that make up the framework of this book and know when each might be called for. For example, when collaborating about schoolwide issues, teachers often are choosing to enter together a new arena of educational methodology or philosophy. Therefore, *support* for this new endeavor, and a means to *facilitate* its acquisition on an ongoing basis, probably are in the forefront. Specific *information* likely is needed, and often a specialist or consultant from outside the school might be brought in to provide that information and work as a facilitator during the period of acquisition. Some forms of direct *prescription* regarding how to proceed methodologically would likely accompany such a major change in curriculum or instruction.

When collaborative problem solving is initiated in response to a classroom problem, other dimensions move to the forefront. First, a pair or small group of teachers and specialists first work together to *facilitate* problem solving on the part of the teacher who seeks assistance and to support the teacher during that time. In this way, joint ownership for the problem and its solution remain with the teachers. If you are a specialist, this means controlling the tendency to be prescriptive and instead working with your general education peers to build on the strengths they already bring to the situation.

In our experience, only rarely should a sequence of steps be *prescribed*. In the case of collaboration used to support ongoing integration of students with significant disabilities, *support* and *information* usually are most relevant, with *prescription* and *facilitation* following closely when a serious challenge presents itself. So we see that not all situations call for the same dimensions of collaboration. But all four dimensions interact to solve the broad range of problems that teachers encounter in their attempts to improve their work with students.

GENERAL FEATURES OF COLLABORATIVE PROBLEM SOLVING

No matter for which purpose it is initiated, each form of collaborative problem solving retains some common features:

- The shared nature of the interaction
- The presence of two or more individuals with various kinds of knowledge and expertise that is recognized as being useful to address the problem at hand
- Joint recognition and acceptance of the need to engage in collaboration as a dependable and effective way to address a specific problem or goal.

This last feature means that participants acknowledge that the results of their joint problem solving probably will be superior to each trying to solve the problem individually. Irrespective of the various titles that participants in collaborative problem solving may have, once they come together for a specific, agreed-upon purpose, they should function as a team and honor and respect the various strengths that each brings.

Further, no matter what the reason for initiating collaborative problem solving, all participants in these interactions can benefit from bringing to the group the basic communication skills addressed in Chapters 3 through 6. Although specific collaborative problem-solving relationships will look different depending upon the teachers involved and the problem in which they are interested, they nevertheless should all be identifiable by these common features. Finally, in addition to these overall common features, collaborative problem-solving interactions rely on (a) the four dimensions of collaboration that make up the framework of this book and (b) a step-by-step problem-solving process.

GENERAL STEPS IN PROBLEM SOLVING

Most problem-solving models, whether they are team or one-to-one models, follow a series of basic steps to help structure the interactions. These steps have become so accepted in practice that they are almost always cited in the collaboration literature as the underlying process for problem solving and usually include: (1) some form of problem identification or description, (2) the development of interventions, (3) implementation, and (4) evaluation. The specific problem-solving model we offer is a variation on this process based on our own work on collaborative problem solving (Pugach & Johnson, 1990) and utilizes the following seven steps:

1. Articulation of the problem.

2. Consideration of contributing factors.
3. Development of a problem pattern statement.
4. Generation of solutions.
5. Selection of the solution.
6. Development of an evaluation plan.
7. Implementation and monitoring of the identified solution.

Articulating the Problem to Be Solved

A problem is a general dilemma, concern, or challenge that a teacher wishes to resolve. This challenge need not be student-centered. It could be curriculum-centered, teacher-centered, or a concern of the broader school community. This step in the process is short and involves developing a brief statement articulating in the most general terms the problem area to be examined. More specific statements should not be forced, nor should they be encouraged, because focusing too quickly on problems tends to inhibit full examination and exploration.

Considering Contributing Factors

One of the most critical components of any problem-solving process is time for reflection, during which an individual can explore all the factors that might be contributing to the problem and reflect on how they relate to the issue being addressed. Using peer collaboration, we facilitated reflection using a structured dialogue in which teachers developed and answered their own questions related to the issue being addressed. A peer partner monitored the questions to ensure that the partner was asking "what, when, where, and who" questions and provided prompts if needed, to facilitate the process.

In this step teachers who initiate the problem-solving process should stay focused on issues over which they have control. Although there may be some merit in exploring contributing factors that don't relate immediately to the classroom over which the teacher has control, in the long run these factors often prove to be distracters. If the teacher is unable to control or change these factors, he or she probably will not be able to develop an intervention that addresses them. If, on the other hand, the primary contributors to the problem are clearly outside of the teacher's control, this should be a clear indication that outside expertise and resources should be brought to bear on the problem.

Developing a Problem Pattern Statement

After exploring contributing factors, the individual experiencing the problem will indicate that it is time to move on and develop a pattern for the problem. The pattern contains three components:

1. A brief description of the problem and its underlying factors.
2. The individual or group response to the problem.
3. A list of controllable areas that relate to the identified problem.

Those who are collaborating with this teacher should take notes to assure an accurate record of the interaction.

Generating Possible Solutions

Once the patterns have been identified, possible solutions can be generated using the notes that have been taken and reexamining the answers to the questions that have been posed. These can be summarized for the teacher or given to the teacher to read so he or she can begin to generate possible solutions. One strategy is to have the teacher generate at least three solutions that he or she can use in beginning to work on the problem. This is a good strategy because it encourages teachers to take ownership and develop strategies within their repertoire of teaching skills.

Sometimes, however, you may wish to access the expertise of the group and can engage in a brainstorming session. In brainstorming, the following rules apply.

1. Criticism is not acceptable.
2. Brainstorming encourages participants to offer ideas freely and willingly, generating many ideas without making judgments.
3. The facilitator combines related ideas to generate more fully developed possible solutions.
4. "Killer phrases" are avoided at all cost. Phrases such as, "That's ridiculous," "but that will cost a lot of money," and the like can derail a strategy or an approach before it is even considered. More important, it can diminish a teacher's motivation for trying something new.

If a brainstorming technique has been used to generate possible solutions for interventions, the teacher should pick two or three interventions from the list. The group should withhold judgment as to the merit of specific interventions.

The teacher with the problem owns the problem and owns the solutions. He or she must have a right to select and implement what in his or her professional judgment seems to be the most appropriate solution.

Selecting a Solution

At this point, the classroom teacher has explored all facets of the problem and now is at a point where he or she must select a reasonable intervention. The group should be playing a background role and the teacher should be most actively engaged in selecting an appropriate solution. One strategy that can be used is to have the teacher predict what is likely to happen when each of the proposed interventions is used in the classroom. Through these predictions, teachers reexamine their biases, fears, and concerns and try to project what's likely to take place in their classroom. Typically, one strategy emerges as more workable than others. Going through this process should help the teacher select a strategy to implement in his or her classroom.

Developing an Evaluation Plan

To promote a successful solution, classroom teachers must develop some plans to establish that the situation has changed as a result of its implementation. More important, they must document that they have implemented the plan as they have stated it. This need not be a rigorous task, but it must be something that can convince the group that the teacher was able to both monitor that he or she had implemented the strategy (process evaluation) and establish that the intervention was successful (outcome evaluation).

Implementing and Monitoring the Accepted Solution

A timeline should be established that identifies when the intervention will be implemented and how long it will be implemented before making a decision about its effectiveness. If everything seems to work out, the follow-up meeting can be brief and the teachers can share their success. If, on the other hand, things are not working as projected, the teacher and the team have to decide whether to bring in the expertise of the consultant or to reexamine steps in the problem-solving process to see if they missed a key issue that could relate to a more successful strategy.

USING PROBLEM-SOLVING STEPS WISELY

In general, this approach to problem solving places the primary emphasis on description of the problem by allowing ample time for the teacher to reflect on the various factors that might contribute to the problem—primarily as a means of seeking appropriate strategies for intervention. This step-by-step process introduces a structure for how professionals might spend the precious time they have in which to engage in problem solving.

Once participants are familiar with these steps and have internalized them, solving problems should begin to feel less like a formal process and more like a conversation—but a highly focused conversation. Further, although the process may seem at first to take a lot of time, the time required becomes shorter with practice. But problem solving does indeed take time—and one of the goals of collaborative schools is to reorganize resources to maximize the time teachers have to work on improving their own practice and the collective practice of their school.

Models of Classroom-Specific Collaborative Problem Solving

In the context of special education and school psychology classroom-specific collaborative problem solving has been practiced for at least two decades. As a result, several models involving varying degrees of structure have been developed to facilitate problem solving as it relates to teachers' capability and willingness to accommodate students with disabilities and other students who seem difficult to teach within a specific classroom. Development of these models burgeoned in the 1980s. They have various names, including but not limited to teacher assistance teams (Chalfant, Pysh, & Moultrie, 1979), intervention assistance teams (Zins, Curtis, Graden, & Ponti, 1988), peer collaboration (Johnson & Pugach, 1991), and mainstream assistance teams (Fuchs, Fuchs, Bahr, Fernstrom, & Stecker, 1990). What these models have in common is the goal of bringing together teachers with other teachers or specialists to improve the school experience for specific students who are having difficulty. Despite this broad common goal, though, the models themselves vary greatly, specifically with respect to how the expertise of specialists and classroom teachers is conceptualized and the roles that various participants play in the process of problem solving.

When schools are moving toward greater integration between special and general education, they often begin by selecting and implementing one of these collaborative models. Because different models of classroom-specific collaborative problem solving place different weights on the roles of the participants, selecting a specific model marks, *de facto*, how collaboration is defined in that building and influences the kind of relationships that develop between specialists and general education teachers in the context of that model.

For example, if the model selected to guide the interaction between specialists and classroom teachers is heavily weighted toward *prescription* on the part of specialists, the classroom teacher's expertise may never be recognized properly. On the other hand, if the model is weighted more heavily toward *facilitation* of teachers' expertise, other relationships and strengths may develop. In our experience, the "default" form of interaction when specialists and classroom teachers get together seems to be the direct dispensing of answers by specialists—no matter how collaborative the interaction is intended to be. Therefore, selecting a model that already fosters the prescriptive approach could limit the growth potential of the teachers in the building.

We would argue that the relationship between creating schoolwide norms of collaboration and selecting a specific collaborative model to enact those goals has to be recognized from the outset—so that the selection of a specific model for collaboration is informed by the school's prior commitments and goals. In this way, each model can be measured against the schoolwide goal before any one is selected—to see if it is consistent with the direction the school wishes to go. With the school as the critical context for developing and sustaining the commitment to collaboration, pairs or small groups of teachers become subunits working toward the same goal with whatever model the school chooses.

Given a prior commitment to schoolwide collaboration, these various models should serve as tools to reach the overriding goal of schoolwide collaboration, and *not* what defines the overall relationship between special and general education. The schoolwide context within which these specific, special education-oriented collaborative models operate is critical to their success. But the school should be considered the primary unit of mutual commitment to collaboration as a means of meeting the needs of all the students in a building.

FOUR EXAMPLES OF COLLABORATIVE PROBLEM SOLVING

We have selected four examples, displayed in Table 1, that illustrate fundamental differences among various commonly used problem-solving models. In your work you are likely to come across various interpretations of these and other models for collaborative problem solving that are initiated in reaction to specific student problems in the classroom. They may operate under the names described here, or under a general rubric such as *prereferral intervention,* discussed earlier, or the district or school may have developed a local name for the process. Notice how each places a slightly different emphasis on various aspects of collaboration.

These four models can be viewed along a continuum of directiveness, with TATs at one end as an example of a highly nondirective approach and MATs at the other end as an example of a highly directive approach (see Figure 7.1). As we have seen, TATs and peer collaboration are both based on the assumption that teachers themselves have a great deal of expertise—expertise that should be recognized and utilized for solving many classroom problems. More specifically, peer collaboration stresses the role of teacher reflection in understanding the problem and creating solutions. The lesson of TATs and peer collaboration is that we cannot always make the assumption that classroom teachers require that specialists be present to address problems. Instead, we need to recognize the extent to which classroom teachers are themselves capable professionals in coming up with solutions for themselves or for their colleagues. As a result, specialists' time may be better used to address more intensive problems.

On the other hand, both the IAT and MAT models require participation of the special education teacher or school psychologist. The assumption underlying these approaches is that problems cannot be solved readily without the specialist's presence and expertise. Unlike MATs, however, the IAT process is not nearly as prescriptive; its proponents stress the need for voluntary teacher participation.

Limitations of the TAT model revolve around the issue of *structure of the meetings* themselves. Typically, the format for problem solving is to brainstorm various solutions. Although TATs do seem to result in usable

TABLE 7.1 Comparison of Four Models of Classroom-Specific Problem Solving

Model	Major Characteristics	Research	Benefits	Limitations
1. Teacher Assistance Teams (TAT) (Chalfant & Pysh, 1989)	• Problem-solving team • General education teachers • 30-minute problem-solving sessions • Teachers self-refer to TAT • Brainstorming format	• Can reduce inappropriate referrals	• High value on expertise of general education teachers • Joint ownership of problems	• Unstructured interactions—may get off track easily
2. Peer Collaboration (Johnson & Pugach, 1991; Pugach & Johnson, 1995)	• Structured, reflective dialogue • Designated roles (initiator and facilitator) • Internal dialogue fostered for initiator; facilitator assists • Requires clarifying questions, summarizing, predicting, and evaluating • Can be used between general or special education teachers	• Most problems identified improved; referral rates of participants were significantly lower than control group	• Structured process; content not prescribed • Values expertise of general education teacher • Active participation, high degree of ownership of problems and solutions	• Structure of dialogue may be confining

TABLE 7.1   (continued)

Model	Major Characteristics	Research	Benefits	Limitations
3. Intervention Assistance Teams (IAT) (Zins, Curtis, Graden, & Ponti, 1988)	▪ Small group (teacher, specialist, administrator) ▪ Follows typical problem-solving steps ▪ Permanent teams are often established; stability of teams encouraged ▪ Uses terminology of "consultee" and "consultant"; promotes a collaborative, not expert, approach ▪ Teams encouraged to develop and disseminate standard operating procedures	N/A	▪ Promotes parity among team members ▪ Brings specialist knowledge to team	▪ Can become overly bureaucratized
4. Mainstream Assistance Teams (MAT) (Fuchs, Fuchs, & Bahr, 1990)	▪ Highly prescriptive ▪ Specialists are consultants, classroom teachers are consultees ▪ Strives for efficiency in changing behavior of classroom teacher ▪ List of prescribed interventions for classroom teacher ▪ Scripts for consultants	▪ 70% of daily behavioral goals met	▪ Efficient ▪ Easy to access specialist's advice	▪ Absence of reflection on practice ▪ Narrow range of interventions offered ▪ Highly structured; little room for dialogue, questioning

interventions, and though the open structure of the meetings may allow for much latitude in developing interventions, more structure than is described in the TAT literature may be desirable to ensure that the meetings efficiently facilitate teachers' thinking about how to approach the problems they wish to address. Peer collaboration provides a structure for the process, but a balance has to be struck between the structure of the dialogue and teachers' freedom to engage in a conversational sort of interaction.

 Under whatever name these interactions take place, what you should be looking for are the underlying assumptions of the model in practice and how consistent they are with the school's prior commitment to collaboration. How are these models alike? How do they differ? With which would you feel most comfortable?

Another issue that clearly distinguishes more and less directive models of collaborative problem solving is *resistance*. Managing resistance is a common theme in the literature on collaboration and consultation (see, for example, Aldinger, Warger, & Eavy, 1991; Friend & Cook, 1992; Zins et al., 1988). Its prominence reveals an overriding concern that many teachers may resist the suggestions of specialists and consultants—suggestions that place on the recipient the expectation for changing his or her classroom practice. In fact, much of this literature on resistance makes reference to the "acceptability" of suggested interventions (e.g., Witt & Elliott, 1985).

In models such as the MAT, commitment to implementing the solution typically is seen as the point of resistance. Resistance is considered to be an

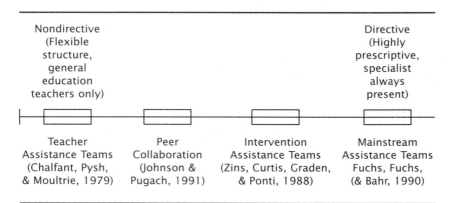

FIGURE 7.1 Continuum of Four Classroom-Specific Models of Collaborative Problem Solving

issue after the solution is developed—a byproduct of the process. In these more directive models, building teacher skills through an efficient and pre-scriptive means precedes the issue of building commitment. In contrast, in less directive models such as TAT's and peer collaboration, building commitment is related integrally to the process itself. Teachers are seen as having the skills and knowledge to generate effective interventions, an assumption that pro-vides a basis for one's commitment to the intervention itself.

In a sense, in less directive models resistance is dealt with at the front end of the process by focusing on the teachers' expertise and willingness to try to work out solutions, and not on their lack of skill. Teachers may need to learn new skills, but they do so in a context in which their contribution and profes-sional commitment is recognized and valued from the outset of the problem-solving process. We believe that resistance is counteracted by having teachers choose to intervene for educational improvement at the classroom level in a manner that is consistent with their own levels of professional development, but within an overall school climate that favors such change.

If the goal of collaborative problem solving is to build teacher flexibility and enhance the teacher's repertoire of instructional or behavioral strategies, the teacher himself or herself must be committed to implementing whatever changes are developed as a result of the collaboration. This is the case whether the process includes a specialist, another teacher, or a small group. Lasting change comes about because teachers feel comfortable taking the risks associ-ated with trying the new teaching behaviors themselves.

This view of teacher resistance is not meant to imply that change comes without conflict. To the contrary, conflict during the process of change can be one indicator of free and open dialogue among a school staff. Our point here is that the schoolwide context itself can intensify or limit resistance to change among the professionals who work there.

CURRICULUM COLLABORATION: THE BRIDGE BETWEEN INDIVIDUAL AND SCHOOLWIDE PERSPECTIVES

As we noted earlier, sometimes the problem isn't really a problem with the stu-dent at all but is a larger problem that is having a negative influence on the stu-dent's ability to be successful in school. Often, one source of difficulty is the standard general education curriculum; this is where many students first expe-rience failure and then are referred for special education (Pugach & Warger, 1996). When the standard curriculum is inflexible, or dull, or dominated by skill and drill, or lacking in adequate opportunity for students to be creative, it should come as no surprise if many students do not do well, resist, and have trouble learning. In traditional special education consultation and collabora-tion, the student nearly always is viewed as the source of the problem instead

AN EMPHASIS ON REFLECTIVE PROBLEM SOLVING: PEER COLLABORATION

In peer collaboration, each participant takes on one role, that of either initiator or facilitator. The initiator is the teacher who has a problem to be addressed; the facilitator's role is to guide his or her peer to reflect on the problem and come up with solutions. To begin the interaction, the initiator prepares a brief written description of the problem as he or she sees it. Then the pair (or triad, as appropriate) begins the cycle of peer collaboration. The four general steps of the process are: (1) clarifying questions, (2) summarization, (3) interventions and predictions, and (4) evaluation.

The steps to peer collaboration illustrate the interactive nature of the dialogue between participants:

1. *Clarifying questions:* The facilitator begins asking questions to assist the initiator in clarifying the problematic situation. To ensure that the initiator is engaging in reflective thought about these questions, the facilitator re-forms the question to make it more meaningful. Then the initiator responds to it. The purpose of this step is to turn over ownership of the process of clarification to the initiating teacher, as he or she has the most information about the situation. The facilitator guides his or her peer to consider basic areas about which good questions might be asked. Once the problem is clarified to the satisfaction of both partners, they move to problem summarization.

2. *Summarization:* This step provides the opportunity for the initiating teacher to reframe the problem based on the clarifying activities just concluded. Often in collaborative problem solving, the assumption is made that the problem as stated by the teacher is an accurate description of what is going on. In peer collaboration, the assumption is that, given the time and structure to clarify multiple aspects of the situation, the problem may look different than it did initially. The format for summarizing the problem anew consists of (1) establishing the pattern of behavior, (2) acknowledging the teacher's feelings about the problem, and (3) identifying classroom and school variables that are under the teacher's control. The last aspect of the summarization focuses attention on things the teacher can do about the situation instead of dwelling on things over which he or she has no control.

3. *Interventions and predictions:* Like many other problem-solving models, the third and fourth steps of this process include identifying possible interventions and developing an implementation/evaluation strategy. In peer collaboration, at least three potential interventions are generated and predictions are made regarding the outcomes of each. After assessing each possibility, the initiator chooses the one he or she is most comfortable in implementing. During this phase, the facilitator may continue to ask clarifying questions about the interventions, models the development of interventions if necessary, and ensures that predictions are made about each.

4. *Evaluation:* Finally, a two-part evaluation strategy is developed. First, it is important to develop an implementation strategy and design a means to keep track of it. Next, a plan for accounting for the student's progress is designed. The partners plan a meeting to take place 2 weeks later to consider progress or to redesign the intervention, possibly taking into consideration the other alternatives generated in Step Three.

Source: "Peer Collaboration: Accommodating the Needs of Students with Mild Learning and Behavior Problems," by L. J. Johnson and M. C. Pugach, in *Exceptional Children, 57*(5), 454–461.

of considering the interaction between the student and various characteristics of the teaching and learning climate in the school.

In shifting the focus of collaboration away from developing individual interventions directed to student "problems" and toward curriculum, we begin to build a bridge between conventional roles for special educators and contemporary roles that acknowledge the relationship between special education and problems in the general education curriculum (Pugach & Warger, 1996). In so doing we take into account the worth of what we are asking students to learn and be able to do in school in the first place, rather than assume they will fail at whatever we are asking them—and everyone else—to do. Focusing on curriculum as the centerpiece of collaboration also begins to align the practice of collaboration more directly with the 1997 amendments to IDEA with respect to the role of the general education curriculum in relationship to inclusive education. Finally, a curriculum focus for collaboration encourages teachers to ask important questions about the quality of their own teaching and the learning that results from it in relationship to the curriculum (Pugach & Fitzgerald, 2001).

Pugach & Warger (1996) developed a curriculum-centered model of collaborative problem solving that places the interaction between the student and the curriculum at the center of the process. Although this model follows a general four stage problem-solving pattern, it represents a significant departure from the typical problem-solving model because of its unyielding concern for the role of curriculum change in improving the learning situation for students who are not successful in school.

In the first stage, *Establishing Rapport and Negotiating the Contract*, special and general education teachers (and other participants as appropriate) clarify the expectations for the purpose of the collaboration. At this point the special educator has to gain a clear picture of the curriculum used in the general education classroom and the curricular outcomes expected of the student.

In the second stage, *Problem Identification*, the curriculum has to be analyzed in relationship to the student's progress (or lack of it). Teachers engage in a process of identifying new curriculum goals, new instructional strategies, and appropriate, authentic assessment techniques. Then they begin to identify new potential relationships among the student, the curriculum, the teacher, and other students. How will the teacher assist the student in reaching the curriculum goal? What difficulties might the student have as a result of possible mismatches between the curriculum or the assignment and the student's abilities that will require modifications on the part of the teacher? The difference between this approach and the conventional problem-solving model described earlier in the chapter is that professionals are not beginning their collaboration based on the assumption that something is wrong with the student. Instead, an adjustment has to be made to the *curriculum* to foster the students' success—possibly leading to a new approach to curriculum altogether.

During the third stage, *Intervention*, participants brainstorm modifications of the curriculum, the teacher's instruction, or assessment. How does the curriculum have to be adjusted, expanded, or enhanced for this student? What steps will the general education teacher take to make and sustain these changes?

The last stage, as with any collaboration, consists of an evaluation plan. In the curriculum-centered collaboration model, the final stage, *Evaluation and Closure,* requires asking oneself the question, "What did the student learn, and how do I know learning took place?" This represents a much different emphasis from evaluation plans directed to, for example, what percentage of the time a student was off task and how that time increased. Instead, a curriculum-centered model promotes looking at the curriculum as a good candidate for the reason the student is off-task or is not achieving in the first place. At the least, those who participate in collaboration should consider any problem that students are experiencing as an interaction between the student's performance/behavior, the demands of the curriculum, and the classroom expectations for what is worth learning.

Placing curriculum at the center of collaborative problem solving begins to build a bridge between collaboration as classroom-based problem solving and collaboration as schoolwide problem solving. Why? Once we move beyond the assumption that the problem is always within the student, we begin to ask questions about the way teaching and learning are organized at a school. The curriculum represents what the school values, as do the instructional methods used to deliver the curriculum and the alignment (or lack of alignment) between the curriculum and the assessments used to document student learning. Once we begin to ask questions about the curriculum, we are asking teachers to consider factors that have implications for the whole school and not just for individual teachers or classrooms. Questions include: "How well is the curriculum serving all of our students?" "How motivating is this curriculum?" "Why are we organizing social studies in this way? Is there a better way to do it?" This leads to collaboration as schoolwide problem solving.

Structures to Support Schoolwide Collaboration and Professional Development

As school staffs begin to move away from the isolated, individualized notion of teachers having responsibility for a single classroom alone, structural changes to facilitate proactive, schoolwide collaboration are being implemented much more frequently than ever before. These schoolwide structures may be either formal or informal depending on the nature of the problem to be addressed, and they are more or less successful depending upon how closely the staff and administrators function according to the philosophy of shared governance and participatory management.

As we noted in Chapter 1, the purpose of participatory forms of school management is to encourage teachers to work collegially to make important decisions regarding how the school operates—both philosophically and practically. Once teachers, administrators, staff, and family members work in a participatory fashion and as part of a unified professional community to make decisions about their school consistent with the vision they set out, real improvement at the school level can take place. One of the foremost goals of these participatory approaches is to enhance the professionalism of the teaching staff and increase teachers' direct responsibility for the quality of the teaching and consequent learning.

Some schools have been managed in a way that fosters participatory decision making and shared responsibility for problem solving, chiefly because of the principal's collaborative leadership style. Others, under the guise of participatory school management, have structures in place in which staff members and administrators meet regularly to engage in what is supposed to be collegial decision making, yet in reality the principal continues to make top-down decisions without a serious commitment to staff deliberation. This invalidates the concept of participatory decision making. Teachers might sit on monthly school management councils, for example, but feel uncomfortable raising questions that arise daily about instructional or disciplinary practices in the school. Therefore, more important than a school that professes to be a participatory work environment is the quality of the professional interactions and workplace structures that exist in a school to make it function as a collaborative, continuously renewing entity.

PICTURING THE COLLABORATIVE SCHOOL

Making a verbal and cosmetic commitment to participatory management characterized by collegial, collective decision making and actually reaching this goal are distinctly different (Conley & Bacharach, 1990). What do schools actually look like where teachers and administrators work together as members of a community to improve the educational program for which they are responsible? In her exemplary study of the organization of schools, Rosenholtz (1989) identified several characteristics of vital, energetic, professionally renewing schools—schools in which schoolwide collaboration was the professional norm:

1. Staff members at these schools had identified clear goals for their students. What went on in individual classrooms was clearly related to a set of mutually defined schoolwide expectations. This means that time

had been taken to talk about schoolwide goals and reach consensus on what they would be.

2. As a means of reaching these goals, teachers provided assistance to their peers without hesitation. No longer were teachers expected to find their own answers to problems or struggle in isolation to acquire new methods. Structurally, this means that time has to be set aside for teachers to engage in professional talk; share technical, methodological knowledge; observe and demonstrate in each others' classrooms; and coach each other in the acquisition of methodology consistent with schoolwide goals.

3. An atmosphere was fostered in which teachers' ongoing learning and professional development was a schoolwide expectation and norm. Structurally, this means that professional growth opportunities must be developed that allow teachers to practice new instructional skills and receive feedback on their progress, rather than just listening to "how to" inservice programs.

4. Principals incorporated an expectation for teacher learning in the evaluation process, chiefly as a means of communicating the importance of this value in the school and recognizing where support for weaker teachers could be marshaled.

With these underlying structures in place comes an increase in teacher commitment, chiefly because the potential for positive change seems attainable and well within the collective powers of the school's teachers and staff. When these basic characteristics of a professionally active school are in place, teachers begin to feel more confident taking the risks that will enable them to solve problems more creatively and try new approaches that can positively affect all of their students. This is the essence of schoolwide collaboration. It is what leads teachers to reconceptualize their work as a shared enterprise. For any specific situation that might arise, the ethos of a collaborative school would dictate that ingenuity, experimentation, learning, and continuous professional growth and improvement on the part of the collective staff is to be expected as a way of reaching the school's goals. In this way teachers can begin to take leadership roles in the process of school renewal and reform.

In schools that practice collaboration, teachers meet regularly to discuss professional issues, and they do so with encouragement for their leadership roles and impunity for challenging the status quo. Staff meetings or other designated meeting times are set aside specifically to reflect on progress toward the school's goals and to identify new issues that require attention. Through the mechanism of open communication, issues to be resolved have a public forum in which to be addressed. In some schools a committee or work group structure might be formed within which smaller groups of teachers collaborate, study an issue, and report back to the entire staff. In other schools, grade or multi-age-level team meetings take place regularly for the purpose of identifying specific issues. The common thread is that these meetings take place at regular intervals for the purpose of improving school practice. The meetings are purposeful and have an eye toward reaching schoolwide goals. Finally, teachers form and re-form such groups as needed.

Although the specific structures that facilitate new outcomes differ from school to school depending upon the relationship that develops between the principal and the teachers, the general qualities we have described—a well-defined common goal, frequent communication, an atmosphere that honors experimentation, and ongoing learning and support for learning in the staff— are found in all schools characterized by proactive collaboration. Lieberman and Miller (1999) identified five "building blocks" that provide newly emerging collaborative schools with a roadmap for thinking about where to begin the work of transforming and improving their schools:

1. Rethinking curriculum and instruction to improve quality and promote equality. *Example: What kind of curricular and instructional changes must occur to build our capacity to serve all students with disabilities in our school?*
2. Rethinking the structure of the school. *Example: Can we realign our staff resources to assign a teacher fulltime to mentoring our new teachers, including conducting demonstration teaching?*
3. Adopting a two-pronged focus: Students and teachers. *Example: What do we as teachers need to do differently to improve our students' learning?*
4. Making professional connections outside of the school. *Example: Teachers are active in professional networks (as opposed to professional organizations)—for instance, Educators for Social Responsibility and local teacher action research networks.*
5. Encouraging more participation by parents/families and the community. *Example: Teachers work directly with parents and family members to discuss and plan for new curriculum and instructional approaches at the school.*

Transforming schools through collaboration is not easy work. If a school practices this level of problem solving and school improvement continually, however, its status becomes "business as usual," a regular part of the work of professionals in schools.

When schools engage in collaborative problem solving, collaboration pervades the school and the entire atmosphere is imbued with a sense of professional support, self-renewal, and interdependence. In a sense, you know it when you feel it—and as a teacher you're painfully aware of its absence when you don't. New teachers are socialized to the norms in place in a specific school. If those norms are collaborative as they pertain to addressing buildingwide problems or challenges, new teachers will easily shed the age-old belief that teachers must "do it alone" and will begin to participate naturally in the various forms of schoolwide collaboration.

COLLABORATING FOR PROFESSIONAL DEVELOPMENT

One of the most important purposes of schoolwide collaboration is to foster the ongoing professional development of teachers. Only when teachers are engaged in continuous professional growth can their schools be places of renewal and reform, and only when teachers work together at this level to achieve school improvement can their students benefit most from the teaching and learning environment.

When teachers and other professionals at a school engage in ongoing growth and development activity, we usually think of these as *staff development* or *professional development* activities. We prefer the term *professional development* because it communicates that teachers are professionals. It also communicates that there is an ongoing expectation that teachers participate as professionals in growth and development activities.

Many people think of professional development chiefly as participating in one-time large-group workshops. The term *inservice training* usually conjures up long hours in a dull but required session after school or on days set aside specially for this purpose. Today, though, the options for engaging in professional development are far more sophisticated and multidimensional than simply sitting in a session and listening to a presenter, or even participating in activities within the large-group setting. Figure 7.2 is an adaptation of an organizational schema for the range of professional development options according to Lieberman and Miller (1999). Their schema indicates that a professional does not need to participate in a workshop to grow professionally; actually, many other intensive in-school or out-of-school options might offer longer lasting growth opportunities.

Whether you are a specialist or a general education teacher, you might be called upon to engage in any of these forms of professional development over the course of your career. Typically, however, you are likely to be asked to implement a workshop on a specific aspect of teaching and learning in which you have expertise. Workshops are beneficial for building awareness of a new approach, strategy, or method, or a new organizational structure. For these new approaches to take hold, however, the staff must engage in one of the in-school forms of professional development as a means of practicing and getting feedback on implementation of the new approach. Workshops alone cannot fill this function. We now offer some brief suggestions for planning a workshop, and

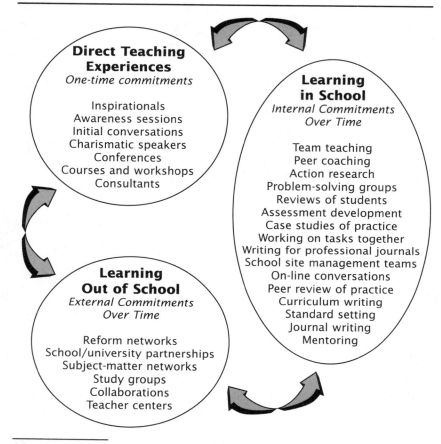

Adapted from *Teachers-Transforming Their World and Their Work* by A. Lieberman and L. Miller (New York: Teachers College Press, 1999).

FIGURE 7.2   Categories of Professional Development

then provide a description of peer coaching as one strategy for following up on a formal workshop presentation.

Creating and Implementing Effective Workshops

A formal presentation such as a workshop can be highly effective for creating awareness and generating enthusiasm. Its success, however, depends on several important things, including:

   1. Knowing your goal

2. Knowing your participants
3. Knowing your material
4. Detailed planning for adult learners
5. Engaging the participants
6. Evaluation and follow-up

In many ways planning a good workshop is like planning a good lesson. You must begin with a specific goal in mind, and then you must have information regarding the knowledge and experience base of the participants in relationship to your goal, as well as the current practices in the school or district. Otherwise you may not pitch the presentation appropriately. You also must know your material well. Sometimes people agree to conduct workshops on topics for which they do not have adequate expertise or experience. This places them at a serious disadvantage and is not fair to the participants.

One aspect that differentiates professional development workshop planning from classroom planning is that the participants are adults. Adult learners, and especially teachers and other school-based professionals, are incredibly busy. They expect workshops to be well designed and well focused and to address the topic they expect to hear about. They have high expectations for whatever workshop you will be presenting and low tolerance for what they perceive to be a time-wasting activity. Therefore, in planning workshops, you should include meaningful activities that engage the participants and not expect the group to sit still and listen for a long time, especially if you are in the unfortunate circumstance of presenting the workshop after a busy school day.

At its conclusion, you must provide participants with an opportunity to evaluate the quality of the workshop you have presented. In so doing, you will gain valuable information and show that you are committed to improving your own professional practice.

In agreeing to conduct a workshop, from the outset plans should be made for following up with specific in-school learning activities such as peer coaching. Let's say, for example, that you have just presented a workshop on conflict resolution to a staff of elementary-school teachers. If no plans were made for follow up, you may find that one or two teachers contact you to get additional information. But if the school is serious about working on student-student relationships, on reducing conflict, and on creating a stronger community of learners among the students, teachers will need many opportunities to practice conflict-resolution skills in their classrooms. Teachers new to this practice are likely to feel uncertain about how to proceed and would benefit either by demonstrations within the classroom or by videotaping their own initial attempts at implementing conflict resolution and working with a group of peers to get feedback and suggestions. This brings us to peer coaching as a form of collaborative professional development.

Peer Coaching as a Professional Development Activity

Peer coaching supports teachers when the school is trying to implement a new method of teaching. Joyce and Showers (1988) made clear that acquiring any new teaching method takes time—much more time than traditional patterns of one-shot inservice education can foster. They recognize the important role of feedback in assisting teachers as they attempt such changes. Once a school adopts a specific direction intended to accommodate student diversity more effectively, teachers can form dyads or triads to support each other as they experiment with new methods or make more substantive, broad-based changes such as changing the curriculum.

The purpose of peer coaching is to provide that support, not in an evaluative manner but, rather, in a manner that stresses the importance of collegial sharing while acquiring new methods. The process begins with the acquisition of knowledge regarding new methods and practice in initial training sessions. Then the emphasis shifts to using the method within the classroom. At this point, "coaching conferences take on the character of collaborative problem-solving sessions, which often conclude with joint planning of lessons the team will experiment with" (Joyce & Showers, 1988, p. 86). The term "coaching" was selected purposefully to denote the gradual development of skill, through practice, with the guidance and feedback so often associated with the coaching role.

Teachers involved in peer coaching relationships learn new methods together, watch each other practice those methods with their students, and critique each other's progress by jointly watching videotaped lessons. The group becomes the support mechanism by which informal discussion related to growth, problems encountered, and variations on method can be shared and discussed. Most important, helping each other learn new ways to work is accepted and valued as a schoolwide norm. This change benefits classroom teachers and specialists alike, because if teachers and specialists are learning new techniques together, they necessarily are functioning as equals within the school. This diminishes the tendency toward creating hierarchies within the school staff.

Research on peer coaching suggests that teachers who participate in coaching use new methods more often, more appropriately, and with longer retention than their noncoached peers (Joyce & Showers, 1988). Most important, coached teachers show greater cognitive understanding of the purpose of the new methods (Joyce & Showers, 1988).

Peer coaching as conceptualized by Showers and Joyce is not meant to be evaluative at all, but instead complements efforts to create a supportive environment for school improvement. The principles associated with peer coaching—namely, support and feedback by peers—deserve a place in a collaborative school as a fundamental means of creating an environment where teachers are willing to try new approaches to meet the needs of the diverse students they teach.

Interactions Between Schoolwide and Classroom-Specific Collaboration

Schoolwide and classroom-specific collaboration are not mutually exclusive. Both forms of problem solving have to occur in a school that is committed to meeting the needs of all of its students. Preventing problems for difficult-to-teach students through schoolwide awareness and planning is the most expeditious way to meet diverse needs. But even with the best curriculum and teaching, there always will be a need to make accommodations for some students, a need for teachers to be flexible in their expectations and demands. Sometimes those demands are specific to the needs of students with disabilities. At other times, they involve children labeled at risk for school failure. In some cases, a specialist may have to be involved to create a successful situation for the student—or for pairs or small groups of teachers to work together to generate creative solutions. But sometimes problems that seem to require one-to-one interaction to meet the needs of a specific student in reality stem from larger issues that require schoolwide attention. To what extent is the problem really the student's problem, and to what extent is it a problem with the way things are conceptualized and operationalized at the school? Collaboration is labor-intensive, and lots of individual, teacher-to-teacher collaborative interaction doesn't make sense if the solution lies in larger changes at the school level.

This distinction is important because it relates directly to the issue of resistance we discussed earlier. Our position on the problem of resistance is that within a supportive context for collaboration schoolwide, resistance to innovation either (a) diminishes, or (b) is part of a series of smaller skirmishes with resistance that can be addressed from a schoolwide perspective and not singularly on the part of a specialist. We recognize that teachers often are reluctant to take the risks associated with trying new teaching approaches. When such changes are expected and supported schoolwide, however, a climate can be created in which the norm shifts from the status quo to one of experimentation. As a result, experimentation and growth stand a better chance of becoming the norm rather than the exception. But when an individual teacher alone is expected to try a different method of doing things—within the relatively lonely context of a one-to-one relationship with a specialist—resistance might well be the result. Therefore, we see resistance more as a problem of the school context in which it occurs and believe that the greatest potential for reducing resistance is to create a school context that regularly supports the risk-taking required to improve one's teaching. If the specific problem a child is encountering is in reality a problem for many of the students, or is a problem with the school's general approach to a specific issue, that issue has to be addressed schoolwide, and all the energy that goes into individual collaborative interactions might better be redistributed around greater change schoolwide.

We can think of three areas that may give rise to confusion as to whether the focus of collaboration is schoolwide or situation-specific:

1. The curriculum
2. Inclusive education as a schoolwide goal
3. Creating conducive environments for teacher change.

These three examples point to the importance of nesting collaboration within the larger context of the school—both for the sake of efficient problem solving and for reducing the potential for resistance. By doing so, short-term change that takes place classroom by classroom is integrated with long-term change schoolwide—to which each classroom teacher contributes. Change within schools will always take place on two levels at once—schoolwide and individual—but building a climate of proactive, schoolwide collaboration prevents the need for so much reactive, situation-specific collaboration.

IS IT THE STUDENT OR IS IT THE CURRICULUM?

One of the most common reasons for initiating a cycle of collaborative problem solving at the classroom level is that a student is "behind" or "can't get his work done on time." Once the student has been determined to be capable of completing the work but chooses not to, an immediate determination must be made as to whether the work is, in fact, worth doing. In his book *Growing Minds: On Becoming a Teacher*, Herbert Kohl writes that one of the most important disciplinary tools a teacher has is the students' desire to be included in the daily activities *because they are worthwhile* in the student's eyes (Kohl, 1984). In the most immediate sense, the problem on which the teacher wishes to collaborate really does exist in the classroom. In the larger sense, if the curriculum is dull, is decontextualized, and requires students to engage in meaningless tasks in which they have no personal investment, one wonders why more students are not getting their work done!

Although not all students who have difficulty achieving in school are victims of a dull curriculum, the emphatic curriculum reform efforts of the 1980s in all of the major subject areas suggest that for the majority of students, the traditional, lock-step curriculum is a big part of the problem. If you are consulting with a teacher who is trying to make a dry curriculum more palatable to a student who is not interested in it, you face a question of principle when you engage in the joint development of interventions. In the short run, plans you develop jointly may put a stop to the immediate problem. But the question you probably want to ask yourself is: "If the curriculum for the grade or the school is the problem, why are we using sophisticated means of developing individual interventions and not attacking the fundamental issue itself?" By failing to address the larger curriculum question, the interventions developed for several students in several classrooms may be duplicating the effort to "make do" with a bad curriculum.

When curricula are based entirely upon mastering basic skills, students often do not see the reason for their labors. Instead, when the study of basic skills—which is often the concern of teachers with students who are having difficulty achieving—is embedded in meaningful academic work (Means, Chelemer, & Knapp, 1991), the motivation for students' getting actively involved is likely to improve. If, for example, students are reading interesting books and writing interesting stories and reports, the messages they are getting about the purpose of schooling are far different from the messages they get when they perceive reading as decoding and mathematics solely as the acquisition of basic facts. Much research going on today suggests that, with adequate curricular reform, students with disabilities can participate and achieve well in highly engaging curricula (e.g., Hindin, Morocco, & Aguilar, 2001).

Until we sort out whether a student's difficulties stem more from the curriculum than from any problems he or she is having, developing an individual intervention simply skirts the larger issue. That is not to say that the intervention might not be an appropriate stop-gap measure. But working proactively on curriculum change and renewal schoolwide, rather than engaging again and again in reactive problem solving, probably is one of the best ways to promote successful learning for diverse learners.

INCLUSIVE EDUCATION AS A SCHOOLWIDE GOAL

Often in one-to-one collaborative problem solving, one of the goals is to broaden the range of student diversity with which a teacher feels comfortable. Teachers might be working together to serve a child with an identified disability more effectively. A particular teacher might be collaborating to learn how to use assistive technology to accommodate a student with a visual impairment. The commitment to inclusive education, however, gains far more power if it is undertaken as a schoolwide rather than an individual goal.

If a teacher is having difficulty developing the flexibility to work with students whose needs differ from those of other students, making those changes within a school context where everyone is addressing the same problems and where there is a group forum for their discussion removes the pressure of being singled out, of being the only one who is trying to change. Questions of students' acceptance outside of the classroom, in special classes, across the school, provide the opportunity to see broader progress toward schoolwide goals.

This is not to say that individual change will be neglected but, rather, that change is more likely when it is part of a buildingwide effort and a stated commitment on the part of the principal and the teachers. Without a prior commitment, the potential for changing norms schoolwide is diminished.

CREATING CONDUCIVE ENVIRONMENTS FOR TEACHER CHANGE

Sometimes teachers request one-to-one, situation-specific, collaborative problem solving but seem uninterested in making real change. This may be a question of academic organization or of classroom management for which a teacher seems to want help, but upon collaboration has difficulty or chooses not to follow through. Sometimes teachers keep asking for more and more help, collaboration, and assistance but seem to make no progress. In these cases the pressure to change is focused entirely on individual teachers and those who collaborate with them.

If this kind of interaction takes place in a school where experimentation and change is not the professional norm, the responsibility lies solely with the two who are collaborating to make progress. If, however, the school itself is a workplace where experimentation, teacher improvement, and professional renewal is the professional norm, teachers who are uncomfortable with change have two choices. *First,* they may decide they have absolutely no interest in changing and look for another school in which to work. They are uncomfortable with the school's changing professional norms. *Second,* and more common, teachers begin to take small steps toward change, venturing out from their comfortable routines rather slowly, trying out new approaches first in the safety of their own classrooms and then discussing them with a colleague. In the second scenario, what is absent is the pressure to change as part of a public yet individual collaborative problem-solving dynamic.

Changing the practice of teaching is slow, and the concept of intervention means different things for each teacher depending on his or her point in their professional development. Just because a pair of teachers or a teacher and a specialist have decided on some course of action does not mean that the action will take place. When the problem is taken out of the context of the individual classroom and placed into a schoolwide context in which improvement in teaching is supported and expected, somehow taking the chance to try something new doesn't seem as intimidating. Given the overall difficulty of fostering improvement in teaching, creating a supportive environment schoolwide seems to be a necessary precursor to expecting change for a single, specific situation.

Achieving a Balance Between Schoolwide and Classroom Problem Solving

We hope that, when collaboration is a valued means of school improvement, a balance between classroom and schoolwide collaborative problem solving can be achieved in schools. We believe that as teachers gain more and more experience with collaborative professional relationships across the range of challenges that each school presents, problems associated specifically with hierarchical rather than collaborative relationships should diminish considerably. As a school becomes more and more collaborative and the professional norm is to work jointly with others to solve problems and improve one's own practice, teachers should have many opportunities to begin to feel comfortable engaging in the four roles that all collaboration requires and not see themselves only in the role of, for example, one who receives the prescriptions of others. By the same token, with experience all teachers should feel comfortable receiving advice in a collegial fashion.

Although solving problems is certainly common when educators collaborate, we pointed out in Chapter 2 that not all forms of collaboration are meant to result in problem-solving interactions. Collaboration designed to solve specific problems is based on the assumption that expertise from different individuals is needed temporarily to deal with the situation properly or fully. Collaboration as problem solving connotes a specific goal on the part of those participating in the interaction. In contrast, team teaching, which we address in Chapter 8, is a form of collaboration in which specific teachers share the direct work of teaching on an ongoing and permanent basis.

Remember . . .

1. Collaborative problem-solving techniques can apply to schoolwide or classroom-specific challenges.
2. Establishing collaborative problem solving as a schoolwide norm provides the capacity for a school staff to identify and solve its own problems and use creative approaches to improve schools.

3. By solving problems jointly, the results can be superior to those arrived at in isolation.
4. Because models of classroom-specific collaborative problem solving differ greatly in philosophy and thus define collaboration differently, the selection of a model should come after a school has established its goals.
5. Problems that seem to require classroom-specific solutions may be a function of problematic practices that should be changed schoolwide.
6. One important outcome of collaborative problem solving is to create a support structure for teachers to improve their own classroom instruction.

Activities

1. Divide into groups of five or six. Using the first initial of each person's name, take the letters and use them to identify an organization with a name and a specific purpose. When this is done, reflect on how well your group collaborated. What skills did you use?
2. Divide into small groups. For each group, select a school (real or fictitious). Generate a list of resources available to you in the school and decide how to reorganize, redistribute, or redesign these resources to help a wider range of students.
3. Divide into groups of four and select one group member to be the problem-identifier. This person should describe a specific problem that he or she is having with a student. Through discussion and asking questions, try to determine whether this is more a schoolwide or a classroom-specific problem. If time permits, repeat the activity with other group members.

8

Team Teaching
as Collaboration

One of the most powerful forms of collaboration is team teaching. When teachers decide to become part of an instructional team, they are making a commitment to open the classroom door, to make their teaching more public, to seek and give ongoing support to their colleagues, and to recognize the strengths they can contribute and the areas in which their colleagues can contribute to improving their work. In contrast to a problem-centered view of collaboration, one in which teachers come together to work on a specific challenging learning situation for a student or a group of students, those who teach in teams collaborate as a regular part of their daily work for the purpose of designing and carrying out educational programs that foster students' growth and, as much as possible, prevent problems from developing. When problems do arise (as they inevitably do), the team itself is an ongoing, ready-made resource and support for problem solving within the context of its larger, yearlong educational goals. That is why we sometimes think of team teaching as *proactive collaboration.*

Team teaching has had a spotty history in the U.S. educational system. Although pockets of team teaching have always been there, in contemporary times the interest in team teaching appeared in the early 1960s and was documented in the educational literature of that era (Cohen, 1981) but slowed soon after. An interest in team teaching emerged again in the 1990s as widespread attempts to restructure and reform education were implemented, chiefly as (a) the foundation of the middle-school concept, (b) teaming between remedial/special education and general classroom teachers, and (c) teaming between teachers in primary grades as a form of reducing class size. Teams can also be found in elementary and high schools, but in these settings it is not as common.

In middle schools, teachers from different subject areas might share responsibility for planning and teaching a specific number of students, often from 100–150—a model that permits teachers and students to build a learning community in which students feel a sense of belonging. Many middle-school teams include a special education teacher. In this model, students have the opportunity to build a relationship with their teachers over time rather than shift from class to class every 45 or 50 minutes. Also, creating student and teacher teams builds on the natural developmental preference that preadolescents and adolescents have for participating in a strong peer culture.

Team teaching increasingly has become a preferred model for collaboration between special or compensatory education (e.g., Title I reading programs) teachers and classroom teachers. This kind of teaming, sometimes called collaborative teaching, co-teaching, or cooperative teaching (Bauwens, Hourcade, & Friend, 1989), has emerged as a reaction to the well documented problems with traditional special and compensatory education models, in which students have been permanently identified as low achievers, have been pulled out of their general classrooms usually decontextualized for basic skills instruction, and have had fragmented social and educational experiences while traveling back and forth between special and general education classrooms. Special education and Title I reading classes are often a form of academic tracking, and teaming is one way of overcoming this problem. Another premise of the team teaching model is that not only students who are labeled as needing special or compensatory education have difficulty achieving in school. Many other students who are not labeled but have trouble academically could benefit from the resources of additional teachers in their classrooms. Team teaching allows teachers to work with more heterogeneous groups of students and, as a result, can assist in eradicating the stigma associated with permanent placement in a lower academic track (for a discussion of tracking, see Oakes, 1985).

Most recently, the goal of reducing class size in the primary grades has also led to team teaching (Laine & Ward, 2000). For example, in the Student Achievement Guarantee Program in Wisconsin (SAGE), team teaching is one of the three most common teaching structures identified to reduce class size to a 15:1 ratio in grades 1–3. These teams may consist of an experienced teacher and a relatively new teacher, two relatively new teachers, or a combination. In each case, teachers report having more time to spend getting to know their students and providing much needed individual and small group interaction (Molnar, Smith, & Zahorik, 1999).

Although team teaching as a form of collaboration originates from different purposes and at different levels within the educational system, many of the dynamics between teachers in any team teaching situation are similar. In this chapter we present principles that characterize healthy team teaching situations. This is not an absolute formula for success but, instead, these principles form a set of criteria against which the practice of team teaching can be judged.

Why Team?

Before deciding to enter into a teaching team, teachers have to consider under what conditions teaming makes sense as an instructional arrangement.

Planning to Meet Student Needs

One of the LD teachers at Central Elementary School, Sally Long, has been reading about the value of team teaching and has talked with a few LD teachers in neighboring districts who raved about team teaching and the relief in scheduling it provides. Sally is brimming with enthusiasm to try this new approach. Because most of her students are third graders, she approaches a third-grade teacher, Angelina Garcia, who enthusiastically agrees to try teaming the following year. Together they design a workable schedule for sharing the teaching load, identifying which subjects each will teach and how they will interact during the lessons. They plan a common daily meeting time and plan to have the LD students assigned directly to Angelina's class from the start of the year. Although they will have 34 students altogether, rather than the standard 26, eight of whom are formally identified as having LD, they believe that the 4 hours per day Sally will be in the room will make up for the larger class size.

As they begin to discuss specific subject areas, Sally and Angelina find themselves spending a lot of time talking about math. Sally is comfortable teaching math, so she wants to take a major role in this curriculum area early on. They discuss how difficult the concepts of multiplication and division are and how hard it is for the students to understand the relationship between them. Sally and Angelina also discuss the problems students have in understanding the concept of fractions and how easy it is for students to fail to see the whole fraction as a number. The teachers agree that both of them will be needed to help the many students they think will have problems in this area. With two teachers in the room, the chance of success for all of the students who are having difficulty with this and other skills should improve. Sally and Angelina believe that together they can assist many more students in achieving the goals of their school's traditional curriculum.

Given these plans, how will teaming improve the overall educational situation for students who have difficulty learning? For students labeled LD in particular? Specifically in mathematics? Do you think this plan is valid? Could these two teachers have planned for mathematics instruction in any other ways? Can you think of analogous situations for other subject areas?

TEAM TEACHING AND CURRICULUM REFORM

In this book we have argued consistently that when students are having difficulty, the root of the problem is often the intractability of the traditional general education curriculum. A clear advantage of team teaching is that it permits students to receive additional assistance in the traditional curriculum. Therefore, even though teachers such as Sally and Angelina might have misgivings about the quality of the curriculum they are directed to use, they see team teaching as a way to make it more palatable. As a structure for teaching, teaming certainly can be beneficial to students in these situations by making two teachers available to assist these students in acquiring skills and small chunks of subject-by-subject knowledge as represented in the traditional curriculum.

The potential of team teaching, however, is much greater than simply making a bad curriculum more accessible by providing two teachers to help students through it (Pugach & Wesson, 1995). The real aim of team teaching should be to create teaching and learning situations that represent the most motivating and effective approaches to curriculum and instruction available to teachers. This means shifting from a decontextualized curriculum based on acquiring separate skills and facts to a curriculum that builds on the natural interests that children and youth bring to school. With this natural motivation as a backdrop, teaching basic skills can be embedded more naturally within a framework of meaningful educational experiences. Team teaching should be the means to provide teachers with the opportunity to create strong, effective classroom communities in which students who previously have had difficulty learning are successful and in which students with significant disabilities are supported as full members of the classroom community.

Therefore, in making the commitment to participate in teams, teachers' primary goal ought to be *a joint effort to improve the teaching/learning process by implementing the most effective contemporary approaches to curriculum and instruction available.* A commitment to team teaching should mean a commitment to improving the whole act of teaching, particularly when existing approaches to curriculum and instruction have led to a lot of children and youth having difficulty in school. With this commitment to improving instruction, teaming has the potential to prevent many learning and behavior problems from developing in the first place—and not just for students whose difficulties stem from a disability.

Finally, teachers who team can engage together in continuously monitoring the extent to which their teaching is contextualized within their students' cultures and communities. The need for teaching that is culturally relevant, or culturally congruent, has been well documented (Irvine, 1990; Ladson-Billings, 1994). What this means is that teachers cannot teach in a vacuum of cultural and community knowledge. Rather, they must be working continually toward connecting their learning goals to the lives of their students and their students' families meaningfully and in ways that foster high levels of achievement. When teachers make the decision to team, they must continue to discuss their obligations and responsibilities to contextualize their instruction for the diverse student populations they teach. When teachers from different cultural or language backgrounds make up the team, dialogue about contextualizing instruction may surface more readily. But no matter who the team consists of, contextual knowledge must have a prominent place in planning and implementing curriculum and instruction.

Why is the commitment to improving curriculum and instruction a concern with respect to deciding to participate in team teaching—and not just a function of each individual teacher's decision to enter the profession? It is because teaming provides the natural support that teachers need to implement new curricula and instructional approaches that have the potential to counteract the rigid educational structure that has led to so much school failure. The resources of two individuals are available on a continuous basis to select, implement, and evaluate improvements based on student outcomes. Team teaching becomes the means by which teachers can challenge themselves and jointly take the risks needed to improve the quality of teaching and learning for their students. It enables teachers to be flexible and to shift their teaching from routine, skill-driven, subject-by-subject instruction to nonroutine and increasingly complex instruction—instruction that challenges their typical, day-to-day routine (Cohen, 1981). The flexibility and support that team teaching afford are squandered resources if these are not used to fuel basic changes in curriculum and instruction (Pugach & Wesson, 1995). With this commitment to change comes the responsibility to communicate the benefits of change to colleagues throughout the school.

The commitment to improving educational practice as a basic principle of team teaching should not be seen as a call for changing everything at once. Rather, teachers who team ought to set specific goals for various curriculum areas, working to gain skill in one and then applying those skills to other areas of the curriculum. Or they may begin by experimenting with one thematic unit and gradually incorporate others. The point is that teaming is only an effective form of professional collaboration if the question "Collaboration for what purpose?" is answered with, "Collaboration to promote the most effective teaching and learning possible for the greatest number of students" (Pugach & Fitzgerald, 2001).

TEAMING AND IMPROVING THE CONDITIONS OF WORK

In addition to the goal of improving student achievement, team teaching has a goal of improving the conditions of work for teachers—conditions that are challenging because today teachers teach more heterogeneous groups of students. In this case, the benefits of teaming include more power to do the job well, a sense of shared responsibility, and a partner with whom to share frustrations as well as successes. Others have identified an expanded sense of survival and power, more freedom, an increased sense of belonging, and simply making teaching more enjoyable (Thousand & Villa, 1990). For a profession that traditionally has been grounded in isolated teaching in separate classrooms, these benefits are important. The collegiality that has to be constructed for teachers who work in isolation in their own classrooms is not an issue for those who team teach. A community of adult learners begins to exist by virtue of the decision to team.

Further, the dimensions of collaboration described in Chapter 2 are integrated because in team teaching members continually move back and forth from direct to indirect support within the context of working as equals—even if their respective backgrounds and professional preparation differ. In this way, teaming naturally resolves some of the problems associated with seeing support teachers as "specialists" and classroom teachers as less worthy "generalists."

Finally, teachers who team also seem to benefit from the synergy generated by their own joint efforts. In one case we know of, the teachers' enthusiasm, expressed openly in their teachers' lounge, caused jealousy among their colleagues who were teaching in isolation. In a fully collaborative school, such exuberance should be honored.

The potential for curriculum reform and improving the conditions of work are two benefits of team teaching. Take a moment to consider all of the other benefits of this approach. What other benefits does it have for students? For teachers? For school improvement as a whole?

Principles of Team Teaching

We obviously believe that team teaching has many benefits and that the benefits clearly outweigh the extra time and effort to participate in this kind of teaching structure. After making the commitment to team teach, the question arises as to how to go about doing it. The following principles for team teaching serve as our basis for its implementation.

1. *Team members challenge themselves to improve their teaching.* Although teachers can challenge themselves to improve their practice when they are not involved in team teaching, they may rise to the challenge more readily with the built-in support mechanism that teaming affords. After making the decision to team, teachers must set a common, broad goal of instructional and curriculum improvement within whatever subject areas the team members select. Improving learning outcomes for all students by improving the quality of teaching is the foundation for the decision to team teach.

2. *Team members share responsibility for all students.* An axiom in team teaching is that the students with whom team teachers work "belong" to all teachers involved. Particularly when classroom teachers and specialist teachers enter teaming arrangements, they might have a residual tendency to see the students as "my" and "your" group. Although for administrative reasons students might still have to be identified by a label or as "belonging" to a certain teacher, these distinctions should not be made during the day-to-day operation of the classroom. One of the most important outcomes of team teaching is to create a sense of community within the classroom, a community to which all students belong. Especially when team teaching is initiated deliberately to reduce various forms of academic tracking or to integrate a student with significant disabilities, the students must be seen as a unified group and the teachers (as well as the students) as having responsibility for everyone in it.

A commonly reported positive outcome of teaming seems to be the inability to distinguish, either initially or over time, students who were formerly segregated from other students, particularly in LD resource rooms. If groups of students are identified as belonging to the special or general education teacher, overcoming the stigma of labeling becomes more difficult, even when the learning and behavior is positive.

Shared responsibility should not be interpreted to mean that all members of a teaching team have to do everything. Clearly, one of the benefits of teaming is that the work of teaching can be divided. This division of labor has to occur within the framework of a unified commitment and sense of responsibility and accountability for student progress. Otherwise, what is really going on isn't teaming but, rather, is parallel teaching, in which teachers work side-by-side but aren't committed to a common goal. When parallel teaching substitutes for real teaming, teachers more readily forget to set common goals and to work toward them jointly. In real team teaching, decision making becomes a shared responsibility.

Invisible Disabilities

Near the end of the school year at Mesa Middle School, part of the sixth-grade team is in the library to use computers to complete a series of assignments in English. This team of teachers was formed the previous summer specifically to integrate students labeled as having learning disabilities. The teaching team consisted of two general education teachers and one LD teacher, who together teach approximately 60 students. The teachers, Rachael, Joan, and Chris, work hard to use instructional methods that enable all of the students to be successful. They use cooperative learning, attend to individual students' needs, and have shifted their literacy program from the traditional basal approach to a more integrated program based on trade books and a lot of writing. The teachers never identified the students who were labeled LD, and the students never raised the issue during the year.

On the day in question that May, Dan was having trouble spelling some of the words for his composition. He was getting a little frustrated and asked his teacher how to spell the word "glass." His classmate, Maria, overheard his question and said in a sassy voice, "You don't know how to spell that word? That's an easy word!" Without missing a beat, Dan replied, "Well, I have a learning disability and spelling is hard for me, so if I need some help, I ask for it."

With an astonished look, Maria said, "You have a learning disability? You can't be in our class! You need to go to a special school!" To which Dan replied, "No, I don't. We're in a special program this year. The LD kids are with everyone else, and we're making it. If I have to go to a special school, so does Carlos. Right, Carlos?" Carlos piped in, "Yeah, I have a learning disability, too. And if I have to go, so do Samantha and Kayla."

Maria was shocked because Kayla was one of the top math students in the class and Maria was among the lowest. Maria said, "I can't believe this. Not Kayla! All of you fit right in." Despite her initial surprise, she went back to work with a shrug of her shoulders. The LD students had made it to May without a problem, and it seemed they would get through the next few weeks in the same way.

3. *Team members share responsibility for instruction.* Sharing responsibility for the same group of students means sharing responsibility for their instruction as well. Instruction can be divided in several ways. Teachers who team may choose specific subject areas in which they excel, or they may share all subjects, taking turns in the leadership role. The most important facet of decision making in the context of shared responsibility for instruction is that all teachers involved in teaming should take major responsibility for some portion of instruction. This is especially crucial in teams where one member formerly was strictly the remedial or special education teacher, and worked exclusively with students who had problems. In these situations, shifting the status of a specialist teacher to one who teaches all students will depend largely on his or her willingness to take on major teaching roles in the various subject areas. If this does not happen, the former specialist runs the risk of always being seen as a "helping" teacher rather than a "real" teacher.

Coordination of instructional responsibilities is a critical feature of teaming. Cohen (1981) and her colleagues discuss two kinds of interdependence in teaching teams, each requiring different amounts of coordination and communication. The first, *throughout interdependence*, takes place when teams of teachers split the instructional tasks, with each taking responsibility for specific groups of students. In this kind of interdependence, teachers do not necessarily have to interact concerning substantive issues of instructional method or philosophy.

The second, *instructional interdependence*, is defined as two or more teachers working with the same group of students in the same subject. This form of interdependence is more demanding and means that teachers spend time directly involved in the development and coordination of instruction. This more challenging form of interdependence, which places teachers in a reciprocal relationship with regard to instructional stimulation and feedback, is far less frequent than interdependence of scheduling, discipline, and other more routine aspects of teaching (Cohen, 1981). Therefore, if teachers who choose to enter teaming arrangements are not conscious of the need to aspire to instructional, or reciprocal, interdependence, they may find themselves simply dividing up the work and never really benefiting from the challenges they can take on as members of a team.

Specifically, then, sharing responsibility for instruction also means identifying challenging instructional goals for the team. Teachers who team should specify in which areas they wish to grow each year, and work together toward those goals. This puts all team members in the position of learning new skills together. For example, in the scenario presented earlier, Sally and Angelina might want to move toward a problem-solving, more conceptual approach to teaching mathematics to replace the approach based primarily on computation. This represents a major instructional change and probably will absorb a lot of their energy. Working together on this goal, however, should provide the support they need to see it through.

Sharing responsibility for instruction also means figuring out the most effective ways to balance the needs of individual students who may be having difficulty with the needs of the group as a whole. Unlike teachers who work in isolation, teachers who team have more flexibility in how they group students. A benefit of this kind of teaching structure is the capacity to form and re-form small groups as needed for instructional support—for both remediation and enrichment (Pugach & Wesson, 1995).

Flexible grouping means that for any given subject, students are pulled together as needed for intensive explicit assistance. What distinguishes this approach from traditional grouping is the concept of flexibility, which Mason and Good (1993) called "situational adjustment," to denote that grouping decisions are temporary depending on the topic, and require constant teacher monitoring to determine group membership.

With shared responsibility for instruction, benefits also accrue to the teachers. One LD teacher who teamed with several middle-school colleagues unequivocally supported teaming because it ended her own isolation as an LD teacher, placed her much more in touch with the regular staff and the curriculum, made her feel like a more valued member of the school, and, finally, seemed to counteract the perception that she was a lunchroom aide!

4. *Team members communicate regularly with each other about the progress of their work.* Although a tremendous amount of communication among team members takes place informally in the day-to-day operation of the class, a regular meeting time must be set aside for discussion and planning. In a job as demanding as teaching, it is tempting to use scheduled planning time to "blow off steam" and wind down from the hectic daily pace. Nevertheless, time must be identified for reviewing progress and for future planning. Of course, the amount of time and energy team members put into their planning fluctuates, but the general rule ought to be to meet regularly, to meet often (at least weekly), and to use the time productively. In one study of collaboration, teachers used a form called the "Meeting Tamer" to give structure to their discussions and to ensure the productive use of time (Ellis, 1990). To maximize your ability to communicate in these meetings, the guidelines in Chapters 3 to 6 should be of assistance.

Setting weekly times for communication is easier if teams are structured as permanent working groups. This becomes more difficult, however, if a Title I reading or special education teacher teams with several classroom teachers. Nevertheless, the communication aspect of teaming is crucial if it is to be successful.

Another critical issue related to communication among team members is what teachers in these teams communicate *about*. If, as suggested earlier, teams set complex instructional routines as their goals, regular meetings would likely serve a real purpose in terms of reflecting on the progress of these efforts. In the absence of prior commitments, time likely may be devoted to routine tasks that may be performed better by a routine division of labor. Every decision, particularly a trivial one, does not have to be made through laborious debate. Instead, energy should be conserved for stimulating discussion about instruction and curriculum issues.

Essential to a healthy team is to be open about problems. These problems may involve how a team member is interacting with students, other team members, family members, or administrators. Or a problem may stem from an instructional difficulty a teacher is having. In each case, ground rules should be set from the beginning. Team members must have the capacity to air problems openly and from the beginning so they don't escalate and cause the team to become dysfunctional.

Another vital aspect of communication is the ability to handle differing viewpoints among team members respectfully. Team members should expect to engage in heated discussions with their peers from time to time about the best ways to approach various classroom situations. These discussions often lead to solutions that are more creative than if they had been developed by just one teacher. A strength of teaming is its ability to promote discussion and debate, pushing team members to the outer limits of their creativity. This aspect of teaching, according to Cohen (1981), is what can save the teaching profession from "fossilizing."

5. *Teachers who team support their teaching partners.* Even though mutual and reciprocal support should be axiomatic in team teaching, it nevertheless should be highlighted as one of the fundamental principles of teaming. Part of the agreement to participate on a team is the knowledge that daily support will be an ongoing feature. When things are going well, support recedes into the background. When things are not going smoothly, support assumes a more prominent role and may take more time. In the latter case, taking the time to support each other is well worth the investment.

Support takes many different forms in a teaching team. It might be as simple as an informal, "That was a great lesson" or, "I'm really glad we tried that new approach—it seems to be working well." Or it could be support in the face of a botched lesson. Still another kind of support is needed when a student is having difficulty or is especially hard to control, or when a testy parent or administrator is part of the picture. Those who elect to teach in teams should anticipate support from their colleagues and at the same time should expect to provide it.

A different kind of support comes when teachers are working actively to acquire a new skill and need to coach each other in their progress. This kind of support usually comes under the general title of *peer coaching,* which is discussed in Chapter 7. Peer coaching is applicable in team teaching when both members of a coaching pair are learning a new instructional method or strategy together. And the general strategies associated with peer coaching also are applicable when one team member wishes to acquire skills in a new subject area or a new instructional approach with which the other teammate is already familiar. Each member brings a different kind of expertise, and an inherent value of teaming is the ability to learn from and coach each other.

6. *Team teaching requires actively working to include all learners.* When teaching alone, one of the standard complaints is the difficulty in meeting the needs of all of the students. As organizations, schools have created ways of alleviating these pressures by introducing various forms of tracking—special education, Title I, ability grouping, and so on. With the inception of team teaching, teachers can work actively to implement curriculum and instructional methods that do a better overall job of meeting the needs of all their students. Teachers who team should make this goal a central part of their work. In one team we know, the teachers decided to target five students a week as a way of attending to every student's individual needs systematically—in addition to the other efforts they were making to improve their overall instructional approaches. Weekly meetings should incorporate time specifically to talk about the progress of individual students in relationship to the group and group needs.

These six principles, then, form the backbone of team teaching:

1. Challenging yourselves to improve your teaching
2. Sharing responsibility for all students
3. Sharing responsibility for instruction
4. Communicating regularly
5. Supporting team members
6. Actively working to include all students.

In the absence of any one of these principles, teachers who team teach will have a harder time meeting the challenge associated with teaching diverse groups of learners.

Team Teaching in Action

How do these principles play out in practice as teachers begin setting up team teaching situations? And what might teaming look like at various levels?

PLANNING FOR TEAMING

If the purpose of teaming is to foster the inclusion of students who have learning and behavior problems, decisions about team teaching may depend upon how many specialists are available to work with classroom teachers in the school. In our experience, specialists include special education teachers, speech and language teachers, Title I reading teachers, district-funded reading and other remedial teachers, and various state-funded teachers. Rather than looking at teaming simply as a function of integrating special and general education teachers, which limits the potential for teaming to the number of special education teachers available, we suggest first looking at the staff schoolwide to determine who might be in a position to begin teaming. In this way, one team teaching situation might be formed at each grade level (for elementary) or one per subject area (secondary), and the team might readily begin to accommodate students who are likely to need assistance with learning and behavior difficulties.

This type of schoolwide approach is effective only when specialists are not tied to a specific category of disability or a specific type of low achievement. For example, if a special education teacher with expertise in learning disabilities works with all students in that grade who are labeled as having learning disabilities, behavior disorders, or cognitive disabilities, another specialist may then be available to work at another grade level or subject with the same range of students. By coordinating the work of most special and remedial/compensatory education teachers, it may become possible to arrange teaming in at least one classroom per grade level. This depends, of course, on the willingness of specialists to work across the groups' categories of low-achieving students.

A related planning consideration is how many students who are formally identified as remedial or as having disabilities are "too many" for a single team and classroom. For example, some districts and schools place all students with mild disabilities within a single team. In these cases the proportion of students with disabilities far exceeds their typical proportions in the school population as a whole. This is a tricky situation, though, because if students who have never had the opportunity to participate in a general education classroom as full participants in the life of that classroom community, the extent to which they will challenge the teachers over time is unknown initially. In planning for team teaching, one cannot make assumptions or set hard-and-fast expectations about the behavior of students labeled as having disabilities until they are given the chance to be educated in an educational environment that is as stimulating, motivating, and supportive as possible (Pugach, 1993). What this does mean, however, is that during the initial year of transition to an integrated setting, students might need a period of supported transition (Pugach & Wesson,

1995) to allow them to gain the confidence they need to function effectively and independently within the larger group.

Also families must be included from the outset of planning a shift to team teaching, particularly when integrating special education students. In the collective experience of the teachers with whom we have worked, families are nearly uniformly supportive of teaming once they see the benefits their children enjoy. This applies to children with disabilities and those without alike. Some districts begin by offering families of children with disabilities a choice of resource room or full integration into a teaching team. Others simply integrate all children at a given grade level.

Many teachers we have talked with suggest starting off slowly, with volunteer teachers who are willing to take the time and effort to make heterogeneous grouping work well. Teachers who resist teaming are often those for whom isolation has become the only professional mode they can imagine or who seem to lack flexibility in instructional planning. Even so, the door should remain open to teachers who previously have doubted the potential of team teaching. Once the benefits become apparent schoolwide, more and more teachers likely will show an interest in becoming a member of a team.

Next, even within the context of teaming, a place should be retained for students who have periodic behavior problems to "cool off." This may be a specific room, or specific students may go to the classroom of another favorite teacher with whom prior arrangements have been made. Some students likely will continue to need crisis intervention. Once students labeled as having emotional/ behavioral disorders have the opportunity to function effectively in optimal general classrooms with peers who have few such problems as role models, the special-needs students may need such a place less and less frequently.

Finally, once a specific grade level shifts to teaming, particularly in situations in which specialists join with classroom teachers, they will have to plan ahead for what kind of classrooms the students will be moving into in subsequent years. If, for example, the fifth grade initiates a team, is there a team of sixth-grade teachers preparing for the coming year so special education students are not placed in the position of returning to a segregated, resource setting the following fall? Unfortunately, situations such as this have occurred, and students and parents alike have been forced to seesaw between segregated and integrated classes because long-range planning did not take place. Ensuring that classes in subsequent grades are prepared to continue team teaching requires long-range planning and the solid commitment of the school's administration at each step of that process. This kind of planning is particularly important when students are making the transition from elementary to middle school or from middle school to high school.

SHARING RESPONSIBILITY FOR INSTRUCTION

The most successful teams we have observed are those in which the teachers take turns working with large and small groups, but all planning takes place jointly. On whatever schedule teachers set up, one teacher takes major responsibility for the lesson as a whole while the other works to monitor student progress or to identify and instruct flexible groupings of students who need assistance—be it remediation or enrichment—associated with that or related lessons.

During actual teaching time, the most effective teaching partners are comfortable when both contribute to the actual lesson, even though one may be taking the lead. The decision on how to divide responsibilities usually is based on the subject matter and the extent to which the specialist teacher feels comfortable with the subject matter. What seems to work best in a new team is to have specialists begin large-group lessons with the subject areas in which they feel most comfortable and to observe and study subjects in which they feel less comfortable.

The goal is to ensure that both adults are unequivocally seen as teachers—and not one as a teacher and the other as only a helper. This difficulty tends to arise when specialists spend all of their time working with small groups of students who are having difficulties with achievement or behavior. Team teachers must alternate in taking responsibility for the lead role in teaching.

Another configuration is to split the class into two groups of equal size for major instruction that is the same for both groups. This enables each teacher to work with a smaller group and thereby reach more students. In this teaching structure both teachers take lead responsibility for teaching and both take lead responsibility for working with students in follow-up activities. A variation on this structure is to have both teachers take the lead, but for entirely different activities within a specific content area. For example, one teacher may be working with a literature circle and another may be holding individual or small-group meetings to work on peer editing with the group while students who are not engaged in peer editing read individually.

In one team we know of, two first-grade teachers in a large urban school district share a class as a function of federal policies on reduced class size. Each week one teacher takes the lead for planning and instruction and the other monitors, works with small groups, and spends some time out of the classroom calling the parents/families of every student in their classes. This approach to team teaching has enabled these teachers to develop strong and lasting relationships with the families of their students, overcoming the unfounded stereotype that parents/families of students in urban schools do not care about or wish to be involved in their children's education.

At certain times teachers who are teaming may decide to have one teacher take the lead and the other carefully observe the lead teaching. This structure should be reserved for times when the team is learning new instructional approaches. Then the observation becomes a form of peer coaching for professional growth and development. The second instance when observation might be appropriate is when both teachers agree that they need specific observational data on the responses or reactions of a certain student or group of students. But if one teacher finds himself or herself taking the lead all the time and the other teacher is not actively involved in teaching and is professing to observe or assist more than is appropriate, the team should renegotiate the joint responsibilities to equalize the load.

VARIATIONS ON TEAM TEACHING STRUCTURES

At the elementary level, team teaching can take various forms. Given the current age-graded organizational structure of most elementary schools, the most common format we have observed is one in which a specialist teacher works at one grade level with a general education teacher. We also know of teams in which one special education teacher formed a partnership with two general education teachers who shared some of the basic academic subjects. This approach means that if teaming is to become the format for serving heterogeneous classes of students, eventually at least one specialist per grade level will have to be part of the team all the way through the school.

Elementary teaming can be conceptualized in two other ways when fewer specialists are available. First, and most preferable, is to form multi-age classrooms in which one specialist teacher works with various labeled students at multiple grade levels. The trend toward multi-age grouping is beginning to appear more frequently nationwide, often in the primary years, when it is known as "ungraded primary." The reason for this approach is that developmentally children are not all at the same point simply because they all end the second grade, for example, on June 15. Ungraded primary settings provide a block of several years for children to develop the knowledge they will need in the intermediate grades. Further, these settings maximize the natural help and modeling that older children provide to younger ones. A natural extension of this educational trend would be to form a teaching team that includes a specialist and that enables a group of students at multiple levels to be assigned to that class.

The other way to structure team teaching at the elementary level is to split the specialist's time between two classroom teachers at two different grade levels. This is less favorable, as it leaves one teacher without a partner for a portion of the school day. Depending on the personality of the class, however, it may be entirely feasible for a specialist to work only in certain subject areas or for certain integrated thematic units.

The structure of true middle schools easily lends itself to teaming between specialists and classroom teachers. Based on the concept of interdisciplinary academic teams, often middle school teachers simply integrate one specialist into their "house" of students. The division of labor depends on the various areas of expertise that the classroom and specialist teachers share. Because peer culture is such a prominent concern for adolescents, team teaching provides the sense of belonging that is often absent in impersonal, decentralized settings and may be felt most vividly by preadolescents and adolescents in the middle-school years.

If teaming is being planned for a high school, team teaching still can take place with each specialist working directly with one or more teachers in specific subject areas. Similar to the set-up in elementary schools, specialists across the various compensatory and remedial programs could be teamed with various teachers or subjects to spread the practice of teaming across the school. Teaming initiated at the middle- or high-school level poses a special challenge with respect to subject matter for specialist teachers who may not have taught advanced skills in, say, science, literature, or mathematics. Typically, a specialist takes at least a semester to begin to feel comfortable with a new subject area. Nevertheless, teaming at the high-school level is becoming one of the hallmarks of reform, exemplified in some well-known early successes such as Central Park East in New York City (for a discussion of secondary school reform, see Sizer, 1989).

In some cases, specialist teachers may run special study halls for their students, especially during the initial transition from a resource room to an integrated team teaching approach. This provides the security students may need until they feel confident in their abilities to perform comfortably in the general school program.

Challenges for Teachers Who Team

Team teaching does have its challenges. Particularly for teachers who have taught in isolation for many years, team teaching represents a major change in their work.

First, someone is watching them teach on a regular basis. This is the greatest change from conventional teaching. Difficulties with this challenge manifest themselves in several ways. Some teachers simply do not know what to do with themselves when their team member is delivering a specific lesson, and they need to structure their tasks in this regard. Grading papers or leaving the room while a team member is teaching violates the intent of teaming in the first place. Others feel uncomfortable asking their teaching partner to do a specific job. Teachers who are used to being in the specialist role—without their own large classroom group—may not take the initiative in the lead role and may consistently put off "taking the plunge" with instructing and managing a whole class of students. Despite the potential initial discomfort when job responsibilities shift in this way, the power of watching and being watched while teaching is more than just a challenge. One LD teacher told us that having someone watch her teach was a luxury because she now receives feedback on her work. Communicating regularly about these aspects of teaming, until all team members feel comfortable, is essential.

Second, teachers who team no longer have their "own room." They now share a room with another teacher. Some teams dispense with teachers' desks altogether, and others move two desks into a single room. Whatever the arrangement, decisions regarding space, traffic patterns, rules, and creating a stimulating physical learning environment are no longer decisions to be made alone. Because at least some of these decisions reflect personal preference—in contrast to those made on the basis of mutual agreement on professional matters—they may cause unease. Each member of a team must be clear on what he or she is not willing to compromise when sharing a classroom. One of the most common problems involves different levels of tolerance for noise. Other problems might involve individual styles of record keeping. A more complex problem relates to different styles of planning. Still another involves disciplinary styles. These are all things that team members must discuss from the outset to avoid unnecessary problems.

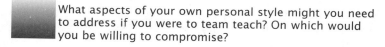

What aspects of your own personal style might you need to address if you were to team teach? On which would you be willing to compromise?

A third challenge arises from philosophical differences. In making the decision to become part of a team, teachers, we assume, either know each other well enough to recognize that they have compatible educational philosophies or at the least have discussed these issues prior to formalizing their commitment. Two teachers often decide to team simply because they already have common beliefs about teaching (Cohen, 1981). If this is not the case, the professionals who will be teaming should discuss early in the planning process their preferences for instruction, management routines, and the extent to which a child-centered or teacher-centered approach dominates their teaching style.

The issue of philosophical differences diminishes in importance once teachers agree to move *together* toward alternative, contemporary approaches to teaching and learning. In some teams we have seen, teachers with diametrically opposed and irreconcilable philosophical differences have been placed together involuntarily and never have been able to find a comfortable way to work together. Therefore, involuntary teaming situations should be avoided, as they lead to dysfunctional teaming. At the same time, teachers who at first may not seem to be likely partners should be given the opportunity to explore the potential that teaming offers. They may choose to participate in good faith on a trial or partial basis and discover that their philosophies are more compatible with those of some of their peers than they had first believed.

A fourth challenge stems from different levels of expertise. As we discussed earlier, one of the functions of teaming is to provide support in acquiring new instructional skills. Teachers who team should expect to learn from and to teach their partners the various skills and knowledge they possess. This does not mean that, as a result of teaming, partners should end up like carbon copies of each other. Instead, teaming should be conceptualized as providing the opportunity to share expertise. The challenge comes when one team member feels threatened by the expertise of his or her partner. Open communication about these issues should dispel many of those potential problems.

What is the array of expertise among teachers who team? If the collaborative teaching situation consists of a group of classroom teachers (as in a middle-school team), individuals might have expertise in specific academic curriculum areas, in contemporary organizational structures such as cooperative learning, or in approaches such as integrated thematic instruction or process writing. If the collaborative teaming situation blends remedial or special education teachers and classroom teachers, classroom teachers are likely to have more expertise in subject matter and large-group management. Specialists, on the other hand, may be knowledgeable in a few of the subject areas, typically limited to reading and mathematics, but may have expertise in individual approaches to management or peer tutoring or providing highly explicit instruction. Specialists for students with significant disabilities are likely to have expertise in communication modes and assistive technology, as well as the array of functional curriculum goals and materials usually associated with students who have moderate to more severe disabilities.

Whatever expertise members bring to the team constitutes a resource upon which the whole team can draw. Unless all teachers see themselves as being able to learn *from* as well as *provide for* their peers, these expert resources run the risk of being lost amidst team members' insecurities about being placed in the position of learning from their teammates.

The Power of Team Teaching as Collaboration

We began this chapter by calling team teaching one of the most powerful manifestations of professional collaboration. We believe this is the case because team teaching changes the basic conception of teaching from an isolated task to one in which collaboration among professionals is built into teachers' daily work. Once some form of team teaching is established in a building, endless possibilities are opened up for developing new configurations of teachers for different teaching goals.

Some school staffs easily make the transition to teaming. Others hold onto the old norms of isolation, resisting the changes that teaming requires. At each stage of the transition, the mutual support of teachers and administrators at varying levels is necessary to emphasize the potential of teaming. Sometimes administrative support builds slowly and only after demonstrated success of team teaching—much like skeptical teachers' buying in after others begin teaming. At other times, administrative support is universal and the challenge is to bring along teachers who lack the confidence to make their teaching more public. In some cases teachers hold onto the isolated mode of teaching as a means of keeping private their skill levels, which may fall below what is considered adequate. Whatever the reasons for resisting the transition to teaming, in our view it is important to continue working toward team teaching as a schoolwide goal and, more important, as a teaching structure that has the potential to transform the basic configuration of the profession.

Each team, of course, will have its own personal character—forged by the personalities of the individual teachers who make up the team. Personal creativity and variation are some of the most important hallmarks of teaching. Teachers need not and should not lose these individual qualities as teaming takes on a larger role in the schools. Instead, the personal and professional strengths of all participating teachers are shared in team teaching. This increases the potential for improving the educational experiences of the children and youth for whom we make these changes in our professional lives.

Remember . . .

1. Team teaching provides a permanent collaborative arrangement to support teachers in their work.
2. Team teaching provides the natural support to challenge and encourage teachers to practice and use new instructional strategies.
3. Teachers who team share full responsibility for all of the students in their classrooms.
4. Team teaching requires a full appreciation for the varying kinds of expertise that each team member has to offer.
5. Team teachers need to build a strong working relationship by becoming familiar with each others' teaching styles and by participating in regular joint planning.

Activities

1. In a small group, have each member identify the personal and professional skills he or she would bring to team teaching. When the list is compiled, decide what other skills, if any, you might need. How could you get access to those other skills?

2. One of the most important issues that teachers face in team teaching is to reconcile different styles. In a small group, plan a week-long or weekend summer vacation together. Afterward, discuss your planning styles, preferences, and so on. Draw analogies to teaching.

3. Make a list of all the things that obstruct progress in school for some of the most challenging students with whom you have worked. Then, in small groups, prioritize which problems you would tackle first if you were in a team teaching situation.

4. With one other person, prepare a brief presentation for your classmates. Begin by identifying your strengths and weaknesses. Then develop the presentation to maximize the use of those strengths and to complement the weaknesses. After the presentation, explain to your audience how you decided to use your strengths and compensate for your weakness.

5. Interview a teacher who has recently entered a team teaching situation. Ask him or her to contrast the job of teaching before and after teaming. What are the pros and cons of teaming for this teacher?

9

Collaboration and School Partnerships

Up to this point we have discussed various ways by which teachers might collaborate on a variety of problems and challenges they face as they work to meet the needs of all of the students in their schools. Another important trend in the broad context of school reform is the development of partnerships between schools and other agencies or institutions. Recognizing that as they attempt to meet their students' complex needs, schools cannot always "go it alone"—nor should they—schools often seek to pool expertise across institutional boundaries, or engage in *cross-institutional collaboration*. Partnerships like these evolve because professionals representing the various institutions that are planning to work together are willing to collaborate across institutional borders to improve the lives of children and youth.

In this chapter we describe two types of school-partnerships that exemplify cross-institutional collaboration: partnerships between schools and social service or health agencies, and partnerships between schools and universities. Partnerships between schools and social service or health agencies represent the belief that children's educational needs do not exist in a vacuum of other basic needs. Partnerships between schools and universities represent the belief that improving the quality of teaching and learning in the schools is an inextricable, reciprocal relationship between the quality of how new teachers are prepared and the quality of teaching and of the professional lives of practicing teachers in the schools. Cross-institutional partnerships require multiple levels of interactions.

For example, some interactions take place directly among practitioners, such as between a teacher and a social worker or between a teacher and a university professor. Others take place among those with a higher level of institutional responsibility for the partnership—for example, between a principal and a director of a local Boys' Club or Girls' Club or between a superintendent and a dean of a college or school of education. Both levels of interaction are essential for the partnership to be successful. Further, although cross-institutional collaboration at the practitioner level may be highly effective in meeting an individual student's needs, collaboration at the higher levels will be needed to make sure that the needs of all students who can benefit from cross-institutional collaboration will be considered in these partnerships.

Partnerships that involve schools and social service or health agencies differ significantly in focus and implementation from those that bring together schools and colleges or universities, but certain common concerns, dynamics, and considerations exist across all cross-institutional partnerships. We now turn our attention to these commonalities.

The Power of Cross-Institutional Collaboration

In the first chapter we delineated several underlying values of collaborative professionals. Several of these values apply to cross-institutional collaboration as well. For example, when a school and a social service or health agency, or a school and a university, work together to meet the goal of improving learning for students in schools, differential expertise is brought together and shared. Collaborating across organizations or institutions is based on the fundamental recognition of the need for one kind of expertise to complement another in addressing challenging problems or situations in schools. Representatives across participants in the partnership understand the limits of their own knowledge and the role that other, complementary knowledge plays in their work. These collaborations are not based on the assumption that one kind of knowledge is superior to another but, rather, that differential knowledge is needed to meet the complex task at hand, however that task is defined.

Partnerships across institutions also are based on the assumption that working together generates synergy in addressing the tasks that partners define as requiring their joint attention. When they operate in concert, representatives of the participating institutions have access to more and better information about the situation than they would have alone. Much like collaboration between individual professionals, collaborating across different institutions should lead to stronger outcomes than are possible when one institution acts alone.

Related to the notions of complementary expertise and synergy is that collaborating across different institutional cultures signifies a willingness to view these different cultures as strengths. Probably the most important consideration in developing partnerships is that each institution (e.g., school, agency, university) has its own ways of operating, its own norms and expectations for what constitutes professional behavior, its own terminology, practices, and primary concerns. Entering into a cross-institutional collaboration enables the partners to expand the boundaries of their individual institutional cultures and to challenge the norms of practice that drive their everyday actions and decisions. Partnerships are by nature inclusive; the partners must be willing to say that their ways of doing things might benefit from the ongoing involvement of another institution and might result in one or both institutions stretching and reaching for new ways of thinking and behaving.

When institutions collaborate, they provide an added benefit. Representatives of various institutions often lay blame for difficult situations on other institutions' lack of effectiveness. We might hear, for example, a social worker blaming a teacher or a principal for a problem with one of his or her clients, or a principal or superintendent blaming the local teacher education institution for not preparing teachers well enough. Joint ownership can create a political safety net to overcome the tendency to blame—which usually comes from frustration with persistent problems. Instead of one institution blaming another for shortcomings, in a cross-institutional collaboration both agree to own and work together to solve sticky, enduring problems. As they expend less energy on blaming the other institution, they can focus more energy on actively addressing the problems that partners have jointly identified as requiring their collective attention and differential, complementary expertise.

Guidelines for Cross-Institutional Collaboration

Partnerships across schools and other institutions or agencies can be initiated in two ways. First, working on behalf of a specific student, a teacher and a professional from outside of the school may work together. In the case of an interaction regarding a student with disabilities, this partnership is likely to include both the general and the special education teacher, as well as members of the student's family. These individual practitioners and family members may work together over time effectively in the absence of any substantial formal agreement or interaction between their respective parent institutions.

In contrast, those with higher levels of responsibility at their institutions may initiate partnerships because they wish to address shared concerns from a more systemic perspective. For example, a county health commissioner might enter into dialogue with a superintendent of a large urban school district to discuss locating health clinics in school buildings. This partnership has implications for collaboration between teachers and health-care workers in the school building. Similarly, a dean of a college or school of education in an urban area may enter into dialogue with a school district's director of human resources to discuss how they might jointly address a persistent teacher shortage and how to increase the diversity of the local urban teaching force. This kind of partnership has implications for advising individuals who may be paraprofessionals, safety aides, or other entry-level school district employees how to enter a teacher education program. As these partnerships are initiated on multiple levels, what guidelines might we follow to increase the likelihood of their success and, more important, their sustainability?

GUIDELINE 1: PLAN FOR COMMUNICATION

For any collaboration to be successful, an open line of communication between the partners is an absolute necessity. Some specific recommendations related to enhancing communication between agencies include (Johnson et al., 2001):

- Developing a proactive approach to communication with all stakeholders, including being "up front" when differences arise
- Making sure that communication is frequent and uses all available communication channels (e.g., meetings, phone calls, email)
- Developing personal links to partners to foster a close working relationship (e.g., occasionally meeting for a cup of coffee or lunch)

This precaution is particularly important in the early stages of interagency collaboration, when representatives of the different organizations are establishing trust. In any cross-institutional partnership, the partners have to recognize the need for a period of trust-building, whether it be a partnership between a school and an agency or one between a school and a university (Pugach & Pasch, 1994). This is essential for getting past the stereotypes that each carries about the other and asking questions such as, "What will we as a school get out of this? What will I as a faculty member get out of this? What's in it for us as partners?" (Goodlad, 1988). Taking time for this stage allows all of the subsequent activities to take place in a relatively positive atmosphere.

GUIDELINE 2: ENGAGE IN CULTURAL LEARNING

One of the greatest challenges in cross-institutional collaboration is learning about the organizational culture of the participating partners. Agencies, schools, and colleges and universities all have different norms of behavior and practice that reflect their unique values and priorities. Each agency has its own organizational culture, including idiosyncratic language, values or priorities, rules and regulations, ways of doing business, and even definitions of collaboration. If they go unrecognized, these organizational differences can obstruct the joint goals of the collaboration and may be the source of much preventable misunderstanding and misinterpretation. You might achieve this goal by having someone from the partnering agency make a formal presentation on its organizational culture, focusing specifically on mission, language/ terminology, and priorities (Johnson et al., 2001). Prior to the collaborative effort, any relevant laws and regulations that may affect the interactions must be reviewed.

GUIDELINE 3: SET COMMON GOALS

In Chapter 1 we emphasized the importance of setting clear goals for collaboration. This holds true for cross-institutional partnerships. Following initial communication and trust-building, common goals have to be set to focus the energy of the participants and to provide a framework for accountability regarding the success of the partnership. In his description of school-university partnerships in particular, Goodlad (1988) specifically warns against setting common goals too soon, as it may prevent the necessary dialogue from occurring in the first place. What is needed, he says, is the development of a healthy tension between engaging in dialogue and goal setting, so that thinking and reflecting carefully before acting becomes the norm for all of the stakeholders.

GUIDELINE 4: PUT TURF ISSUES INTO CONTEXT

No matter how much we would like to think we can bypass this characteristic of collaboration through careful communication, turf issues are bound to arise in any cross-institutional collaboration and cannot be ignored. The best way to minimize these issues is to anticipate them and to develop a plan for addressing them as they emerge. This might include providing the staff with a positive view of the collaboration by highlighting its potential positive outcomes, disseminating examples of the positive outcomes of previous collaborations that have worked effectively, and implementing a system of rewards and consequences for individuals participating in the collaborative effort (Johnson et al., 2001).

GUIDELINE 5: INVOLVE KEY DECISION MAKERS

As we stated earlier, cross-institutional collaboration can begin at the micro-level of the classroom, or it can begin at the macro-level among the participating institutions' highest levels of authority and responsibility. In Johnson et al.'s (2001) study, stakeholders noted the necessity of upper management's involvment in and committment to the collaboration. At crucial points in the partnership the active participation of key decision makers who are truly representative of the collaborating agencies is essential. Without this element partnership is likely to diminish over time. It is critical to involve someone who really understands the agency's position and priorities, can make decisions on behalf of the agency, can provide immediate and direct assistance when problems arise, and is authorized to apply the resources of the organization as a fiscal or human resource for the joint effort.

Key decision makers also are essential to maintain a successful collaboration, because they are in the most powerful position to provide individuals in their respective organizations with the support needed to engage in activities of the partnership. For example, they can assure that participants have regular opportunities for dialogue within the scope of the collaboration. Further, they can provide additional resources for those engaging the collaboration, as well as seek additional funding sources to avoid asking individuals to engage in a difficult task while still being held accountable for the full load of responsibilities they had before the collaboration began (Johnson et al., 2001).

The participation of key decision makers also communicates the level of commitment to the collaboration. Without a strong mutual commitment to the goals and visions of the collaboration, it eventually will fail. Suggestions related to building and maintaining commitment between collaborating agencies include developing a way to compromise on important differences, making clear the issues that cannot be compromised, and being sure not to lose sight of the goals and the potential positive outcomes of the collaboration (Johnson et al., 2001).

GUIDELINE 6: IDENTIFY POINT PEOPLE IN EACH PARTNER ORGANIZATION

Yet another task is to identify point people at multiple levels in the partnership to broker the interactions between the two institutions and their resources. Once agreements are in place among administrators, it falls to the various players at the school and agency or institutional sites to develop the relationships that enable children and youth to gain from the partnership. The different levels of the partnership must maintain good lines of communication. Let's say, for instance, that a specific project within the partnership requires specific human, fiscal, or academic resources not currently available. The teacher and the collaborating partner need to know that they can raise this issue with key decision makers and have a fair hearing for their ideas. Equally important, the level of school implementation is often where new goals are set and initiated as the partnership develops.

GUIDELINE 7: TEMPER COMMITMENT WITH A LITTLE PATIENCE

One other guideline has to be mentioned as essential in promoting healthy cross-institutional collaborations. Participating in a partnership means making a commitment to changing the way the system serves children and youth. This is a long-term commitment. Those who take part in cross-institutional partnerships have to be aware that change can come slowly. The action orientation of most teachers suggests that if things are not changing quickly, they tend to believe the partnership is not working. This is precisely when a more reflective, long-term view may be helpful, though. As long as progress toward change is taking place, stakeholders can feel good about the work they are doing together. That being said, acknowledging the pace of change is not to be confused with keeping common goals front and center and pushing for everyone to keep reaching for these goals, even when the pace of change seems slower than desired.

FROM GUIDELINES TO PRACTICE

These guidelines provide a general road map for establishing and maintaining cross-institutional collaborative partnerships. But how do these partnerships actually play out in schools and in the lives of those who participate in them? Next we offer two examples, one from the perspective of collaborative partnerships with community and social service agencies, and one from the perspective of collaborative partnerships between a large school district and a multipurpose university.

Partnerships Between Schools and Social Service and Community Agencies

The University of Cincinnati's Child Development Program at the Arlitt Child and Family Research and Education Center is a demonstration, inclusive, early childhood education and child care program for children ages 3 to 5. It is funded by tuition, the College of Education, grants, and partnership agreements with a series of community agencies. Over the past 75 years, the center has engaged in numerous collaborative partnerships. None have been so strong and long-lasting, however, as the partnerships the center has with Head Start and the local Board of Mental Retardation and Developmental Disabilities (MRDD). The center serves 154 children, 83 funded by Head Start and 16 funded by MRDD; the families of the remaining 55 children pay tuition. These collaborative partnerships have overcome many challenges to become pillars of the Child Development Program.

As you read this section, write down examples that relate to the guidelines for partnerships. Can you find examples that relate to all seven guidelines?

One of the most important underpinnings of these partnerships has been the commitment to a common goal. All partners are committed to the children and families served at Arlitt. This commitment has enabled participants to set aside turf issues and develop a set of services that best serve the children and their families. We also have found that the cultures of the various agencies differ and we must work continually to understand these differences. The cultural differences are overarching and include everything from notions of best practices to expectations regarding workload and holidays. For example, the calendar must be worked out with respect to each program's holidays, inservices, number of required attendance days, and so on.

All of our classes are inclusive and serve children supported from different funding sources (Head Start, MRDD, College of Education, parent tuition). Each of these agencies has different rules and regulations regarding employees. We have had to involve key decision makers from these agencies in developing a common set of rules that cut across funding sources. Money issues must be addressed to determine who pays for what and what percentage of salaries and fringe benefits are allocated for employees. These resource issues are easier to tackle if all stakeholders value the partnership and commitment is evident at all levels of both organizations.

The Arlitt Center has been a Head Start Delegate since 1972. Funding from the Hamilton County-Cincinnati Community Action Agency, the Head Start grantee, is a major source of the Child Development Program's operating budget. While staff at the center fully embrace the Head Start philosophy, they have struggled and continue to grapple with Head Start initiatives that conflict with the constructivist theoretical underpinnings of the Arlitt curriculum, staff perceptions of best practice, and staff workload. How these challenges have been met and addressed resembles a slow dance between partners who occasionally step on one another's toes. A tremendous amount of work and compromise have gone into building and maintaining a relationship that works for both partners. For example, during one era of the Head Start partnership, the administration at the Arlitt Center believed that we should ignore initiatives or rules that we didn't agree with.

Although we were able to maintain the partnership, a great deal of tension and distrust were present. We decided that this was not healthy, and we began to address differences in an open manner. We had to work hard at communication and had to listen, understand, and at times compromise. We also have tried to be active partners at local, state, and national levels to influence policy. The following are a few ways in which the Arlitt Center staff took the initiative locally to become part of the Head Start program—instead of being an unhappy delegate.

1. The Arlitt director engages other directors in presenting workshops and research endeavors.

2. The disabilities coordinator at the Arlitt Center continues to meet regularly with all other Head Start disabilities coordinators and the local education agencies to assist in developing protocol for serving children with disabilities.
3. Arlitt teachers and other staff members have served on committees at the Head Start agencies, such as the Health Advisory Committee and the Curriculum Framework Committee.
4. The Arlitt staff assists with Head Start recruitment efforts, volunteers to take on projects, helps to develop new forms, and invites other delegates and Head Start staff members to workshops and events held at the Arlitt Center.

The keys to the Arlitt Center's current success are listening to ideas and concerns, hearing what is being said without too much bias, determining how staff perceptions hinder or help the partnership, and establishing the Arlitt Center as part of Head Start and not just as an outside entity getting funding. Moreover, we work hard at trying to develop solutions to problems. Because of successful collaboration in recent years, the Arlitt Center has expanded its program to include a Head Start child care partner and is considering implementing Early Head Start in partnership with the grantee.

If an Early Head Start partnership comes about, the collaboration with the Hamilton County Board of MRDD may change to early intervention instead of preschool. Although the Arlitt Center has served children with disabilities since the late 1920s, the center has had a partnership with MRDD only since 1992. The 2001 school year will mark the end of the partnership as it now exists. The positive aspect of ending the preschool relationship is that preschool children with disabilities in the county now are being served in their home schools. On the other hand, the Arlitt Center will lose an MRDD teacher and related service personnel who have become part of the Arlitt family.

Although the start of the MRDD partnership was difficult, subsequent years have gone much more smoothly. Still. it has its challenges. The agreement between the Arlitt Center and MRDD is to serve preschoolers with disabilities in an inclusive environment. A teacher from MRDD serves as an Arlitt preschool teacher half-days and also is the liaison between service providers, families, and both agencies. Related service personnel—occupational therapists, physical therapists, speech therapists, adaptive physical educators, specialists in visual impairment, and others—have become part of a program committed to serving all children.

The main challenge in collaboration with MRDD has been implementation of practices within the constructs of constructivism versus behaviorism. This historically is true for many early childhood educators and early childhood special educators. At the beginning of the partnership, Arlitt teachers felt threatened by and uncomfortable with practices that took a behaviorist approach. MRDD teachers and related service personnel perceived the Arlitt teachers as being too extreme in their approach and unwilling to really "meet the needs of the children." The process of blending these approaches involved much dialogue about what was being done for individual children and why. Changes did not come about until relationships were steady and trust was established among all stakeholders.

Bimonthly staffing meetings with teachers and service providers were instrumental in developing a truly blended, collaborative partnership. At first the Arlitt staff did not understand or value the relevance of these staffings. They perceived the time taken away from the classroom as an intrusion into their day. The staffings, however, were part of the teachers' responsibilities as written in their job description. As the staff and related personnel met on a regular basis, the relationships among stakeholders that began to emerge enhanced the dialogue about the whys and hows of intervention and the foundations of the curricular model at the Arlitt center. Role sharing became a major piece of the staffing dialogue. This led to increased awareness of instructional strategies and the value of early childhood education and early childhood special education practices and, eventually, role release in the classroom.

MRDD related-service personnel began to try out strategies that were less behaviorist and to collect anecdotal data on literacy development, cognitive and social development, and math skills as they interacted with children in the classroom. Arlitt teachers began to extend therapeutic interventions throughout the week when related-service personnel were not present, documenting children's progress in speech and physical development related to the goals of the speech therapist and the occupational therapist. These written anecdotes were shared at staffings, and information about progress was related informally when the therapists were in the Arlitt Center. The outcome of this collaboration was evident in the children's progress as well as involvement of families in the program.

Families of children with disabilities at the Arlitt Center have written testimonials to the caring attitudes and commitment to their children by all Arlitt staff members. Families always include our MRDD partners as part of the staff. Families who have been part of this collaborative partnership volunteer at the center at proportionally higher levels than do their peers who do not have children with disabilities. They attend meetings about their children and in addition are more likely to attend events, sit at the cookie sale table, and help out in the classroom.

To summarize, successful collaborative partnerships at the Arlitt Child and Family Research and Education Center have been built on commitment, relationships, trust, and dialogue. Although complete agreement about practice among stakeholders is not imperative, commitment to children and families *is* imperative. Ongoing communication and understanding of differences require constant care and work. Key decision makers must be willing to compromise on policies and rules when they conflict. In the end, the outcomes of the work necessary to make a collaborative partnership successful are tremendous. The children and families have benefitted greatly from the increased resources that have emerged from this cross-institutional collaboration.

School-University Partnerships: From Preschool to "Grade 16"

Historically the relationship between schools and universities was characterized by periodic interaction in which, in general, university faculty sought research sites or placements for student teachers but had little interest in long-term commitments to improving schools. They might visit every few weeks to supervise a student teacher or to collect research data. Similarly, schools called upon the university faculty to provide "one-shot" inservice workshops, expected teachers to change their practice as a result of these minimal interactions, and were disappointed when change did not take place. Schools often accused universities of being far too distant from the world of practice and the needs of the teacher and students in the schools. This kind of episodic relationship had one fundamental fault: the absence of a common goal that could form the basis for a cross-institutional partnership and contribute to unifying the efforts of schools and universities alike under the goal of improving the quality of teaching and learning in the schools.

Recognizing the serious nature of the problems facing schools beginning in the early 1980s, schools and universities began to enter new forms of partnership as a means of linking the reform of teacher education to the reform of schools. One basic tenet of these emerging partnerships was that schools and universities would collaborate to link the development of preservice teachers and practicing teachers alike, thereby stressing that teachers are in a continuous state of professional development across the continuum of their careers and that without continuous development, the kinds of changes needed to improve our schools are not likely to happen. According to Fullan and Stiegelbauer (1991), teacher development then "becomes an overall strategy for professional and institutional reform" (p. 321), inextricably linking schools and institutions of higher education as a means of improving teaching and learning.

This new concept of school-university collaboration probably was, early on, best known under the name *professional development schools* (Holmes Group, 1990) or *professional practice schools* (Levine, 1992). As partners, each contributes a unique perspective to these common efforts. If they are to work, they represent a new way of life, not just another project. In the process, the culture of the school and the culture of the university change and begin to overlap in organic ways" (p. 323). Consider this: Teacher education students learn both at the university and in the world of schools. The quality of teaching in schools—and in the classrooms in which they learn to teach—directly affects the quality of their preparation.

Meant to parallel the idea of teaching hospitals, in professional development schools teachers, administrators, teacher education students, and university faculty are present and working together at the school site on a regular basis. The concept of professional development schools has been aligned with the national accreditation of teacher education through the Professional Development School standards project of the National Council for the Accreditation of Teacher Education (2001). In many communities nationwide professional development schools represent vital relationships between schools and universities and often are active centers of teacher activity, reflection, and professional development.

In PDSs, for example, inquiry into the problems and processes of education may be conducted as a collaborative effort with teachers and administrators, who are equally interested in improving educational practice and who have critical contributions to make in terms of conceptualizing, implementing, and interpreting classroom-based research. Given the intention of the PDS structure to overcome the traditional separation of teacher education, research, and school improvement, at the least the potential exists to have much more interaction between prospective and practicing teachers. Further, the experiences gained in schools ideally should be used as a basis for reflecting on, and thereby learning from, practice itself.

Nevertheless, professional development schools are limited in their potential because (a) a single school cannot accommodate (and therefore have a positive effect on) all the preservice students in a given university's teacher education program, and (b) improving one school through such partnerships, though extremely important for that school, does not represent systemic change, which is the goal of school reform. Today the scope of school-university partnerships is broadening significantly to encompass the goal of systemwide change. What has become apparent is that school-university partnerships must emanate from the more fundamental idea that the quality of schools is tied directly to the quality of life in a community and that schools and institutions of higher education bear a joint, mutual responsibility for working together to ensure the quality and vitality of the local schools. These newly defined partnerships are beginning to take place under the auspices of *P-16 councils*, spanning preschool to "grade 16," in which grades 13–16, so to speak, represent the four years of undergraduate college education.

Obviously, professional development schools can be an important component of P-16 efforts. But where responsibility for a PDS might be located within a given school, college, or department of education in a postsecondary institution in relationship to a single public school, P-16 councils are cross-institutional collaborations across several institutions and institutional cultures that bring together administrators and leaders on a much higher level to look at a broad range of systemic issues and challenges. For example, in the Milwaukee Partnership Academy, a P-16 council constituted to improve the quality of teaching and learning in the Milwaukee Public Schools, the following high-level administrators convene monthly:

- University chancellor
- School superintendent
- Chief executive officer of the local teachers' union
- School board president
- Vice-president of local community college
- Local business partners
- Deans of education and liberal arts

These individuals represent significant power brokers who together, through the P-16 council, can consider a broad range of issues that affect the quality of teaching and learning in the schools, and take action on those issues. Obviously, P-16 councils must encompass the continuum of teacher development as a reform strategy, but they might also concern themselves with recruiting and retaining teachers or the impact of various reforms on teaching and learning and the relationship of these issues to the quality of the teaching force.

In addition to joint ownership, a critical operating principle for school-university collaborations is achieving mutual respect for the contributions of each partner. Because university faculty and K-12 teachers and administrators historically have been deeply divided in any school-university partnership, whether it is a PDS or a P-16 council or any other partnership, mutual respect must be a public part of the joint agenda.

Although the tendency has been to lay blame upon one another, the university faculty, according to Goodlad and Sirotnik (1988), provide constructive criticism and insist on reflection on practice, whereas school staffs tend to be more action-oriented in their goals. By bringing together these approaches—rather than using them as a source for mutual backstabbing—the potential for real reform, rather than just cosmetic changes or small improvements, can be increased significantly. We might measure the success of such collaborations when we no longer hear this age-old comment: "Forget everything you learned in the university; this is the real world." Instead, we must understand that if experience in the schools were the only path to success, we would have no poorly qualified veteran teachers in the schools. By the same token, universities must understand the day-to-day pressures under which schools operate and must consider how to bridge theory and practice in a practical manner. We must value the complementary expertise we bring to the goal of improving the quality of teaching and learning in the schools.

There are many specific strengths universities bring to the schools and the schools bring to university-based teacher education. Take a minute to think about what these strengths are. Make two lists, one defining university strengths and one for the schools.

What Do P-16 Councils Mean for Teachers?

What are the implications of cross-institutional collaborations such as P-16 councils for the day-to-day lives of teachers in schools? What demands related to collaboration do these partnerships require? We are going to consider two situations: the *professional development school* and *teachers as clinical teacher education faculty*. Collaborative activities can be constructed in infinite ways in the context of P-16 councils. The two we describe here are perhaps two of the more commonly recognized forms of school-university partnerships.

A DAY IN THE LIFE OF A PROFESSIONAL DEVELOPMENT SCHOOL

First we share an example from a PDS that defined improving literacy instruction as the initial goal of the partnership (Jett-Simpson, Pugach, & Whipp, 1992). The philosophy adopted jointly was that of a strategic approach to learning based on the overall goal of developing independent, lifelong readers. The scenario on pages 194 and 195 describes what you, on any given day, might observe taking place with respect to the goal of improved literacy instruction.

As you read the scenario, look for the various ways in which collaboration is taking place. Specifically, write down all the things that went on in the building that day that seem different from "business as usual" in a school. Then note specifically all the different instances of collaboration that occurred at this PDS. Between whom did they occur, and for what purposes?

This PDS scenario represents one instance of a contemporary approach to cross-institutional collaboration. Several examples from the scenario illustrate the interactions between teachers, faculty members, administrators, and prospective teachers that contribute to a climate of ongoing professional growth and development. These include collaboration between prospective and experienced teachers, between beginning teachers and university faculty, for building internal leadership among literacy instructors, for direct increases in teachers' knowledge, and to facilitate the process of action research. Although each instance of collaboration is important, what is most important is the changing nature of the school as a place to work. Experimentation, reflection, and open discourse about instruction characterize all the various kinds of collaboration that may be encountered in this school. Many opportunities for professional growth have become a regular part of what happens in this highly collaborative school.

Action Research as a Collaborative Professional Development Strategy

One of the collaborative activities mentioned in the PDS scenario is *action research*. When teachers think of inquiry, or research, they often visualize university faculty members working alone in their offices, poring over statistical analyses, or figuring out how to establish a relationship with a school so data can be collected for their study. Teachers often do not think of themselves as being involved in research or as capable of being researchers themselves. The research tradition called *action research* adopted in this PDS, however, has as its explicit purpose collegial, collaborative inquiry into classroom practice by teachers themselves.

Coined by Kurt Lewin (1946), the term *action* implies that research in the social sciences should be linked to social action and directly involve those who practice in social institutions in the study and improvement of their own work. The purpose of action research is to inform action, and the process belongs to the practitioners—in this case, teachers—themselves. In this process teachers study problems that are meaningful to teachers. Problems for study are not defined in isolation by university researchers.

Action research has the potential to "demystify" research. Holly (1991) has called it "the missing link in the creation of school as centers of inquiry" (p. 133). As teachers participate collegially in systematic inquiry into their own teaching practice, they are better able to see, own, and implement the kinds of changes that may best improve education in their own school. Action research, then, is based on the belief that teachers themselves can and should be undertaking research on their practice, and that their practice-oriented research can inform the improvement of education as much (if not more) than traditional research (Cochran-Smith & Lytle, 1993).

Collaborating at a PDS

On Tuesdays at Central City Elementary School—a school of about 650 students ranging from kindergarten through fifth grade in a large metropolitan district—literacy learning is apparent everywhere. Students are busily reading books, writing their own stories, having them typed on computers so they can be "published," or preparing for a multicultural literature competition. Each week two faculty members from the partnership university, called liaisons, spend about a day and a half each in the building in lieu of one course taught at the university; Tuesday is their full day at the school. In the morning they stop in the office to talk briefly with the principal or vice principal.

Because this year is the first year in which Title I reading teachers have been working directly with the teachers in their classrooms each morning, their discussion focuses on planning a half-day professional development session on team teaching. The principal, reading teachers, and faculty members believe they need to develop and discuss guidelines for team teaching and role play what it looks like now that everyone has had the chance to get started. They also have a brief conversation about the need to secure a substitute teacher in the near future, as one of the teachers is making a presentation at a professional conference with one of the two faculty members who work in the building.

At the same time, 15 teacher education students are working directly with students in reading and writing as part of their methods courses and, later in the morning, meeting with their professor (one of the two assigned to the building) to reflect on what they've been working on during the past week by reviewing videotapes of their teaching. Teachers in whose rooms these students work have volunteered to host them because they themselves are interested in implementing the techniques the students are learning in their reading methods class. Later in the semester these teachers participate in evaluating their students' professional portfolios for reading methods together with faculty members from the elementary teacher education program. As it is close to the end of the semester, several of the literacy students are requesting to return to the building for student teaching in the coming semester.

This semester the school also is hosting three student teachers. In most cases, student teachers and their cooperating teachers work as members of a team rather than the traditional arrangement. Sometimes the host teachers are relatively new themselves, and the opportunity to team with a student teacher helps them move toward their instructional goals in literacy more systematically. Although a student teaching supervisor is formally assigned to the school, the faculty members visit the student teachers regularly and talk with them and their host teacher often, as they do on this day.

In the teachers' lounge is a sign-up sheet where teachers have requested informal meetings with the faculty liaisons. Some want to meet during their preparation time to discuss their action research projects in literacy. Others have requested that a certain reading or writing technique be demonstrated in the classroom. Still others have prepared to teach a lesson jointly as a means of gaining confidence with a new method. Also located in the lounge is a professional development library with recent professional journals in all subject areas, and in particular many recent books that serve as resources about contemporary approaches to literacy teaching.

Throughout the day teachers and faculty liaisons can be found talking about the progress that Central City's students are making, about problems they are having implementing a new approach, about courses they might take the following summer related to literacy learning. These informal discussions also take place during lunchtime. In the afternoon one of the professors and the school's lead reading teacher together teach an informal class for the building's paraprofessionals on specific roles related to individual reading with students consistent with the school's literacy learning goals. After this class the two meet to discuss a session they will hold at the university with the school's Title I reading teachers to provide them with time to gauge the progress of the team teaching model they instituted for the first time that year, and also to discuss the support that various teachers need as they continue to try to alter their literacy curriculum.

Twenty additional preservice students are participating directly in classrooms as part of their first field experience in schools. They are greeted by the professor who instructs the course for which this field assignment is required. Their informal conversations on Tuesdays allow the students and the professor alike to get a sense of their progress. Their professor also checks with their host teachers to see if things are going smoothly. As part of their work, these students interact with family members, community members, the principal, and the vice principal. One is assisting with a special project being run by one of the teachers and university professor liaisons to prepare a group of fourth and fifth graders to act as guides when guests come to visit the school. Once or twice during the semester this group meets to discuss the structure of their students' experience and ways to improve it in coming semesters.

After school the two faculty members work with a group of volunteer teachers who are particularly interested in portfolios as a means of assessing their students' progress in literacy learning. This group meets about once a month and prior to these meetings reads professional articles related to this topic. On their way out of the building, the faculty members make plans to return to see a special performance that several classes will be presenting later in the week related to a thematic unit on the rainforest. The faculty members then return to their office and meet to discuss their work for the coming week related to their school responsibilities.

Action research promotes collaboration on two levels.

1. Teachers are encouraged to participate as a teacher partner or in action research study groups to work on practice-oriented investigations. This aspect of action research means that teachers collaborate to discuss the kinds of issues about which they need to know more, various ways of studying these issues, and the impact of their school context on the study of a specific problem. Ongoing support for the work is embedded in the process of participation itself.

2. Teacher researchers work regularly with academic researchers to acquire the skills they need to formulate problems skillfully, investigate them in meaningful ways, and share the work and recognition of writing up findings and presenting them professionally (Cochran-Smith & Lytle, 1993; Oja & Pine, 1989).

Sometimes action researchers organize themselves into more formal "study groups" (Kyle & Hovda, 1987) with the participating faculty members. These are in essence informal graduate courses that may have credit attached to participation. The periodic meetings, whether formal or informal, are essential if action research is to encourage the goal of reflection, which is an important outgrowth of the action research process.

Because action research is designed to foster teacher inquiry and professional interest in school improvement, it indeed can be integral to the goal of ongoing professional growth and development. When teachers inquire regularly into what they themselves are doing at both the classroom and the school level, they are creating intellectual interest in and responsibility for what goes on in their workplace—one of the hallmarks of a healthy collaborative school. And when they do this collaboratively, as action research is intended to be carried out, the process of inquiry becomes a collective act to be supported and shared. The school as a workplace then becomes a community of inquiry, where all participants are encouraged to raise the level of discourse about their work, including its improvment through systematic study. Equally important, the faculty begins to see research as linked intimately to school practice and takes a major role in assisting teachers to develop the skills they need to carry out classroom and school-based studies.

 If you were to have the opportunity to study some aspect of your teaching in an action research format, what would it be? What do you want to know more about? What do you want to change? How might faculty members from a local university help you?

Action Research and Collaboration Between Special and General Education

Because one of the most common types of professional interaction takes place between special and general education teachers, we must give some thought to the relationship between action research and one-on-one collaboration between a special education teacher and a classroom teacher. Typically, the purpose of these one-on-one interactions is to work with classroom teachers to assist and support them in changing their teaching so it becomes more accommodating of students who have difficulty in school—in either academics or behavior. Although the reason for initiating such a collaborative relationship usually is a specific problem the classroom teacher is having with one or two students, more often than not some general practice in the classroom is the root of the problem.

Elsewhere (Pugach & Johnson, 1990b) we have argued that when the problem to be solved affects more students than the one a particular teacher might target, action research holds great potential for real, consistent change. Action research places ownership for change squarely with the teacher, which minimizes the potential for teacher resistance. Further, if special and general education teachers together participate as members of an action research study group, they instantly are on equal footing as colleagues supporting each other's action research. As a result, both are in the position of inquiring into the quality of their own practice—and are working to improve it.

As we discussed in Chapter 7, resistance to change is a lot less likely when a group of teachers are working on change together and creating a school climate in which change is the norm. We see action research as one important way of shifting from the status quo to norms of experimentation, bypassing the need for some of the formal one-on-one interaction that now goes on between special and general education. Particularly when problems affect many students—for example, motivational problems based more on the problematic nature of the instructional activities than on the student's inherent unwillingness to participate—action research can provide a safe, supportive context in which to address improvements in teaching practice.

TEACHERS AS CLINICAL TEACHER EDUCATION FACULTY

In the PDS example, university faculty members were assigned to a public school as an essential part of the collaborative partnership. Another example of school-university collaboration is to have experienced teachers serve as clinical teacher education faculty members. With regard to teacher education, the traditional role of skilled, veteran teachers has been to serve as cooperating teachers during the student teaching semester. But a new trend is emerging in which, as a result of collaborative arrangements between schools and universities, veteran teachers are beginning to participate directly in the day-to-day delivery of teacher education programs. This arrangement is sometimes known as *teacher-in-residence*. Often this arrangement consists of only one or two teachers, sometimes called Distinguished Teacher(s)-in-Residence. The University of Wisconsin–Milwaukee has a cadre of 20 Teachers-in-Residence on special assignment from the local school district to the university for 2 years (University of Wisconsin–Milwaukee, 2001).

Teachers-in-residence typically retain their employment in their school districts but are assigned to the local university through a special arrangement. This means that local school districts and universities must collaborate on practical issues such as coordination of pay, verification of days worked, different schedules, and requisite evaluations. They must make plans for replacing funds to the schools districts whose teachers are participating in the program. Prior to the start of any such program, the partners must discuss criteria for selection, participate jointly in the selection process, and work with the teachers(s) in the transition from school to university in terms of different norms and expectations. For example, most teachers are not used to the flexible scheduling that is a hallmark of university culture, and initially may have difficulty structuring their time. Also, when a teacher-in-residence visits a school within his or her own district in this new role, other teachers may not understand their role and their concomitant desire to be affiliated with a local institution of higher education.

As a function of cross-institutional collaboration, the concept of teachers-in-residence serves two important functions (University of Wisconsin-Milwaukee, 2001):

1. When teachers are regular participants in all aspects of teacher education, from co-teaching to program development to supervision in the field to program research, a strong link is established between practical experience from the schools and university experiences. All participants gain greater mutual understanding of the complementary roles of the schools and the university.
2. Serving in the role of a teacher-in-residence is a different, long-term form of professional development that can be linked to the development of teacher leaders

Revisiting Cross-Institutional Collaboration

As these examples of cross-institutional collaboration illustrate, partnerships create unprecedented opportunities to support real and lasting change in schools. Creating a climate in which teachers and other institutional partners explore and act together on the problems of educational practice maximizes the potential to find better ways of organizing schools and classrooms to meet the needs of a diverse student population. In the context of school-agency partnerships, expanded services to students can be achieved. With school-university partnerships, joint support for asking difficult questions about educational practices, structuring ways to solve them, and building bridges between schools and institutions of higher education for mutual benefit can result from the collaboration.

Remember...

1. Cross-institutional collaboration is an important strategy for school improvement.
2. Like any other form of collaboration, cross-institutional partnerships pool different, complementary kinds of expertise.
3. Collaboration is based on the development of mutual respect for the contributions of schools and partner institutions to the improvement of schooling.
4. Cross-institutional collaboration can foster the development of a climate in which teachers feel free to experiment and are supported in their efforts.
5. School-agency collaboration can ensure that children with disabilities receive the range of services they require within the context of their school.
6. Action research is a form of collaboration that encourages inquiry into the improvement of teaching.

Activities

1. As a group, record all the school-university partnerships in your area. Which ones exemplify the goals of collaboration advanced in this book?
2. Assume that 20 student teachers are going to be assigned to your school, which has 18 classrooms (three each at grades K–5). How will you organize their semester-long activities to promote the greatest professional collaboration schoolwide?
3. Revisit the four dimensions of collaboration. Which dimensions would be best facilitated by a school-agency partnerships? A school-university partnership?

10

School–Family Collaboration

One of the most important goals that schools can undertake is to develop healthy partnerships with families. A truly collaborative school can be achieved only through active and positive partnerships with families. Our students are all members of families first and students second. Family members are so interrelated that any individual experience that affects one member will affect all. Families are going to have the most lasting and powerful influence on the development of the students with whom we work. Consequently, to be able to lay the groundwork for effective collaborative relationships, we must understand families.

Traditionally, the image of family was perceived as father, mother and two or more children living together. Actually, few American families now fit the traditional image (Zinn & Eitzen, 1993). Fewer than one in five families currently fits the more traditional notion of two parents and children. The U.S. Bureau of Census (Scoon-Rogers, 1999) reports that over the past 25 years, the number of families headed by single men has increased from 1.3 million to 3.2 million and families headed by single women has increased from 5.8 million to 13.6 million. One explanation is a divorce rate that has doubled, along with widowing and adoption. Many families consist of step-parents and step-siblings, extended families, common-law families, communal families, serial families, or some combination thereof (Beirne-Smith, Ittenbach, & Patton, 1998). Our notion of the family has to expand to acknowledge the unique pressures of the various types of family units with which teachers will come in contact. The new types of living arrangements often bring unique problems that include everything from blatant discrimination to social stigma (Edwards, 1995).

In this chapter we provide a framework from which to interpret and understand the unique demands being placed on the family. We must understand families and their unique dynamics as a foundation for our efforts toward developing collaborative relationships with the families of the students. Unless we understand families and their unique needs and pressures, attempts at collaboration will be susceptible to misunderstanding. After we have provided this foundational context, we explore real and perceived barriers that can inhibit collaboration among teachers and families. Finally, we provide practical suggestions regarding ways to collaborate more effectively with the families of students.

 As you read this chapter, take a minute to think about the different types of families with whom you have had more than casual contact. How do they interact, solve problems, experience joy, and so on? They could be families of close relatives, your family, or the families of friends. As you think about these families, identify three or four families with different structures and styles. As you read about families, ask yourself how the issues discussed relate or play themselves out with each of these families. Focus on similarities and differences as you think about these families.

The Family

The basic unit that defines and sustains our society is the family. The family consists of two or more individuals who meet the collective and individual needs of family members. These people may or may not be related by blood or marriage and may or may not usually live together (Turnbull, Turnbull, Shank, & Leal, 1995). The family unit is one of the most basic forms of human organization. Although the family has changed dramatically over the last 25 years, it continues to have as its primary purpose meeting family members' needs to nurture their fullest development. Although families differ across cultures, commonalities among family units worldwide are far greater than their differences. As Moles (1993) has asserted, what parents want for their children is universal.

The family can be defined as a network of people who live together for an extended time because of mutual commitment to the family unit. This commitment can be by blood, marriage, legal means, or otherwise. The type of commitment or how this commitment is made is less important than the fact that a commitment has been made. What is important is the mutual partnership among family members. Families exist in a number of forms or varieties, all of which are able to meet the needs of family members. Some forms are:

1. *Traditional nuclear family:* parents and children.
2. *Single-parent family:* one parent or guardian (male or female) and children. That parent might be single as a result of many factors: death, divorce, never married, adoptive, or desertion.

3. *Blended family:* adults (married or not) and children from previous marriages or unions.
4. *Extended family:* nuclear family unit plus grandparents, aunts, uncles, cousins, and so on.
5. *Same-gender couples:* with and without children.

Family Systems

As a system, the family is made up of members and a series of subsystems that are internally and externally related. If anything affects one family member, it will affect the rest of the family system. Similarly, changes in the broader structural system of the family also will affect the family. For example, a bad economy can create stress that can strain the family system and influence how a child functions in the classroom. In a similar fashion, what happens at school can affect the broader family unit. For example, a child who receives a detention or some kind of school discipline also may be disciplined at home. If one of the adult members of the family considers this discipline to be too harsh, the marital subsystem is stressed. More specifically, when we ask family members to spend extra time with one of their children supporting classwork, the additional time they are spending with this child will detract from other activities within the family. Although requests for support typically have positive outcomes, the extra time we ask family members to work with the child can do more harm than good if the family is already stressed by spending long hours supporting the family.

As stated previously, the idea of a typical family is no longer applicable to today's family unit. Nevertheless, a framework is in place for understanding the family as a series of subsystems. We propose the following four subsystems, modeled after Turnbull and Turnbull (2001):

1. Adult-adult subsystem: partner interactions between the adults in the unit, whether married or not
2. Parental subsystem: parent and child interactions
3. Sibling subsystem: child and child interactions
4. Extended family subsystem: interactions of nuclear family relatives and others who are regarded as relatives.

The interaction between subsystems depends greatly on the structure of the larger family unit. For example, single-parent families have no adult partner subsystem, and families with only one child have no sibling subsystem. A discussion of these subsystems follows.

ADULT-ADULT SUBSYSTEM

The adult-adult subsystem is composed of the two primary adults within the family unit, regardless of their marital status. These adults have needs and roles as adult partners. They plan for the family, support one another, play together, and share intimacy.

PARENTAL SUBSYSTEM

The parental subsystem is composed of the adult primary caregiver(s) and the children. The caregiver(s) assume a wide variety of roles as they interact with the children within the family. Roles include counselors, financial advisors, chauffeurs, disciplinarians, tutors, and so on. These roles can be explicit or implied and are fluid and constantly changing. The primary adult caregiver may be a single individual, a couple of individuals, or more.

SIBLING SUBSYSTEM

The sibling subsystem is made up of interactions between children within the family unit. According to Powell and Gallagher (1993), siblings are socialization agents who provide children's first and most intense peer relationships. A sibling sometimes takes on a parental role within the family and interacts more like a parent than a sibling. Siblings may be step-siblings, half- siblings, natural siblings, or adoptive siblings.

EXTENDED FAMILY SUBSYSTEM

The extended family subsystem consists of members of the family beyond the immediate family members. Interactions with extended family can be a source of support or they can be a source of additional stress. Some extended families provide a great deal of support, and others have become estranged because of their geographic location or for other reasons. As a result, these families do not have a natural support system upon which to rely. Families without extended families must create an analogous support system from friends and neighbors. Unfortunately, some families are unable to create such a support system.

Next we are going to discuss basic family needs. As you read this section, think about the families of students in your class or practicum. Are some families having trouble meeting their basic needs? How does this affect children at school? Could the school do anything to help the family meet its needs? Is the school responsible for helping families meet their needs? Are there any pitfalls for schools providing resources to enable families to be better able to meet their needs?

Family Functions

The tasks in which families engage to meet the needs of family members are called *family functions*. Each family function is affected by every family member. This influence may be positive, negative, or neutral (Barnett & Boyce, 1995; O'Conner, 1995). Turnbull and Turnbull (2001) have described seven family functions:

1. Economic needs
2. Daily care needs
3. Recreation needs
4. Socialization needs
5. Self-esteem needs
6. Affection needs
7. Education-vocation needs.

Families implement these functions to meet their current and individual needs and to transfer the responsibility of meeting those needs from the older generation of the family to the younger generation of the family. We as professionals must understand these family functions and how they relate to the family. All too often we focus on families' educational and vocational needs and ignore their other needs. Families are extremely complex, with diverse needs that must be met for the family to be effective. These needs are explored next, along with ways in which professionals can help families meet those needs.

ECONOMIC NEEDS

All families must make decisions about how to obtain and spend money to meet the family's needs. Difficulty meeting economic needs places tremendous stress on the family unit. This stress can accentuate negative behaviors of family members and strain their interactions. Maintaining a supportive environment is difficult when basic needs are not being met. If a family has a child with a disability who requires special needs and care, the consumption demands on the family can increase greatly as a result of additional costs associated with medical care or restrictions on the ability of family to generate resources.

Schools can do many things to help. A school can collect information and resources on financial planning and place these in a family resource library. A school can contact appropriate local resources to provide parents with unique information in the community, such as employment services and financial planning. The school's parent organization could identify special speakers to address financial planning and saving for college and other economic concerns that may be causing concern to parents within the schools. Parents who have been successful in addressing issues such as planning for college could be asked to speak to other families that are experiencing similar problems. Secondary schools can help families become aware of scholarships and other ways to help with planning for college.

DAILY CARE NEEDS

Perhaps the most important function that a family performs is meeting the daily care needs of family members. Cooking, cleaning, doing laundry, transporting, obtaining appropriate medical care, and so on, typically dominate the family's life. As with economic needs, if the family's medical and domestic care needs are not being met, the family will have trouble focusing on other issues. When parents are trying to meet the daily care needs of their family, they often overlook their own needs and become exhausted.

When a family is having difficulty meeting daily care needs, the school might provide information on health care services in the area as part of its resource library. This information should include resources for psychological information as well as physical health care needs. The school can introduce health promotion into the curriculum. If the school has a school nurse, he or she could work with parents to develop programs for the family. Some schools have washers and dryers to assist families in the most serious need. A simple but effective action is to investigate food served at the school to ensure that it is consistent with best thinking about nutrition. Parents who have been successful in juggling the many demands placed upon them to meet daily care needs of their children can share with other families actions that have helped them be successful.

SOCIALIZATION NEEDS

The ability to socialize is a critical component of the quality of life in any family. Families with children who have disabilities or behavior problems can be severely limited in their options to socialize because of the stress the family faces when the child is in public.

School professionals can do several things to aid families' socialization options. Respite options can be developed for families that have a child with severe disabilities. People who are skilled in dealing with the child's disability might provide child care as well as provide socialization and recreation options. The school could provide workshops on behavior management, focusing on strategies to deal with inappropriate behavior in public. Schools can encourage family support groups as a means for families to socialize with other family members. Finally, the school can reconceptualize itself as a community center and offer workshops and other community activities, providing a way for families to interact with other families in the community.

RECREATIONAL NEEDS

We all need activities to unwind and divert our attention from the routine of our daily lives. The family is a primary source of recreational opportunities for family members. Recreational needs are met through everything from planned structured vacations to simple walks or conversations during dinner. The school's efforts to provide for families' social needs can double as a venue for meeting their recreational needs.

SELF-ESTEEM NEEDS

A sense of confidence and self-worth are integral to our identity as individuals. The family is perhaps the most important system to help people develop their sense of self-identity. We must realize that the self-identity of parents is tied heavily to the abilities of their children. For example, if a child is having difficulty in school, family members might internalize a sense of responsibility for the problem and have feelings of inadequacy themselves. Helping parents identify and pursue their own interests is one way to help them nurture their self-identity. Finding ways for parents to participate and be successful within the school is important, too. Family support groups again can help families address their concerns in relation to other families experiencing similar concerns.

AFFECTION NEEDS

Families provide a vital environment for individuals to experience affection and physical intimacy. The family provides physical as well as emotional messages that communicate unconditional regard and love to members. These messages are communicated through both verbal and nonverbal means. Nonverbal actions such as touching, hugging, kissing, or just being with one another are extremely powerful.

Although we are inclined to believe that meeting the affection needs of families is beyond the scope of schools, the school can do some things to help families address these needs. For example, schools can make accurate information on sexuality accessible to students and families. Information on AIDS and other sexually transmitted diseases is especially important for students. Counselors or support groups can be helpful to students as they confront issues of affection.

EDUCATION AND VOCATIONAL NEEDS

The educational and vocational needs of the family probably represents the area most often emphasized by professionals. Many demands are being placed on families for their time and efforts. We must be sensitive to the kinds of demands being placed on the parents and recognize that the child is only one of those demands. As a result, families must be able to choose their level of involvement within the school. If the educational/vocational needs of the family are not being met, it is extremely difficult for the family to be more involved in the school. The actions described in the section related to addressing a family's economic needs could easily be expanded to include educational and vocational needs.

Elements of Family Interactions

The extent of cohesiveness or adaptability of the family has a significant impact on the quality of interactions within the family subsystem. Cohesion is the emotional bond between members of the family, and adaptability is the ability of a family to modify or change in response to outside pressures (Olson, 1980).

COHESION

Cohesion can be conceptualized along a continuum, with high disengagement at one end and high enmeshment at the other end. A healthy family maintains a delicate balance between the degree of disengagement and enmeshment, and this balance often shifts as new issues confront the family. For example, when a family is confronted with a crisis, it typically becomes more enmeshed. On the other hand, when a high school graduate is trying to strike out on his or her own, the healthy family becomes more disengaged.

ENMESHMENT

Families that are highly enmeshed often are characterized by overinvolvement and overprotection of family members. Typically, family members are allowed little privacy, and most activities of family members take place within the family. A family that becomes too enmeshed will have a difficult time functioning effectively. In particular, members will have trouble developing a sense of individuality. A certain degree of enmeshment is healthy and positive, providing a safety net that allows individuals within the family to feel supported and bolstered by the other family members. This environment can provide a foundation to encourage risk taking and growth. If the family's level of enmeshment becomes stifling, however, it will stifle risk taking and inhibit members from growing as individuals.

DISENGAGEMENT

Families that are highly disengaged are characterized by under-involvement, few common interests, excessive privacy, and long periods of separation. These families rarely discuss individual decisions, and activities of family members are seldom family-focused. Disengaged families typically have rigid subsystem boundaries, and members of the subsystem have difficulty interfacing with another subsystem. For example, one of the children may have a new girlfriend whom the siblings are aware of, but the parents have no idea of this relationship.

As with enmeshment, some disengagement is healthy for family members. If individuals within a family are to develop autonomy and independence, they must have interests outside of the family. This is particularly true as children reach their teen years and are making the transition into adulthood. Recognizing that each member within the family needs time away from other family members enables younger family members to grow. If a family becomes too disengaged, though, family cohesiveness can be seriously compromised, resulting in family members' not feeling bolstered or supported by other family members.

ADAPTABILITY

Adaptability refers to the family's ability to adjust family roles and routines to new situations. Like cohesiveness, adaptability ranges along a continuum from rigid to chaotic. Some families are extremely rigid and have great difficulty adapting to new situations. Other families are extremely chaotic and have little structure or apparent planning. In a functional family, as the needs of the family evolve, the family becomes more rigid or more chaotic to be able to better address the situation. A family must develop a balance between structure and chaos.

For example, rigid families typically have many strictly enforced rules and a clear power hierarchy. Roles within the family are extremely well defined and inflexible. The emphasis on power and control can stifle the individuality of family members and inhibit appropriate risk taking. This type of family also has difficulty dealing with crises outside of the family's rules and expectations.

Some structure and predictability, however, help children develop self-discipline. Children must learn that their actions can have negative or positive consequences. For this learning, consequences must be applied in a consistent and predictable manner. Actions that warrant negative consequences must result in negative consequences, and actions that warrant positive consequences must result in positive consequences. Through structure and predictability children develop an internalized set of limits that contribute to their self-discipline. If, however, the rules become rigid and unbending, children learn a narrow view of justice, often equated with external controls. Rigid family systems stifle risk taking and inhibit development of self-discipline and worth. Children within such a system typically become dependent upon external rather than internal controls for their behavior.

In contrast, chaotic families have little control and structure. They have few rules, and those rules seldom are reinforced. Promise and commitments often are not kept, and family members learn at an early age that they cannot count on one another. This type of family lacks a hierarchical role structure of family members and subsystems. As a result, roles and role expectations are uncertain and confusing. This ambiguity around roles can be a source of tension among family members.

On the other hand, appropriate chaos within the family is healthy. The most positive aspect of chaos is flexibility. The notion that roles can change within the family and that rules can be negotiated help children learn a greater sense of fairness that takes into consideration the unique circumstances of a situation. Without clear leadership and distinct roles, however, children sometimes learn a sense of helplessness or fail to develop self- reliance and self-regulatory behaviors because they have an *external locus of control* (Beirne-Smith, Ittenbach, & Patton, 1994). They believe they have little control over things that happen to them; no matter what they do, it doesn't seem to make a difference because outcomes seem to be independent of their actions.

Effective Family Interactions

Although functional families vary greatly in general structure and organization, certain characteristics of families do seem to enhance their ability to be functional. These characteristics, described by Luterman (1991), are as follows.

1. Communication among family members is clear and open. They discuss issues clearly, and direct personal comments to the appropriate individual. Messages are congruent with content and feeling.

2. Although roles and responsibilities of family members are clearly delineated, the family has the flexibility to address unique situations. For a family to run effectively, it must have clear boundaries that members of the family understand. Expectations and roles must be clearly articulated and fulfilled. At the same time, the family must be flexible enough so roles can be shifted to meet unique challenges of the family.

3. Family members accept limits and participate in resolving conflicts. Conflict is a healthy part of any family, and effective families resolve conflict at an individual level through fair and open means. Conflict is not denied, nor are the needs of one individual considered paramount to the needs of the family unit or other individuals within the family. Rather, resolution is sought in which all family members can feel committed. Often these families have successful face-saving mechanisms that allow all family members to feel as if they were partially successful in resolving the conflict.

4. Intimacy is prevalent and is a function of equal power transactions. A primary feature of the family is to provide intimacy to members. Human beings need an environment of closeness and caring with other humans. Intimacy must be based on an equal power transaction and is not something to be demanded. Everyone within the family must feel free to share intimacy based on their own individual needs as well as the needs of the family unit as a whole.

5. There is a healthy balance between change and stability. Families must provide a stable foundation for members within the family and at the same time be willing to adapt to new challenges. A healthy family makes changes to accommodate challenges facing the family while still providing stability for members within the family.

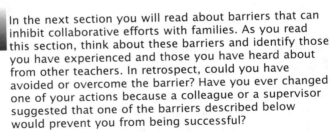

In the next section you will read about barriers that can inhibit collaborative efforts with families. As you read this section, think about these barriers and identify those you have experienced and those you have heard about from other teachers. In retrospect, could you have avoided or overcome the barrier? Have you ever changed one of your actions because a colleague or a supervisor suggested that one of the barriers described below would prevent you from being successful?

Barriers to Family Participation

Serious barriers must be overcome if we are to collaborate effectively with the families of our students. Many of these barriers are merely perceived, and others are grounded in fact. Lynch and Stein (1987) studied these barriers from both a parent and a professional perspective. Parents identified barriers to participation with schools related to issues including logistics (work, time conflicts, transportation problems, and child care), communication problems, misunderstanding of schools that creates feelings of inferiority, and uncertainty about their child's unique problems. Professionals identified barriers that related to issues such as parent apathy, lack of release time and other time, lack of expertise of professionals, and feeling overburdened and devalued. A discussion of some of these perceived barriers follows.

PARENT-IDENTIFIED BARRIERS

Logistical Problems

Families sometimes have substantial logistical problems in trying to arrange for transportation, babysitting, or time away from work to attend conferences or meetings within the schools. These are serious problems that, if recognized, schools can help families overcome. For example, rather than having family members meet within the school, teachers might consider going to the family's home or meeting in a community center near the family's home. Or the school could arrange transportation for a family member to come to the school. The school could provide child care so family members could bring their children and attend meetings or observe in their child's classroom. Child care is relatively inexpensive and is an important means of support for parents who wish to be more involved in the school. Meetings can be held at times that are easiest for parents, such as during the lunch hour or in the evening. Another factor that alleviates time concerns is to conduct meetings efficiently. We must recognize that families have many serious time demands and, by using time efficiently, we can maximize the time spent with parents and families.

Communication Problems

Families often come from cultural or socioeconomic backgrounds different from school personnel—which can make communication more difficult. Given current demographic trends, these differences are likely to increase. When educational jargon and abbreviations enter the mix, teachers and family members might well be speaking two related but different languages with different vocabularies and styles. As a result, we may think we understand each other but actually have completely different understandings of the same conversation.

Compounding the differences are the different communication styles within a family. Some represent individual differences, and others are culturally defined. For example, some families are loud and emotional in their responses to one another, and other families are reserved and restrained. A teacher might interpret a mother's loud and emotional response as aggression, for example, whereas if the teacher were to understand the family's communication norms, he or she might interpret the mother's responses as demonstrating concern for her child.

When attempting to create and maintain effective communication with families, nonverbal communication (facial expressions, body language, eye contact, amount of personal space required, and the way one listens) must be considered. Listening is an especially important part of communication with families because it can relay the value that school personnel place on input from the family, as well as how much effort the listener is giving to understanding what the family believes is important.

As we have stressed in several chapters of this book, developing good communication skills and developing rapport and understanding with the families in your school's community are pivotal. In this way, family members and school personnel can enter a trusting partnership centering on student growth and achievement.

Lack of Understanding of Schools

Schools are complex organizations that have both overt and covert rules of operation. Rules can be formal (including the rights of parents of children with a disability), or they can be subtle and covert (such as the ways by which parents can influence who will be the teacher of their child). If a family member does not understand these rules, he or she may be confused and can get lost in the bureaucracy. As a result, the family member will be unable to use the system to meet the family's needs, or more specifically the child's needs, thereby compounding the sense of disenfranchisement. Having a diminished sense of control in decision making creates a feeling of inferiority and contributes to families' vulnerability to intimidation. Often, families of low-income students and students of color are the ones who feel this diminished sense of control.

To become family-focused, schools must make public their rules of operation and work to ensure that families understand these rules. A first step to becoming more family-focused is for schools to examine what it is about their typical way of doing business that is preventing parents or other family members from being full partners in the educational process. Emphasis must be placed on encouraging families to be an integral part of what is happening within the school. In many cases this means teaching families how to access all of the resources schools have to offer. It also means recognizing that nearly all families represent an educational resource that can enrich the school experiences of all students (Moll, Amanti, Neff, & Gonzalez, 1992), and valuing this resource.

We must create an environment and structure that empowers families. We must recognize that when we are talking to parents about concerns and challenges their children are facing, parents have a sense of responsibility that can affect their interpretation of what we are communicating.

BARRIERS IDENTIFIED BY PROFESSIONALS

Parental Apathy

Although in a few schools parents may be apathetic or indifferent about being involved, school personnel often seriously exaggerate this attitude, particularly with respect to families of minority students. Sometimes the experiences that parents have had with schools have not been positive, so the parents avoid interactions because they expect all interactions to be equally negative. Second, parents may believe that they have very little influence or power over what is going happen to their children, that no matter what they do, it won't make a difference, so why bother (Beirne-Smith et al., 1998). Third, cultural norms may dictate that the teacher is to be respected above all and that teachers know what is best. Therefore, what could families have to say about school to the experts? Finally, what we are interpreting as apathy on the part of parents might actually be exhaustion from the many demands on the family in addition to school.

To combat what is perceived erroneously as apathy, educators must get their own biases under control and not use stereotypes as an excuse to exclude parents. To say "families don't care" is easy when, in fact, scheduled meetings are not responsive to demands placed on families in terms of finding child care, taking time away from work, and getting transportation to attend meetings. When schools are unresponsive to families' day-to-day pressures, the families might say that "schools don't care." Educators must try to make schools family-centered so the activities associated with the schools generate a positive feeling with positive outcomes. If parents experience schools as positive places where positive things happen, they are much more likely to become actively engaged.

Finally, and most important, families' lack of involvement can be overcome by having families be real decision makers within the schools. To give families the appearance of being involved through representation on committees and attendance at key meetings is not enough. We must do everything we can to empower them to be vital decision makers within our schools. As families see that their participation has positive outcomes, they will be less likely to feel uncomfortable participating in the schools.

Professional Time Constraints

Like parents, professionals have a limited time to meet with parents during the school day. As a result, schools are regularly scheduling alternative meeting times such as after school and on weekends. An often overlooked concern for these meetings is the burden placed on teachers to be away from their own families for evening or weekend meetings with family members. We must get creative and develop unique ways to meet the needs of both the teachers and the families they serve. We must begin to think of new ways for teachers and parents to get together. In addition, as previously discussed, efficiently conducted meetings greatly enhance the limited time available for meetings.

We also must check and be honest about our true attitudes toward family participation. We have not always valued the input that families have to offer. Although we have consistently claimed that families are important members of our "team," our actions often convey a very different picture. When families make suggestions that are contrary to the school's views or are critical of the school, these families are often characterized as problem makers. This is particularly true if the family culture is not White and middle class or if family members are assertive in their input. By scheduling meetings at inconvenient times, we communicate to families that they are not important. How meetings are conducted also can communicate to families that they have lower status than the other participants.

For example, in a typical IEP meeting everybody brings and shares formal information about the child. This information might include test scores, observation data, work samples, and the like. All participants at the meeting then make a formal presentation of this information to the other members of the group. Family members typically are not asked to bring any formal information, nor are they asked if they have anything to add. This communicates clearly that family members are not full participants. The structure of the committee and the information required from the members sends the message that family members have a different, less important role than the other participants.

Our actions and words regarding family involvement often communicates an incongruent message. Our actions suggest that families are not equal members while our words suggest that they are. We must work extremely hard to ensure that our actions and words are consistent. If families are equal members of the team, they should be treated as equals.

Professional Expertise

Throughout this book we have argued that working with colleagues in a collaborative manner is hard work that requires a special set of skills to facilitate communication. Working with and supporting families is equally difficult and requires specific skills. Unfortunately, these skills have not always been part of our teacher preparation programs. Becoming proficient in the communication skills delineated in this book will provide the foundational skills necessary to be an active partner with families. We must recognize the important role of families in providing professionals with the expertise and knowledge

Fostering Family Involvement
by Meeting Family Needs

The James E. Biggs Early Childhood Education Center is located in Covington, Kentucky, across the Ohio River and essentially part of the Cincinnati, Ohio, metropolitan area. This is an urban neighborhood populated largely by families of low socioeconomic status and of diverse backgrounds. People in the community have many problems and concerns but, like all people, they care a great deal about their children and have many hopes and dreams for their future. Traditional approaches to involving families in their child's program generally have not resulted in long-term, positive effects in this community. As a result, the administration at the James E. Biggs Center decided to take a different approach to involving families and began to take steps to conceptualize and implement a family-centered program.

Rather than being child-centered, the administration decided that activities of the center must be directed to the whole family. As they began thinking about the family as its responsibility, the nature of the center began to change. The center developed a program for medical and dental care support and a family room to which parents and their children could come. Child care and transportation are provided for parents who want to volunteer or participate in an educational program. A whole series of programs and activities emerged to support families, including make-up classes, Dad's night out, weight classes, GED classes, a clothing exchange, and parent-teacher training. As a result of these efforts, families are actively involved in the program.

On any given day, one can find parents in the classroom, children receiving day care, and parents just dropping by the center to sit a while in the parent room. Clearly, families are actively involved in the program and the program is responsive to their needs. The school has become more than a school and is thought of as a central component in the community. Where many others have failed, the James E. Biggs Center has been successful by letting go of old approaches and embracing new thinking. Rather than focusing on how to get families more involved, they worked to meet the needs of families in the community. As a result, more families got involved.

required to work effectively with families. Until schools become truly family-centered, any reform effort is likely to fall far short of its potential. Although we have a long way to go, many notable examples can guide us.

In this example, an early childhood center has made the transition successfully from a student-centered to a family-centered program. The dominant theme at this school is the mutual respect and partnership between the family and the school. The center was able to make this transition by directing efforts toward meeting the needs of families in the school and avoiding the trap of engaging only in traditional forms of parent involvement. The strategies we discuss next can be used to help establish and nurture an environment that encourages mutual respect and cooperation.

Strategies for Communicating With Families

Several strategies have been set forth for communicating with families. Although all of the strategies we describe below are important, none will be successful unless you first build a good relationship with students' families. Handbooks, announcements of special occasions, newsletters, regular progress reports, occasional notes, and telephone conferences (Turnbull & Turnbull, 2001) are all effective only to the extent that you have worked hard to connect with families and have made the relationship between teacher, school, and family a priority for all. Therefore, we begin with strategies for establishing relationships at the start of the year, then continue with other strategies for communication. In any communication with families whose first language is other than English, you will have to translate written materials or have a translator present for face-to-face or telephone interactions.

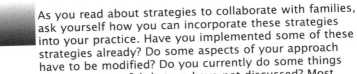 As you read about strategies to collaborate with families, ask yourself how you can incorporate these strategies into your practice. Have you implemented some of these strategies already? Do some aspects of your approach have to be modified? Do you currently do some things that are successful that we have not discussed? Most important, how can these and other strategies help you to nurture an environment that encourages mutual respect and cooperation between you, the school, and the families your school serves?

ESTABLISHING INITIAL RELATIONSHIPS WITH FAMILIES

The most important foundation for communicating with families is to establish relationships with them as soon as the school year begins. There is simply no substitute for teacher's taking the time initially to introduce themselves to their students' primary caregivers and to communicate their desire to be in touch. Initial phone calls also provide teachers with an opportunity to ask family members if they wish to share anything special with the teacher about their child as the new school year begins.

Although phoning each child's family at the start of the year may seem like a daunting task, it is an essential part of every teacher's job. If a family does not have a telephone, you can send home a personal letter in the mail at the start of the school year. Some teachers send each student in their classes a postcard a few weeks before school begins. This communicates to families your level of commitment and caring even before their child steps into your classroom. If you cannot reach family members by phone and have trouble getting family members to respond to letters, you might plan a home visit with the school's parent liaison, social worker, or another teacher.

Collaboration can be successful only if lines of communication are open. Waiting to make a first family contact until a problem arises is a sure-fire way to create negative feelings. Teachers who are serious about collaborating with families take the time to establish positive relationships based on open lines of communication as soon as the school year begins.

HANDBOOKS

Another way to help families understand what you will be doing with their child and how they can support you at home is to give them a handbook describing your rules, philosophy, major activities, a typical day in your class, and so on. Going over this handbook at the beginning of the year gives families an overview of the classroom and a concrete basis for them to ask questions.

ANNOUNCEMENTS FOR SPECIFIC SITUATIONS

When you have special activities or special events within your classroom, sending home an announcement describing the purpose of the activity and how family members can expand upon the activity is a good way to communicate with them. You also can send out announcements periodically about classroom activities and points of interest that might be useful to families. These might include upcoming local education events or other tips that can extend school activities.

NEWSLETTERS

One of the most time-honored ways of communicating with families is a regular newsletter. Newsletters can be developed by the teacher, the class, the school, or other family members of students in the classroom. Newsletters are a means of providing information on upcoming events and highlighting specific accomplishments of children or a class.

REGULAR PROGRESS REPORTS

Another way to communicate with the families is to send home progress reports. These can be done as frequently as once a week or as infrequently as once a month. They offer family members a systematic way of getting information about the accomplishments of their children. One way to go about this is to have students keep a log of activities for the day and provide a place for family members to sign the activity or have teachers put an entry in the log and have the parents sign the log.

OCCASIONAL NOTES HOME

Teachers also can send notes that point out a child's unique accomplishments. These notes could be simple forms of communication such as "happy grams," which talk about a specific accomplishment, or a little sticker that the child can wear home. The notes may be simple and brief, mentioning something the child has done that the families might like to hear about.

TELEPHONE CONFERENCES

Communicating by way of the telephone should be reserved for short conversations. Long conversations are better done in person and are not appropriate by telephone. Although the telephone is convenient and can be useful in addressing family concerns quickly, it precludes nonverbal messages. When calling a family member, the caller should always identify himself or herself and ask if this is a convenient time to talk. The telephone should not be a regular means to relate negative information about the child. Those communications are delicate and require great effort to ensure good communication. When sending s delicate messages, eye contact and the body language of the parent aid communication. Telephone calls should be planned carefully, and the key issues jotted down prior to making the call. In doing this, you can concentrate on the conversation and ensure that you don't forget to bring up an important item. Parents should be allowed time to respond to or answer questions.

Formal Family Conferences

In virtually all schools in the United States, conferences are the primary vehicle to communicate with families. Conferences with family members are held to accomplish the following (Turnbull & Turnbull, 2001):

1. To share information about the home and school environment.
2. To work together to help the child develop and share information on the child's progress.
3. To develop rapport and mutual commitment to the child's optimal development.
4. To cooperate in alleviating problems or concerns.

Turnbull and Turnbull (2001) also identify three phases to follow in planning and carrying out a conference: (a) preconference planning, (b) conference implementation, and (c) postconference follow-up.

PRECONFERENCE PLANNING

Good planning can help ensure a successful conference. Kroth (1985) identifies three basic steps to a preconference: (a) notify, (b) prepare and (c) arrange.

Notify

The first step in preconference planning is to notify key family members of the upcoming conference. Sometimes schools have predetermined conference procedures, including scheduling conference time and space and sending notification through school calendars and reminders that the conference will be held. Each family must be considered, and individual strategies developed when needed, to ensure that family members are aware of the conference and able to attend. The notification must be as nonthreatening as possible. If parents feel threatened, they may find a convenient reason for not attending the conference. School personnel also can alleviate anxiety by being as clear as possible about the purpose of the conference. In schools with large populations of students whose families' first language is not English, all materials must be translated into the appropriate languages.

Prepare

In preparing for the conference, you must be well aware of the issues to be addressed. Several steps may be considered (Turnbull & Turnbull, 2001).

1. Prior to the visit review the student's cumulative folder and samples of student work that indicate progress, such as portfolios.

2. Have a clear assessment as to the student's current progress or the issue to be addressed.
3. Have examples of the student's work.
4. Prepare an outline of topics to be addressed.
5. When appropriate, meet with other professionals to gain additional information about the child.

Arrange

The final step in the preconference is to prepare the environment. Consider implementing the following (Turnbull & Turnbull, 2001):

1. If no one else will be in the classroom, it is an ideal place because it enables families to see the context of their child's learning. If the classroom is equipped with only small chairs, however, consider bringing in a table to sit around, or meet in another room. Having adults sit on small chairs is uncomfortable and can be distracting.
2. Gather all the important information prior to the meeting so you are ready to go when the family members arrive.
3. Try to schedule a time or place where interruptions are unlikely.
4. Make sure the room is comfortable. An uncomfortable setting can inhibit concentration and communication.
5. If the topic for discussion is sensitive, have tissues available in case someone becomes emotional during the meeting.
6. If the family does not speak English fluently, provide for an interpreter.

CONDUCTING THE CONFERENCE

In conducting any conference, good communication skills are essential. Start with broad opening statements and do not get into the essence of the information too quickly. Use active listening to help clarify the issues and concerns that family members raise. Follow the agenda and do not allow the conference to stray. If critical new information is raised at the conference, make a judgment as to the merit of changing the planned agenda to address the new information. Make every effort to adjust when needed without becoming so distracted that the task at hand gets lost. Once the conference is over, summarize it so everybody knows what was decided in the conference.

POSTCONFERENCE FOLLOW-UP

Depending on the purpose and length of the conference, summarizing the notes and providing a written copy to participants is a good way to facilitate understanding and to ensure that everyone has the same interpretation of the meeting. Depending on the outcomes of the conference, the teacher might want to make a follow-up phone call to the family to see how the implementation of any plan is progressing. Also, it's a good idea to follow up with other key members to see if any new information or new actions have to be developed.

UNPLANNED CONFERENCES

Unplanned conferences with family members will inevitably arise (Turnbull & Turnbull, 2001). Recognizing this reality, these unplanned conferences should be anticipated, and some actions thought through before they take place. Although it is unrealistic to expect that as a teacher you will never be caught off guard, you can do some things to help you to be ready for an unexpected conference.

First, keep good data on the students in your classes. If your files are well organized, you can quickly retrieve the information needed to answer questions. If you are asked a specific question and you don't have the information, it is better to tell the family members that you don't have the information readily at hand but will get it and get back to them immediately than to bluff a response. You might even want to anticipate being caught off guard and come up with a standard phrase such as, "I'm really glad you took the time to talk to me. Let me make sure I get the right information for you and get back to you as soon as possible."

At times, however, parents may come to see you because they are upset about something their child has said or something that has happened in your class or in the school. Unfortunately, the parent may be very angry when he or she approaches you. You must not do anything to escalate the situation. In this case, here are some things you can do to help deflate the aggression:

1. Listen! Do not try to interrupt the family members. Let them get off their chest whatever they came to say.
2. Don't argue, don't become defensive, and don't try to promise something that you may not be able to deliver.
3. Write down the key phrases, and when the family member calms down, repeat these phrases to him or her to be sure you have heard the concerns accurately. Then tell him or her that you will try to get the information needed and schedule a meeting with the appropriate individuals to address their concerns.
4. Speak softly. This often calms family members and encourages them to tone down their voice.

Most unplanned conferences are pleasant occasions for sharing information spontaneously. Although you certainly are likely to encounter upset family members, this type of unplanned conference is the exception rather than the norm.

Working With Families—Well Worth the Effort

Without an active partnership with families, schools always will be limited in what we are able to accomplish. Developing partnerships is one of the most important goals that our schools can undertake. Most of the individual primary needs of our students are met through their families. A collaborative school must include active partnerships with families. Our students are all members of families first and students second. Consequently, families are going to have the most lasting and powerful influence on their development. Forming meaningful partnerships with families is one of the most important collaborative partnerships teachers can develop.

Remember . . .

As you work to develop these partnerships, remember:

1. The family is the basic unit of our society.
2. Family configurations in our culture are diverse, and teachers must be cognizant of this diversity. Also important to consider are the values, decision-making styles, family roles, languages, background knowledge and influences of significant others (Turnbull & Turnbull, 2001).
3. Families are complex systems made up of a series of subsystems. Anything that impacts any subsystem will impact the entire system.
4. One of the biggest challenges in forming strong school-family collaboration is to ensure that school personnel confront their own stereotypes regarding families of students whose race, ethnicity, socioeconomic level, or language differs from their own.
5. The tasks in which families engage to meet the needs of members of the family are called family functions. The seven family functions are: (a) economic, (b) domestic and health care, (c) recreational, (d) socialization, (e) self-definition, (f) affection, and (g) educational/vocational.
6. The extent of cohesiveness, or adaptability, of the family has a significant impact on interactions within the family system. Cohesion represents the emotional bonds between members of the family.

Adaptability is the capacity of a family to change in response to outside pressures.

7. Families have identified logistics, communication problems, and misunderstanding of schools as concerns that inhibit their ability to be full partners with schools.

8. Professionals have identified parent apathy, lack of time, and the expertise of professionals as concerns that inhibit their ability to be full partners with schools.

9. Once a sound relationship is established at the start of the year, other strategies for ways to communicate with parents must be developed. These include: (a) handbooks, (b) announcements for specific situations, (c) newsletters, (d) regular progress messages, (e) occasional notes, and (f) telephone conferences.

10. One important way to communicate with families is through conferences. In planning and carrying out a conference, the three phases that should be followed are: (a) preconference planning, (b) conference implementation, and (c) postconference follow-up.

Activities

1. Break up the class into several groups. Assign each group one or more of the areas of family functioning. Ask each group to develop strategies the school can use to help the family within the areas of family functioning assigned to the group.

2. Have each class member plan and implement a mock conference with a family member. The conference could be videotaped for small-group discussion and peer feedback. If students have their own class or are in a practicum experience, the conference could be real instead of mock.

3. Have students identify a traditional, blended, and single-parent family that has school-age children. Have the students interview the adults in these families to get a sense of their experience with schools and how their unique family configuration inhibits or enhances their experiences.

4. Have students design a brief questionnaire or set of interview questions regarding family perceptions of their relationship to the school. Include questions about the resources that family might represent. Have the students work in groups and present their findings to the class.

5. If students have their own class or are in a practicum experience, have them implement and evaluate one or more of the strategies other than a conference for communicating with families.

References

Abelson, M. A., & Woodman, R. W. (1983). Review of research on team effectiveness: Implications for teams in schools. *School Psychology Review, 12*(2), 125–136.

Aldinger, L. E., Warger, C. L., & Eavy, P. W. (1991). *Strategies for teacher collaboration*. Ann Arbor, MI: Exceptional Innovations.

Artiles, A. J., & Trent, S. C. (1994). Overrepresentation of minority students in special education: A continuing debate. *Journal of Special Education, 27,* 410–437.

Barnett, W. S., & Boyce, G. C. (1995). Effects of children with Down syndrome on parents' attitude. *American Journal on Mental Retardation, 100*(2), 115–127.

Barth, R. S. (1990). *Improving schools from within: Teachers, parents, and principals can make the difference.* San Francisco: Jossey-Bass.

Bauwens, J., Hourcade, J., & Friend, M. (1989). Cooperative teaching: A model for general and special education integration. *Remedial and Special Education, 10*(2), 17–22.

Bean, R. M. (2001). Classroom teachers and reading specialists working together to improve student achievement. In V. J. Risko & K. Bromley (Eds.), *Collaboration for diverse learners: Viewpoints and perspectives* (pp. 348–368). Newark, DE: International Reading Association.

Beane, J. A. (1990). *A middle school curriculum: From rhetoric to reality.* Columbus, OH: National Middle Schools Association.

Beirne-Smith, M., Ittenbach, R. F., & Patton, J. R. (1998). *Mental retardation* (5th ed.). Columbus, OH: Merrill/Prentice-Hall.

Bennis, W. (1984). The four competencies of leadership. *Training and Development Journal, 38*(8), 14–19.

Blake, R. R., Shepard, H. A., & Mouton, J. S. (1964). *Managing intergroup conflict in industry.* Houston, TX: Gulf Publishing.

Bowen, M. (1976). Theory in the practice of psychotherapy. In P. J. Guerin (Ed.), *Family therapy in clinical practice* (pp. 337–387). New York: Gardner Press.

Butler, A. S., & Maher, C. A. (1981). Conflict and special service teams: Perspectives and suggestions for school psychologists. *Journal of School Psychology, 19*(1), 62–70.

Chalfant, J. C., & Pysh, M. V. (1989). Teacher assistance teams: Five descriptive studies on 96 teams. *Remedial and Special Education, 10*(6), 49–58.

Chalfant, J. C., Pysh, M. V., & Moultrie, R., (1979). Teacher assistance teams: A model for within-building problem solving. *Learning Disabilities Quarterly, 2*(3), 85–96.

Cochran-Smith, M., & Lytle, S. L. (1993). *Inside, outside: Teacher research and knowledge.* New York: Teachers College Press.

Cohen, E. G. (1981). Sociology looks at team teaching. *Research in Sociology of Education and Socialization, 2,* 163–193.

Cole, A. L. (1991). Relationships in the workplace: Doing what comes naturally? *Teaching and Teacher Education, 7*(5–6), 415–426.

Combs, A., Avila, D., & Purkey, W. (1971). *Helping relationships: Basic concepts for the helping professions.* Boston: Allyn & Bacon.

Conley, S. C., & Bacharach, S. B. (1990). From school-site management to participatory school-site management. *Phi Delta Kappan, 71*(7), 539–544.

Covey, S. R. (1990). *The seven habits of highly effective people: Restoring the character ethic.* New York: Fireside/Simon Schuster.

Cuban, L. (1989). The "at-risk" label and the problem of urban school reform. *Phi Delta Kappan, 70*(10), 780–784, 799–801.

DeDettmer, P., Thurston, L. P., & Dyck, N. (1993). *Consultation, collaboration, and teamwork for students with special needs.* Boston: Allyn & Bacon.

Dewey, J. (1933). *How we think: A restatement of the relation of reflective thinking to the educative process.* Boston: Heath & Company.

EDC. http://www2.edu.org/fsc/

Edwards, R. (1995, September). Psychologists foster the new definition of family. *APA Monitor,* p. 38.

Elliott, J. (1991). *Action research for educational change.* Philadelphia: Open University Press.

Ellis, N. E. (1990). Collaborative interaction for improvement of teaching. *Teaching and Teacher Education, 6*(3), 267–277.

Friend, M. P., & Cook, L. (1992). *Interactions: Collaboration skills for school professionals.* New York: Longman.

Fuchs, D., Fuchs, L. S., & Bahr, M. W. (1990). Mainstream assistance teams: A scientific basis for the art of consultation. *Exceptional Children, 57*(2), 128–139.

Fuchs, D., Fuchs, L. S., Bahr, M. W., Fernstrom, P., & Stecker, P. M. (1990). Prereferral intervention: A prescriptive approach. *Exceptional Children, 56*(6), 493–513.

Fullan, M., & Stiegelbauer, S. (1991). *The new meaning of educational change* (2d ed.). New York: Teachers College Press.

Galvin, K. M., & Brommel, B. J. (1982). *Family communication: Cohesion and change* (2d ed.). Glenview, IL: Scott, Foresman.

Garrett, A. (1972). *Interviewing: Its principles and methods* (2d ed.). New York: Family Service Association of America.

Goodlad, J. I. (1984). *A place called school: Prospects for the future.* New York: McGraw-Hill.

Goodlad, J. I. (1988). School-university partnerships for educational renewal: Rationale and concepts. In K. A. Sirotnik & J. I. Goodlad (Eds.), *School-university partnerships in action: Concepts, cases and concerns* (pp. 3–31). New York: Teachers College Press.

Goodlad, J. I., & Sirotnik, K. A. (1988). The future of school-university partnerships. In K. A. Sirotnik & J. I.

Goodlad (Eds.), *School-university partnerships in action* (pp. 205–225). New York: Teachers College Press.

Hames, C. C., & Joseph, D. H. (1986). *Basic concepts of helping: A holistic approach* (2d ed.). East Norwalk, CT: Appleton-Century-Crofts.

Hargreaves, A., & Dawe, R. (1990). Paths of professional development: Contrived collegiality, collaborative. *Teacher Education, 6*(3), 227–241.

Hebert, E. A., & Miller, S. I. (1985). Role conflict and the special education supervisor: A qualitative analysis. *Journal of Special Education, 19*(2), 215–229.

Himley, M., & Carini, P. (Eds.). (2000). *From another angle: Children's strengths and school standards.* New York: Teachers College Press.

Hindin, A., Morocco, C. C., & Aguilar, C. M. (2001). "This book *lives* in our school." Teaching middle school students to understand literature. *Remedial and Special Education, 22,* 215–223.

Holly, P. (1991). Action research: The missing link in the creation of schools as centers of inquiry. In A. Lieberman & L. Miller (Eds.), *Staff development for education in the '90s: New demands, new realities, new perspectives* (2d ed., pp. 133–157). New York: Teachers College Press.

Holmes Group. (1990). *Tomorrow's schools: Principles for the design of professional development schools: A report.* East Lansing, MI: Author.

Huinker, D., & Pearson, G. (1997). *The journey begins: First-year activities of the MUSI mathematics/science resource teachers.* A report on the Milwaukee Urban Systemic Initiative, University of Wisconsin-Milwaukee, Center for Mathematics and Science Education Research, sponsored by the National Science Foundation, Arlington, VA. (ERIC Document Reproduction Service No. ED 439 943)

Idol, L., Paolucci-Whitcomb, P., & Nevin, A. (1986). *Collaborative consultation.* Rockville, MD: Aspen Publishers.

Irvine, J. J. (1990). *Black students and school failure.* New York: Praeger.

Jett-Simpson, M., Pugach, M. C., & Whipp, J. (1992, April). *Portrait of an urban professional development school.* Paper presented at annual meeting, American Educational Research Association, San Francisco.

Johnson, L. J., & Bauer, A. M. (1992). *Meeting the needs of special students: Legal, ethical, and practical ramifications.* Newbury Park, CA: Corwin Press.

Johnson, L. J., & Pugach, M. C. (1991) Peer collaboration: Accommodating the needs of students with mild learning and behavior problems. *Exceptional Children, 57*(5), 454–461.

Johnson, L. J., & Pugach, M. C. (1992). Continuing the dialogue: Embracing a more expansive understanding of collaborative relationships. In W. Stainback & S. Stainback (Eds.), *Controversial issues confronting special education: Divergent perspectives* (pp. 215–222). Boston: Allyn & Bacon.

Johnson, L. J., Pugach, M. C., & Hammitte, D. (1988). Barriers to effective special education consultation. *Remedial and Special Education, 9*(6), 41–47.

Johnson, L. J., Tam, B. K. Y., Zorn, D., Makis, M., LaMontagne, M., Oser, C., Peters, M., & Sugarman, B. (2001). *Factors that inhibit or promote successful interagency collaboration.* Manuscript submitted for publication, Arlitt Child and Family Research and Education Center, Cincinnati, OH.

Joyce, B., & Showers, B. (1988). *Student achievement through staff development.* New York: Longman.

Kahn, R. L., Wolfe, D. M., Quinn, R.P. & Snoek, J.D. (1964). *Organizational stress: Studies in role conflict and ambiguity.* New York: Wiley and Sons.

Kohl, H. (1984). *Growing minds: On becoming a teacher.* New York: Harper & Row.

Kolb, D. M.,& Glidden, P. A. (1986). Getting to know your conflict option. *Personnel Administrator, 31*(6), 77–89.

Kroth, R. L. (1985). *Communicating with parents of exceptional children: Improving parent-teacher relationships* (2d ed.). Denver: Love Publishing.

Kyle, D. W., & Hovda, R. A. (1987). Teachers as action researchers: A discussion of developmental, organizational, and policy issues. In D. W. Kyle & R. A. Hovda (Eds.), The potential and practice of action research [special issue]. *Peabody Journal of Education, 64*(2), 80–95.

Ladson-Billings, G. (1994). *The dreamkeepers: Successful teachers of African-American students.* San Francisco: Jossey-Bass.

Laine, S. W. M., & Ward, J. G. (Eds.). (2000). *Using what we know: A review of the research on implementing class size reduction initiatives for state and local policymakers.* Oak Brook, IL: North Central Regional Educational Laboratory (NCREL).

Lane, V. W., & Molyneaux, D. (1992). *The dynamics of communicative development.* Englewood Cliffs, NJ: Prentice Hall.

Levine, M. (Ed.). (1992). *Professional practice schools: Linking teacher education and school reform.* New York: Teachers College Press.

LeVine, R. A., Miller, P. M., & Maxwell West, M. (1988). *Parental behavior in diverse societies.* San Francisco: Jossey-Bass.

Lewin, K. (1946). Action research and minority problems. *Journal of Social Issues, 2*(4), 34–36.

Lieberman, A., & Miller, L. (1984). School improvement: Themes and variations. *Teachers College Record, 86*(1), 4–19.

Lieberman, A., & Miller, L. (1999). *Teachers—Transforming their world and work* (The Series on School Reform). New York: Teachers College Press.

Lilly, M. S. (1971). Forum: A training based model for special education. *Exceptional Children, 37*(10), 745–749.

Little, J. W. (1982). Norms of collegiality and experimentation: Workplace conditions of school success. *American Educational Research Journal, 19*(3), 325–340.

Lortie, D. (1975). *Schoolteacher: A sociological study.* Chicago: University of Chicago Press.

Luterman, D. (1991). Counseling and the diagnostic process. *Counseling the communicatively disordered* (pp. 80–82). Austin, TX: Pro-Ed.

Lynch, E. W., & Stein, R. (1987). Perspectives on parent participation in special education. *Exceptional Education Quarterly, 3*(2), 56–63.

Lyons, C. A. (2001). Developing successful collaborative literacy teams: A case study. In V. J. Risko & K. Bromley (Eds.), *Collaboration for diverse learners: Viewpoints and perspectives* (pp. 168–187). Newark, DE: International Reading Association.

Maher, C. A. (1982). Time management training for providers of special services. *Exceptional Children, 48*(6), 523–528.

Margolis, H., & Shapiro, A. (1988). Systematically resolving parental conflict with the goal-output-process-input procedure. *High School Journal, 71*(2), 88–96.

Mason, D. A., & Good, T. L. (1993). Effects of two-group and whole-class teaching on regrouped elementary students' mathematical achievement. *American Educational Research Journal, 30*(2), 328–360.

McGrath, J. E. (1976). Stress and behavior in organizations. In M. D. Dunnette (Ed.), *Handbook of industrial and organizational psychology.* Chicago: Rand McNally College Pub.

McNiff, J. (1988). *Action research: Principles and practice.* London: Macmillan Education.

Means, B., Chelemer, C., & Knapp, M. S. (Eds.). (1991). *Teaching advanced skills to at-risk students: Views from research and practice.* San Francisco: Jossey-Bass.

Moles, O. C. (1993). Collaboration between schools and disadvantaged parents: Obstacles and openings. In N. F. Chavkin (Ed.), *Families and schools in a pluralistic society* (pp. 21–51). Albany: State University of New York Press.

Moll, L. C., Amanti, C., Neff, D., & Gonzalez, N. (1992). Funds of knowledge and teaching:Using a qualitative approach to connect homes and classrooms. *Theory Into Practice, 31*(2), 132–141.

Molnar, W., Smith, P., & Zahorik, J. (1999, December). *Executive summary: 1998–99 results of the student achievement guarantee program (SAGE) evaluation.* Milwaukee: University of Wisconsin-Milwaukee.

Molyneaux, D., & Lane, V. W. (1982). *Effective interviewing: Techniques and analysis.* Boston: Allyn and Bacon.

National Council for the Accreditation of Teacher Education. (2001). Website [www.ncate.org]

Noddings, N. (1992). *The challenge to care in schools: An alternative approach to education.* New York: Teachers College Press.

Oakes, J. (1985). *Keeping track: How schools structure inequality.* New Haven, CT: Yale University Press.

Oja, S. N., & Pine, G. J. (1989). Collaborative action research: Teachers' stages of development and school contexts. In D. W. Kyle & R. A. Hovda (Eds.), The potential and practice of action research. [Special issue.] *Peabody Journal of Education, 64*(2), 96–115.

Olson, R. A. (1980). *Evaluation as interaction in support of change.* Grand Forks, ND: University of North Dakota.

Palincsar, A. S. (1986). Metacognitive strategy instruction. *Exceptional Children, 53*(2), 118–124.

Pisha, B., & Coyne, P. (2001). Smart from the start: The promise of university design for learning. *Remedial and Special Education, 22,* 198–204.

Powell, T. H., & Gallegher, P. A. (1993). *Brothers and sisters: A special part of exceptional families* (2d ed.). Baltimore: Paul H. Brookes.

Pugach, M. C. (1993, October). *Twice victims: The struggle to educate children in urban schools and the reform of special education and Chapter One.* Paper presented at National Center on Education in Inner Cities Invitational Conference on Making a Difference for Students at Risk, Princeton, NJ.

Pugach, M. C., & Fitzgerald, M. A. (2001). Collaboration as deliberate curriculum decision making. In V. J. Risko & K. Bromley (Eds.), *Collaboration for diverse learners: Viewpoints and perspectives* (pp. 70–86). Newark, DE: International Reading Association.

Pugach, M. C., & Johnson, L. J. (1988a). Peer collaboration. *Teaching Exceptional Children, 20*(3), 75–77.

Pugach, M. C., & Johnson, L. J. (1988b). Rethinking the relationship between consultation and collaborative problem solving. *Focus on Exceptional Children, 21*(4), 1–8.

Pugach, M. C., & Johnson, L. J. (1990a). Meeting diverse needs through professional peer collaboration. In W. Stainback & S. Stainback (Eds.), *Support networks for inclusive schooling: Interdependent integrated education* (pp.123–137). Baltimore: Paul H. Brookes.

Pugach, M. C., & Johnson, L. J. (1990b). Fostering the continued democratization of consultation through action research. *Teacher Education and Special Education, 13*(3–4), 240–245.

Pugach, M. C., & Johnson, L. J. (1995). Unlocking expertise among classroom teachers through structured dialogue: Extending research on peer collaboration. *Exceptional Children, 62*(2), 101–110.

Pugach, M. C., & Pasch, S. H. (1994). The challenge of creating urban professional development schools. In R. Yinger & K. Borman (Eds.), *Restructuring education: Issues and strategies for communities, schools, and universities* (pp. 129–156). Cresskill, NJ: Hampton Press.

Pugach, M. C., & Seidl, B. L. (1998). Responsible linkages between diversity and disability: A challenge for special education. *Teacher Education and Special Education, 21*(4), 319–333.

Pugach, M. C., & Warger, C. L. (Eds.). (1996). *Curriculum trends, special education, and reform: Refocusing the conversation.* New York: Teachers College Press.

Pugach, M. C., & Wesson, C. (1995). Teachers' and students' views of team teaching of general education and learning-disabled students in two fifth grade classes. *Elementary School Journal, 95,* 279–295.

Risko, V. J., & Bromley, K. (Eds.). (2001). *Collaboration for diverse learners: Viewpoints and perspectives.* Newark, DE: International Reading Association.

Rock, M. L. (July/August, 2000). Parents as equal partners: Balancing the scales in IEP development. *Teaching Exceptional Children, 32*(6), 30–37.

Rosenholtz, S. J. (1989). *Teachers' workplace: The social organization of schools.* New York: Longman.

Schrage, M. (1990). *Shared minds: The new technologies of collaboration.* New York: Random House.

Schmidt, P. (1993, July 14). District wide approach enables border system to defy low expectations for IEP students. *Education Week, 12*(39), 6–7.

Scoon-Rogers, L. (1999). Child support for custodial mothers and fathers: 1995. *U.S. Census Bureau Current Population Reports* (Publication No. P60–196). U.S. Department of Commerce.

Seligman, M. E. (1975). *Helplessness: On depression, developmental, and death.* San Francisco: W. H. Freeman.

Sirotnik, K. A. (1988). The meaning and conduct of inquiry in school-university partnerships. In K. A. Sirotnik & J. I. Goodlad (Eds.), *School-university partnerships in action: Concepts, cases, and concerns* (pp. 169–190). New York: Teachers College Press.

Sizer, T. R. (1989). Diverse practice, shared ideas: The essential school. In H. J. Walberg & J. J. Lane (Eds.), *Organizing for learning: Toward the 21st century.* Reston, VA: National Association of Secondary School Principals.

Skrtic, T., Summers, J., Brotherson, M., & Turnbull, A. (1984). Severely handicapped children and their brothers and sisters. In J. Blacher (Ed.) *Severely handicapped young children and their families: Research in review* (pp. 215–246). New York: Academic Press.

Slavin, R. E. (1991). Synthesis of research on cooperative learning. *Educational Leadership, 48*(5), 71–82.

Teachers with National Board Certification outperform others in 11 of 13 areas, significantly enhancing student achievement, study finds. (2000, Fall). *Professional Standard* (official newsletter of National Board for Professional Teaching Standards), *1*(1), 1, 8. [available on-line at www.nbpts.org]

Thomas, K. (1976). Conflict and conflict management. In M. Dunnette (Ed.), *Handbook of industrial and organizational psychology.* Chicago: Rand McNally College Pub.

Thousand, J. S., & Villa, R. A. (1990). Sharing expertise and responsibilities through teaching teams. In W. Stainback & S. Stainback (Eds.), *Support networks for inclusive schooling: Interdependent integrated education* (pp. 151–166). Baltimore: Paul H. Brookes.

Tuckman, B.W., & Jensen, M.A.C. (1977). Stages of small-group development revisited. *Group and Organization Studies, 2*(4), 419–426.

Turnbull, A. P., Summers, J. A., & Brotherson, M. J. (1984). *Working with families with disabled members: A family systems approach.* Lawrence, KS: University of Kansas, Kansas University Affiliated Facility.

Turnbull, A. P., & Turnbull, H. R. III. (1990). *Families, professionals, and exceptionality: A special partnership* (2d ed.). Columbus, OH: Merrill.

Turnbull, A. P., & Turnbull, H. R. III. (2001). *Families, professionals, and exceptionality: Collaborating for empowerment* (4th ed.). Columbus, OH: Merrill/Prentice Hall.

Turnbull, A. P., Turnbull, H. R., Shank, M., & Leal, D. (1995). *Exceptional lives: Special education in today's schools.* Englewood Cliffs, NJ: Merrill/Prentice-Hall.

University of Wisconsin–Milwaukee, School of Education. (2001). Website for teachers-in-residence [http://www.uwm.edu/SOE/TIR/]

Warger, C.L., & Pugach, M.C. (1993). A curriculum focus for collaboration. *LD Forum, 18*(9), 26–30.

Will, M. C. (1986). *Educating students with learning problems—A shared responsibility.* Washington, DC: U.S. Department of Education, Office of Special Education and Rehabilitative Services.

Witt, J. C., & Elliott, S. N. (1985). Acceptability of classroom intervention strategies. In T. R. Kratochwill (Ed.), *Advances in school psychology* (Vol. 6, pp. 251–288). Hillside, NJ: Lawrence Erlbaum.

Zander, A. F. (1971). *Motives and goals in groups.* New York: Academic Press.

Zinn, J. E., & Eitzen. (1993). *Diversity in families* (3d ed.). New York: Harper-Collins.

Zins, J. E., Curtis, M. J., Graden, J. L., & Ponti, C. R. (1988). *Helping students succeed in the regular classroom: A guide for developing intervention assistance programs.* San Francisco: Jossey-Bass.

Using Technology to Enhance Collaboration

The practice of collaboration today, in the 21st century, has relatively new resources in the vast technological advances that have been made in the recent past. How can these advances in technology help to foster collaborative relationships? We suggest three important roles for technology as it relates to collaboration.

First, because communication is fundamental to collaboration, electronic forms of communication have the potential to enhance any collaborative relationship. Email can improve the frequency of communication among professionals and between professionals and families. Listserves can be created to connect various stakeholders in collaborative relationships that have been developed between agencies and schools or universities and schools. Teachers who find it difficult to spend time together during the school day can communicate about the progress of students for whom they share teaching responsibilities, about coordinating the curriculum, or about methods and processes that have been especially effective for students. Using electronic forms of communication still means adhering to the fundamental practices of good communication described in this text—with the understanding that new conventions for electronic communication do exist (for example, the informal tone that is adopted in email messages). Furthermore, despite the growing popularity of electronic communication, we must remember that it is not readily available to all families. These considerations must be taken into account in expanding collaboration electronically.

Second, technology can more easily enable those participating in collaborative relationships to identify and learn about other successful collaborations via the World Wide Web. Educators often feel isolated and constrained by the day-to-day demands of their very challenging work. Not only can teachers learn about what is going on in other collaborations through the Internet, but also they can participate in cross-site discussions and study groups that support collaborative activities and engage in cross-site problem solving surrounding several dimensions of collaboration. For example, use of technology enables teachers who are teaming for instruction in one location to identify teams in other locations and see how they have organized and structured their work, how human resources have been redistributed across the school or district, and so on.

Third, technology can be used to enhance teachers' personal productivity, thus reducing time spent on administrative tasks and freeing up time for substantive interaction with colleagues concerning issues of collaborative teaching and learning. Lack of time is nearly always cited as an impediment to collaboration. In planning new collaborations, teachers can set specific technology learning goals to increase the time available to them to engage in the real work of teaching and learning. And the resources to reach these goals should be supported by administrators.

Finally, and most important, technology is as yet not tapped nearly enough to enhance instruction in the schools. As teachers enter into collaborations to improve students' learning, the skilled use of technology can support this goal significantly. Teachers use technology to enhance written expression, research skills, and presentation skills—as well as use it as a natural means of supporting project-based learning that can include varying levels of student ability and interest. Further, technological advances that specifically support the integration of students with disabilities into general education are a natural support for collaboration between special and general education. Advances in communication technology for students with hearing or visual impairments, or supports like spellcheckers for students with specific learning disabilities or mild cognitive impairments, or much more widespread technological advances like universally designed electronic texts (Pisha & Coyne, 2001), can support higher levels of learning in students who in earlier eras could not participate meaningfully in instruction.

Clearly, practicing collaboration in the year 2001 is not the same as practicing it in 1990, and technology can be an important resource in advancing the varied goals of collaboration.

We end this appendix with a short list of websites that may provide helpful information about collaboration.

Selected Websites Related to Collaboration

■ http://www.ncrel.org/sdrs/areas/rpl_esys/collab.htm/
  This site provides ideas about establishing collaborative classrooms and includes guidelines for teacher roles in these classrooms.

■ http://newhorizons.org/
This site focuses on fostering educational change and includes a section of special education and collaboration.

■ http://teachers.net/
A comprehensive site for teachers, including several chatrooms on current topics that are related to collaboration.

■ http://www.teachervision.com
This site was created by teachers for teachers. Similar to http://teachers.net/, this site includes a wide range of issues, discussions, and resources for teachers, including collaboration.

■ http://www.ccsso.org/intasc.html/
This is the website for the Interstate New Teacher Assistance and Support Consortium of the Council of Chief State School Officers. It includes the new 2001 standards for what all beginning teachers need to know and do to work effectively with students with disabilities.

■ http://www.nbpts.org/
This is the site for the National Board for Professional Teaching Standards, standards for the voluntary certification of accomplished teachers. Many of the assessments for National Board certification include demonstrated knowledge and skill in collaboration.

■ http://seriweb.com/
This site contains a collection of Internet accessible information resources of interest to those involved in the fields related to special education. This collection exists in order to make online special education resources more easily and readily available in one location.

■ http://www.cec.sped.org/
As the official website for the International Council for Exceptional Children, this site includes news, articles, jobs, and current issues in the field of special education.

■ http://www.closingthegap.com/
This is a major site for advances in the use of technology with students with disabilities.

■ http://www.ericec.org/

This site is part of the federally funded national system of educational information known as the Educational Resource Information Center, or ERIC. This particular site is the clearinghouse for data about special education. The general site for the ERIC system is http://www.eric.ed.gov.

Index

A

Action research, 193, 196, 197
Adaptability, 211–212
Adjourning stage, group, 100, 102
Adult-adult subsystems, 206
Advice giving, 80–82
Affection needs, 209–210
Announcement fliers, 220
Arbitration, 107–109
Arlitt Child and Family Research and
    Education Center, 185–189

B

Bilingual education specialists, 119–120
Blended families, 205
Block scheduling, 124–125
Brainstorming, 129
Butler, A. S., 104

C

Child Development Program (University
    of Cincinnati), 185–189
Clarification, 69–71
Class size, 156
Classroom-specific collaborative
    problem solving. See also
    Problem solving
  background of, 118–119
  balance between schoolwide
      collaborative problem solving
      and, 151
  bilingual education or content area
      specialists and, 119–120
  features of, 127

interactions between schoolwide
    collaborative problem solving
    and, 147–151
models of, 130–139
schoolwide collaborative problem
    solving vs., 125–127
special education and, 120–121
steps in, 127–130
student progress reviews and, 119
Clichés, 87–89
Clowning, 106–107
Cohen, E. G., 163, 165
Cohesion, 219
Collaboration. See also Classroom-
    specific collaborative problem
    solving; Schoolwide
    collaborative problem solving
  as schoolwide commitment, 32–33
  challenges of, 22–23
  communication for, 57
  cross-institutional, 179–199
      (See also Cross-institutional
      collaboration)
  curriculum, 136, 138–139
  facilitative dimension of, 38–39
  historical perspective on, 27–33
  in contemporary educational
      practice, 6–11
  in practice, 117
  information-giving dimension of,
      39–40
  multidimensional, 34–36, 41
  overview of, 5, 27
  prescriptive dimension of, 40–41
  professional development through,
      143–147